The Real Poland

THE REAL
POLAND

An Anthology of
National Self-Perception

Edited by Alfred Bloch

CONTINUUM • NEW YORK

To Mrs. Bianca Rosensteil
and Mrs. Ewa Szumanska Walker
of the American Institute of Polish Culture
in Miami, Florida
for their generous support for the study
of nationality conflicts

1982

The Continuum Publishing Company
575 Lexington Avenue, New York, N.Y. 10022

Printed in the United States of America

Library of Congress Cataloging in Publication Data

Main entry under title:
The Real Poland.

1. Poland—History—Philosophy—Addresses, essays,
lectures.   2. Polish literature.   3. Poland—Literary
collections.   I. Bloch, Alfred, 1922–
DK4155.R4   943.8   82-1559
ISBN 0-8264-0060-4   AACR2

Contents

The Peasants   181

The Epilogue as Prologue   193

Introduction

The Poles seek Poland above all, not the Kingdom
of God, and that is why they have no Poland.
——*Pope Pius IX, 1863**

You must carry into the future the whole experience
that is "Poland." It is a difficult experience, perhaps
the most difficult in the world, in Europe,
in the Church . . .
——*Pope John Paul II, 1979***

The purpose of this book, part interpretation, part literary anthology, is to share with the reader a "historical experience" that, as John Paul II said, is perhaps "the most difficult in the world."

History, according to British historian E. H. Carr, is an ever-changing dialogue of the present with the past. In Poland this dialogue has a constant theme: the search for a way for Poland to be free and for the Poles to live their lives in the dignity their humaneness deserves. They have a collective historical memory of when such conditions prevailed, but that memory is now five centuries old. Since then it has been a fight to regain what was, followed by defeat, followed by a renewal of strength, and followed by yet another fight and another loss.

For a modern Pole to continue living in the security of his or her identity, the past has to be continuously in the present, because the realities of the present are a conspiracy aimed at the survival of any Pole as a Pole.

The first three chapters of this book consist of panoramic views of Polish history. One view is representative of what many Poles believe

---

* Quoted from Adam Pickarski, *The Church in Poland* (Warsaw: Interpress Publishers, 1978), p. 57.
** Homily delivered in Czestochowa, Poland, during 1979 visit.

to be the ethos of their history. The other view is the reality of that history. The third chapter identifies the main currents of contemporary Polish history and indicates the rebirth of a new ethos whereby, in the social composition, workers assume most of the role previously played by the gentry. The Catholic church has also contributed actively to the struggle for social justice. Yet the gap between the ethos and the reality is still enormous, a fact that can be explained only by understanding the passions of a people whose conscious struggle for national liberation, freedom, dignity, sovereignty, and the recognition of human rights is, in modern times, second only to the struggle of the Jewish people.

The anthology section of the book includes selections from the writings of political theoreticians who diagnosed the conditions that made Polish history so difficult. But the greatest emphasis of the anthology is on literary works that illustrate the salient components of the ethos of Poland's history and occasionally break through to the reality of Poland.

For a people engaged in a prolonged struggle, the ethos, which encompasses their emotions, hopes, expectations, and values, which feeds the energies needed to maintain a fight that more often than not is foredoomed to failure—this ethos is far more important than reality. The reality of oppression, exploitation, and fear of death need not be described for the people who live under it. They know it, they see it, and they do their best to transcend it.

Usually when the subject is the history of a people, the substantiation of that history should come from the usual sources available to historians and from other historians. But in Poland, where more histories of that country were written than is the case of most other nations, the historians wrote for purposes other, perhaps even more important, than rendering an explanation of the past. Many historians wrote to tell the story of Poland's greatness and glossed over the many faults. Their transcendent motive was to uphold national pride and form national consciousness. Another school of historians wrote accusations and rendered verdicts to explain why Poland, that permanent highway of vulnerability, was condemned to the fate that befell it. Lastly, there was a group of historians who wrote to justify that which was or that which is. The members of this group followed the dictates of whatever the "official line" for Poland or of Poland's government was.

Many writers did the same. But a good novelist can draw a more fascinating living picture through which to illustrate his or her social perceptions. A great writer contributes insights, perceptions of social relations, which the uniqueness of his or her talent discovers among the welter of facts. A prime example of this kind of writer is Tolstoy, whose epic work *War and Peace* contains a deeper understanding of the ethos and reality of Russian history than can be found in most history books. The same can be said about the writings of Pasternak and Solzhenitsyn.

No Polish writer ever attained international recognition equaling Tolstoy's, but that is not due to a lack of talent. Polish literature was, generally speaking, also an underground literature. It had to be either written or published in exile. Or if it was written in Poland, the author had to adopt a style and tone that would enable his or her work to pass the scrutiny of a censor. In the past two centuries, Poland's writers were only semifree to choose their themes and express their views for only about twenty-five years. Before and after, the Polish artistic community was granted only fleeting moments of self-expression.

The basic reason for relying on writers is their unique ability to come to grips with the intangibles of history, with the values that make that particular history unique. They can render the atmosphere, show values in action, and plumb the depth of the conscience of the principal actors. Historians who have to rely on facts, on things that can be proven, on data that can be quantified, do not have this luxury.

Artists, poets, novelists, and composers are free to roam from reality to imagination, from the abject concrete to the beauties of the loftiest experience. Sir Lewis Namier, born a Pole but made famous in England, was a superb historian who said that emotions make history while history writes the libretto. Since Poland's history is emotions based on dreams, the field of Polish history truly belongs to the artist, the communicator of emotions.

POLISH

HISTORY

THE ETHOS

The academic discipline we identify today as the history of peoples, states, and their doings emerged in Europe very late in the eighteenth century and actually has its roots in the early decades of the nineteenth century. At that time, Poland no longer existed as a sovereign state. Thus, Polish history was born and instantly saddled with the task of explaining how and why Poland lost its independence and assessing what was left with which to regain this independence. Polish history had a twin task: to diagnose the past and maintain a vision of the future.

Although Poland's historians disagreed violently on why Poland had the distinction of being the first European state to disappear from the political map of Europe, and disagreed even more on what the future of Poland should be, they were unanimous on one basic theme: Poland had to regain its independence. Obviously, this intention on the part of Polish historians, as well as its novelists, poets, composers, and painters—all of whom were actually historians— made them a dangerous element to the German Empire, Austria-Hungary, and Imperial Russia, the powers that divided Poland among themselves. Therefore, all writing that had as its theme Poland—what it was and how it again could be—had to go "underground" as far as the occupying powers were concerned.

The term *underground* is an apt euphemism for active resistance of an oppressed people against foreign powers. Resistance is an act and that act is the central theme of Polish existence and thus the central theme of Poland's history writers. Resistance is easy to describe but very difficult to understand. Although outwardly similar to a revolution is in its essence, resistance is the opposite of revolution. In a revolution there is always a vision of a future based either on the City of God or on a man-made "city of God." At the core of resistance lies a dream of the past, a dream nourished by emotions, protected by lives, paid for in terms of exile, prison, torture, and death—above all death.

Given these ingredients, it is not surprising that Poles talk best about themselves through poetry, music, and the arts, and least well through the stilted language and convoluted prose of professional historians.

The first king of Poland was converted to Christianity in 966 and that date marks the official recognition of Poland as an independent national entity, subservient only technically to the Holy Roman Emperor of the German nation, who represented, or was supposed to represent, through Europe, the secular power of the pope.

From the very instance of its birth, Poland grew in all directions as if searching for natural frontiers that could bind it into a defensible cohesive entity. It found them on the shores of the Baltic Sea in the north and along the Carpathian mountain range in the south. But neither to the west nor to the east was there any natural obstacle to prevent the Poles from spilling into other lands except the power of their occupants. Westward expansion was soon stopped by the knights of the Holy Roman Empire of the German nation. In the east, however, there is nothing natural or man-made to stop the Poles. When the winter winds begin to blow in the Ural Mountains, thousands of miles away from the nearest Polish hamlet, there is nothing, not even a significant hill, to stop it from freezing the small window panes of a Polish peasant hut.

When there is no geography to help, a frontier becomes a line of men advancing and retreating in the constant, violent rhythm of confrontations with others who suffer from the same consequences of a lack of a natural container for their national identity. In the case of Poland, from the origins of the state in the tenth century until the beginning of its decline in the late sixteenth century, these "others" were the marauding bands of Tartars and cossacks, the military forces of the Mongol hordes, the organized armies of the principality of Muscovy. Since the seventeenth century, the identity of the "others" became the unified Russian Empire and subsequently the Soviet Union. As late as 1969–70 there was yet another adjustment of the frontier between Poland and the Soviet Union, although as far as the exercise of Soviet power is concerned that frontier does not really exist.

Poland, lying at the heart of Europe, was born to war. For one thousand years no single generation of Poles lived its lives without either a war, an uprising, or a rebellion of some sort. Quite a few times Poland was victorious in its armed struggles, but all of its rebellions and uprisings, and most of its wars, were uniquely tragic stories of perpetual losers. Their uniqueness was to be found in the essentially Christian moral considerations that provided the emotional impetus for these expressions of violence and despair.

The process of conversion of Poland to Christianity, which started in 966 and was probably not completed until the thirteenth century, resulted in a marriage of state, nation, and religion, which was never dissolved. No matter what the vagaries of Poland's history, faith was and remains there, even when the vicars of Christ on earth more often than not betrayed these steadfast followers. The Polish people and the rulers of Poland were mostly willing tools in the hands of papal and curial manipulators.

When Rome called for defenders of the faith threatened by the Tartar hordes under the command of Genghis Khan and Kublai Khan, who in the thirteenth and early fourteenth centuries threatened to overrun central Europe, the Poles fought and sacrificed more than any other Christian nation. For their exploits the Poles gained the distinction of being referred to as the "shield of Christendom."

When the Turks began to expand their empire and their victorious armies occupied the Balkans, the Poles again were enlisted by the papacy to fight wars that lasted centuries and bled their kingdom of its people and treasure. And in the early decades of the seventeenth century, when the pope's suffering from secular megalomania conspired with the Hapsburg emperors to destroy Greek Orthodoxy, which radiated from distant Muscovy, they again called upon Poland's armed might to crush the Russians and capture the golden throne of the czars—a throne they inherited in their struggle against the Mongol yoke. For a fleeting moment, ten years before the first Pilgrims landed at Plymouth Rock, a Polish puppet king sat on the throne of the czars.

Yet when unemployed Crusaders robbed, killed, and raped provinces of Poland, the popes kept quiet—and they remained quiet whenever Poland was in dire need of help and wordly recognition. No Pontifex Maxims, no infallible exponent of the evangelical commandment to love, ever officially condemned those who tortured the Polish people. No pope ever came to Poland until a Pole became a pope. And yet Poland, the Polish people, kept sending their treasure to Rome and their sons to death for the faith they embraced.

The reasons for this passionate attachment to Catholicism are to be found in the harshness of peasant life and linked to the absence of a clear demarcation line where Western civilization ends and Russian civilization begins. In a peculiar way beyond the scope of this work to explain, Poland's history is influenced by the echoes of the struggle between the Eastern and Western Roman Empires. Where did one end and the other begin? The inheritors of the Eastern Roman Empire (Greek Orthodoxy) were the Russians; the most Eastern exponents of the Roman Empire (Roman Catholicism) were the Poles; and the demarcation line was never clear. This schism had profound effects on Russian history and obviously on Polish history.

Peasants remain faithful to the very first religion that inspired them with hope—no matter what that religion might be. They will only change their religion if it massively and visibly betrayed their hope, as was the case in Germany during the Reformation and Counter-Reformation. It cannot be overemphasized that peasants may change religion, but they do not eliminate faith as the very foundation of their existence. All movements for social justice for peasants have their roots in faith, in an interpretation of the Scriptures that reenforces their faith. There is no peasant anywhere within the limits of what we identify as Western civilization whose life is not ruled by faith. And once studies are made of peoples of the rest of the world it will be established beyond any dispute that those who exist in a permanent, life-sustaining relationship with earth look at the world through a prism of values at whose foundation is religion. The dictates of that religion, the orders of those who assume rightly or wrongly the positions of leaders of that religion, will be obeyed. Since peasants furnish most of the cannon fodder for wars, all wars assume the outward form of "crusades," even if their objectives are the height of the opposite of the morality of all of the great religions. Roman Catholicism gave the Polish peasant hope and the sense of moral righteousness, and thus the church commanded Polish history.

It is difficult today, when there are so many Christian and pseudo-Christian sects and cults abounding in the world, to understand that Roman Catholicism is the direct successor of the civilized unity that was the Roman Empire. It is through the One and Only Apostolic Church of Rome that Roman legal and political institutions, and Roman social organization persist throughout Western civilization—no matter what descriptive label they chose to adopt. The essential strand of the continuity of Western history was woven by Rome and frozen into eternity by the Roman Catholic church. Neither the Church of England nor any of the Protestant faith could outlive by a split second the end of the Church of Rome. If that edifice falls, so does Western civilization. The Polish Kingdom from 966 to 1794, the Polish Republic of 1918–39, and the Polish People's Republic of 1981 are the Eastern legions of the Church of Rome. The Polish Kingdom was, and the Poles of today feel, a direct link to the Messiah with his face and sword pointing to the East.

In front of the royal palace in Warsaw stands the statue of King Sigismund I with a raised sword. Prior to 1939, he used to face east and his sword pointed in the direction of Moscow. His statue and the marble column on which it stood were destroyed by the Nazis during the Warsaw uprising of 1944. The column and statue were carefully reconstructed after the end of World War II. But, allowing for the political reality of Central Europe being dominated by Stalinism, the statue was slightly turned in a southerly direction. This was the kind of adjustment of Polish history that the Poles, whose history is constantly being adjusted, accept with a bemused smile. They know that the truth has not changed and that "if you scratch a Russian you will find a brutal Tartar lurking behind the skin."

Usually when the term *messianism* is used in a political context it implies aggressiveness, a sense of mission, and an oppressive intolerance. Although some of these characteristics surface in the history of Poland, Polish messianism was primarily defensive. This is a paradox. Yet the Messiah Poland defended against the forces of the "anti-Christ"—meaning the Mongol hordes of Genghis Khan, the golden horde of the Tartars, the Turks, the Russian Empire, the Soviet Russians—was a Messiah totally fused with the essence of being Polish. He was and is a Brother to all the Poles because His Mother was crowned the Virgin Mary, Queen of Poland. Poland's first national anthem, dating back to the early fourteenth century, was dedicated to her and is still being sung today by the workers of Solidarity, the independent labor union fighting for the democratization of their state.

No nation can survive on faith alone and the recognition of that fact surfaces in Poland's second and now official national anthem. It is dedicated to Napoleon, the rationalist emperor of romantic Europe. Behind this glorification of Napoleon lies a very deeply ingrained Polish myth, or more precisely a myth shared by many members of the Polish gentry. It convinced itself that in some fashion they represented the noblest virtues of Rome, both republican and Cesarian. It is symbolic of Poland's conscious universalism that both of the great forces of Western civilization—faith and rationalism—are the essential components of the songs that identify Poland.

Both of Poland's national anthems are resistance songs. The first one commemorates Poland's resistance against all declared enemies of Roman Catholicism; the second one establishes forever Poland's resistance to tyrannies of secularism—be they dynastic or ideological. In the eyes of Poles, Napoleon was a liberator.

Yet the existence of two anthems is not a blessing. The dynamics of faith and the dynamics of reason most often pull a nation in opposite directions. They polarize. Whereas most modern states have developed a working synthesis between faith and secularism (which sometimes becomes unstuck or perverted as in Nazism and Sovietism), the Polish people permanently and consciously struggle with the attractiveness of both. However, since the Polish people have not enjoyed any significant periods of peace, the elements of faith have consistently gained the upper hand. Religion, as the essence of resistance and as the constant element of hope in a nation that has to live on hope, is the core of Poland's internal and external politics. Reason—its needs, demands, and power—surfaces in the history of Poland very rarely and ironically. When it does gain dominion, the "Polishness" of the Polish people begins to suffer.

For example, in the 1770s, when Poland's leading patriots recognized the need to create a constitutional monarchy and began debating the kind of a constitution they wanted, their dialogue reflected the debates current in the United States at that time. Influenced by them and very aware of the day-to-day problems confronting the constitutionalists in the United States, the Poles wrote and adopted in their Parliament the Constitution of the third of May, 1791. It was a magnificent, national document of tolerance, enlightenment, and judicious politics. Yet as soon as it was proclaimed, the Russians, under Catherine the Great, invaded Poland and in 1795 Poland ceased to be. Its people had to return to resistance, faith, and their own historical romanticism.

For seven centuries prior to that fatal data Poland's resistance, fed by faith, was most successful. It developed a geographic momentum and eventually the Polish Kingdom, united in a federation with the Grand Duchy of Lithuania, expanded to the north shore of the Baltic Sea and to the Black Sea. Its eastern frontiers generally paralleled the Dniester River, while on the west it included parts of Prussia. Poland was the largest kingdom on the European continent. When Poland's king called a summit meeting, emperors came.

This expansion of Poland was a function of resistance and not aggression. Although naked aggression and national security are most frequently rationalized in terms of defending the national interest and an "objective case" could be made that Poland's expansion between the fourteenth and seventeenth centuries was no different, in the perception of a Pole and in the context of defending Western Catholic civilization, it was. Poland grew by resisting the forces of the anti-Christ.

Resistance as an activity that spans centuries is an unusual bonding agent among the elements that tie and hold a society together. In the case of Poland, where it became the most important of the elements assuring unity, resistance had, and continues to have, a unique, baffling, and frequently contradictory impact on the social, political, intellectual, and cultural evolution of the Polish people.

The right to participate in resistance is open to all who wish to act in that capacity. The proof of participation is usually self-evident. The notion of resistance creates a sense of community and a sense of responsibility for the community whose common good is the ability to continue to resist until the time is ripe to implement the vision that sustained the resistance. However, no member of a resistance community can decide to cease resisting and still expect to be regarded as a member of that community. The simplistic adage "If you are not with us you are against us" is a basic operating principle of a resistance community. Furthermore, anyone, any group outside that community, is either suspect or regarded as an outright enemy. Thus, internally, the resistance community is very tolerant and inherently democratic, while externally it is hostile, suspicious, and closed. That type of democracy is based on a simple fact of resistance, namely that if a life depends on the "action of the other," the "other" cannot be denied his rights.

Yet resistance, as admirable as it may appear, acts with a forked tongue. It "silently kills" the enemy, and while doing so also kills the consciousness of those who engage in it. The history of Poland offers one of the best illustrations of the double-edged-sword effect of resistance as a way of life.

From the early fifteenth century until the mid-sixteenth century, the Polish Kingdom, which was officially known as the Commonwealth of Poland and Lithuania, was secure and the most tolerant democratic power of Europe. There were no religious wars in Poland, while the rest of Europe was bleeding for the varieties of interpretation of the "good word." The Jews fled to Poland from Spain and its Inquisition, and from Germany and France and their recurrent pogroms. There were no significant disturbances of an anti-Jewish nature on ethnically Polish lands until 1881.

Europe's humanists of the fifteenth and sixteenth centuries admired Poland, and the Jagiellonian University, founded in 1364, became famous for its liberal tradition, open access, and flourishing departments of philosophy and theology.

Moreover Poland, "the shield of Christendom," resisted the centralization of power in papal hands, championed the supremacy of church councils over the pope (the conciliar theory), and was so repelled by the intolerance and corruption of Rome that for a short time most of the leadership of Poland, together with much of the gentry, renounced Catholicism in favor of Protestantism. This was an act of resistance and not a real conversion. The popes and the Curia never forgot or forgave this lapse.

The Jesuits, the soldiers of Christ created as an order by Ignacius Loyola in 1539 and charged by the pope, who gave them their charter in 1540 to fight the Reformation, descended upon Poland. They came in 1565 and very rapidly gained control of the Commonwealth. They brought with them the black wave of repression, intolerance, and obscurantism. The Poles called them the "black wave" because the hassocks worn by the Jesuits were and still are black.

Under their influence and their prompting, the Commonwealth fought battles against the "infidels"—the Turks, the Tartars, the Russians, and anyone else the Jesuits or their minions so designated. Coincidentally with the Jesuits' invasion of Poland, the Polish throne became elective. The electors were all the members of the gentry (*szlachta*), whose number is estimated at about eight hundred thousand. An electorate of eight hundred thousand was unheard of in western Europe (in France, Germany, England) until the middle of the nineteenth century. The fact that Poland had this number as far back as the sixteenth century gave rise to the notion that Poland was a "gentry democracy." This gentry, under the tutelage of the Church of Rome and the Jesuits, was imbued with the ethos of resisters; they were resisting the forces of the anti-Christ.

Although resistance as action is responsible for some of the noblest pages of human history, unemployed rebels have a remarkable tendency for anarchic, lawless, antisocial behavior. The social bond that unifies rebels so strongly in action evaporates in moments of peace. Resistance fighters, accustomed to assuming responsibility for life and death, do not accept the notion of having it taken away from them. Resistance breeds a sense of personal power, which cannot long remain dormant.

On the individual level, the expression of that power in times of peace takes the form of brutal intolerance directed against all who try to curb this power. Thus, the same resistance offered by the Poles to the forces of the "anti-Christ" also filled the pages of Poland's history with the ugliest stories of rape, slovenliness, corruption, and despicable intolerance. History knows no viler creature in its annals of human monsters than unemployed Crusaders, useless rebels, and inspired zealots without a cause.

These were the characteristics of the individual members of most of the so-called "gentry democracy." They wrote the political history of Poland—magnificent in battle, fearless in resistance, and totally incompetent, venal, and shortsighted in formulating policy in those times when Poland was free to do so. Yet this bitter truth was obscured by the reality of their nobility in resistance. This reality became a legend glorified in the writings of Henryk Sienkiewicz, Poland's greatest historical novelist.

It has to be acknowledged that this gentry as a social stratum defended Poland's national identity, forged national consciousness among the illiterate masses who did not have one, and as a group resisted all the efforts of the occupiers to erase Polishness.

The gentry were the architects of the ethos of Poland's history and they made themselves into the subject of that ethos. In reality, as will be shown in the following chapter, they and the magnates (the large landholders) bore the single greatest responsibility for Poland's loss of independence. Why? Because they could not obey laws even if they wrote them. They elected as kings those who bribed them most generously and that meant permission to live outside the law without any responsibility toward the state, except that which they voluntarily assumed. Most of the time they agreed to fight.

In 1795, when the Prussian, Russian, and Austrian powers divided Poland among them, many of the gentry and quite a number of their peasant followers left Poland. Ever since that time Poland has existed mainly as a fiction, a link in the chain of titles attesting to the majesty of an emperor, a colorful costume to be worn at a masked ball given by dukes and princesses and a magnificent uniform to be worn by Poles fighting and dying for causes they hardly understood, rarely identified with, and frequently scorned.

In the two hundred years that separate Thaddeus Kosciuszko's valiant struggle to maintain Poland's independence and Solidarity's attempt in 1980 to affirm at least an aspect of national independence, Polish soldiers fought black freedom fighters in Santo Domingo (1796), participated in all of Napoleon's magnificent yet inglorious campaigns, fought Imperial Russian battles waged against the Turks and the Japanese, and died in remote Italian mountain passes protecting the interests of the Hapsburgs, the ruling house of Austria.

During World War I the Poles fought in the armies of all belligerents. Polish soldiers were drafted into the Austrian army to fight the Russians and into the Russian army to fight the Austrians. Polish legions, recruited from among emigrés living in France and the United States, joined the French and Americans to fight against the Germans and were forced by the Germans to fight the French and the Americans. Each of the belligerent powers promised the Poles that in return for their faithful service they would receive some sort of independence. Most of the Poles believed it.

In addition to fighting in wars that, as citizens of the powers that occupied them, they were legally bound to fight, and in addition to being involved in conflicts of powers whose help the Poles were expecting in their own wars of national liberation, the Poles also rebelled to gain their freedom.

The first major insurrection directed against Imperial Russia occurred in 1830–31. At that time the Poles held a unique position within the Russian Empire, a position equal to that of the Finns. The Poles and the Finns were actually semi-independent. They had their own armies, their own universities, and a great degree of self-rule. The grand duke of Poland was the brother of Czar Alexander I and in that position was the major indication of a Russian Imperial overlordship. The duchy, actually known as the "Congress Kingdom," had its own constitution and the citizens enjoyed more freedom than their counterparts within the Russian Empire proper. Moreover, Alexander I swore to obey and uphold the constitution of the Congress Kingdom, just as he swore to uphold the constitution of the Grand Duchy of Finland. The Finns never rebelled, and the Romanoff czars down to the last one never violated that oath.

The Poles, and more specifically the Polish gentry and the veterans of the Napoleonic wars, decided to provoke an armed insurrection because they felt that the czar's brother Constantine, who was an ineffective drunkard, offended the honor of Poland when he ruled in the name of his brother. The patriots never took into consideration the international situation of a Europe in which conservative policies prevailed, never thought that there was no power in whose interest it would have been to help them, and never really calculated their chances of winning an armed struggle against the might of the Russian Empire. On the contrary, they thought that Russian rebels (who surfaced briefly and ineffectively in 1825 and were known as the Decembrists) would somehow help. By the time the Polish insurrection did occur, Russia was already under the heavy-handed rule of

Czar Nicholas I, the successor of the more liberal Alexander I. The insurrection relieved Nicholas I and all the succeeding czars from honoring the provisions of the constitution of the Congress Kingdom. Thereafter, the Poles in that area existed at the whims of czarist policies.

This insurrection typifies Poland's method of resisting and Poland's love of a fight, frequently without regard to cost and consequence. A people does what it knows how to do, and Poland's history conditioned the Poles to fight and to rebel. Since the Poles did rise, they lost their position, their cultural autonomy, and the right to their own armed forces. Although the name Congress Kingdom was maintained for a few decades, Poland was actually referred to as the lands along the Vistula (Poland's main river).

The second Polish rebellion, directed against the Austrians and the Germans, took place in 1848. At least that rebellion was part of the national liberation struggles and constitutional demands that shook the entire political edifice of all the central and western European states. The Poles could expect a certain amount of success, and they did get concessions from the Hapsburg Empire that made that part of Poland occupied by the Austrians into the most liberal section of the former Polish Kingdom. It allowed Polish language and learning to survive, and it eventually enabled Polish aristocrats to become members of the elite ruling the Hapsburg Empire. The effects of the 1848 rebellion against Prussia proved to be ephemeral successes as they were soon obliterated by Bismarck—not only in Poland but throughout the German Empire he created.

The third national liberation struggle, again directed against the Russians, took place in 1863. This was an insurrection of despair. Due to the loss of the autonomy the Poles enjoyed prior to 1831, the Russians were beginning to systematically destroy Poland's culture. They ruthlessly exterminated the Polish intelligentsia and ruled the Congress Kingdom through the most gruesome police measures possible at that time. The uprising of 1863 never had a chance, especially since the Polish peasants refused to participate or even aid the rebels. The peasants were granted ownership of their land by Alexander II and could not care less who governed Poland. The Poles expected Napoleon III, like his illustrious uncle, to come to their aid. He did not. As a consequence of the failure of 1863, the Poles massively populated Imperial Russia's Siberian labor camps and helped swell the ranks of emigrés living in western Europe. Thereafter, the Polish resistance changed its political direction and became among the most active elements in the Russian revolutions of 1905 and 1917.

The next chapter in the history of Polish rebellions was written during World War II, when the Poles wanted to liberate their own capital, Warsaw, and failed while Soviet armies stood idly by and watched Poles die and a city reduced to a pile of rubble not higher than three meters. The Western Allies (England, France, and the United States) sent ineffective help and politely pressured the Russians to do something, but in reality did not care what happened.

From 1945 to 1948, the Poles fought each other and finally the Stalinists won. Poland became a reluctant satellite but nevertheless a satellite of the Stalinist empire. In 1956, the Poles rose against the oppression of Soviet imperialism and gained a visible measure of independence, similar to that which they enjoyed in the Congress Kingdom prior to the 1830–31 uprising.

The last chapter of the resistance started in 1956 is being written now, in 1980–81, when the Poles are again attempting to complete the work of autonomy and rule themselves at home according to their own laws and visions. The danger lurking in these visions became obvious when martial law was declared in the winter of 1981. The Soviets will not accept an independent Poland. The Poles know this, yet they have already indicated that this is what they are after. If that turns out to be true, Poland of 1982 will resemble the Congress Kingdom of 1863—a people under total repression.

In every decade since 1794 Poles have fought bigger or smaller battles. They have fought without ever winning but, paradoxically, as a nation they have never lost.

The fatalistically regular rhythm of wars, rebellions, failures, destruction, and death acted as a powerful conditioner in a nationwide behavior-modification process. History taught an overwhelming majority of Poles to despise authority, all authority, even if it is in the hands of Poles. Most of the Polish population, which today numbers more than thirty million, views laws as obstacles to survival. Poles utilize the rare periods of tranquility granted them by history as unique opportunities to obtain material gains by any means possible. Goods are either voraciously consumed or shamelessly hoarded. In the nineteenth century, only the gentry had the aura of romantic anarchists. Today anarchy as a social value is the norm of existence, and, despite appearances, an orderly existence is the exception.

Life, joy, education, earning a living, investment plans large or small, establishment of national priorities—all were in Poland ad-hoc formulations. They continue to be so today due to the current realities of Poland's history.

Whereas nearly all modern nation states can take the continuity of their history for granted and can expect it to continue into the foreseeable future, Poland and its people have no such experience. Whether strong or weak, large or small, countries and peoples assume ownership of their own time. They take their historical time for granted. It is a given that only a cataclysm can take away from them. The availability of time to develop social, economic, and educational policies is the foundation of the modern state.

The Poles do not plan, not because they are inherently incapable of it, but because they never owned their own historical time, at least not in the period when Europe's nations were modernizing and industrializing. As a matter of fact, planning for the Poles was and remains a luxury engaged in by many as a sought-after fantasy. The Poles produced and articulated more social and economic plans than those nations, who have "their" time to implement plans and policies. Polish history, however, taught the Poles, demanded that the Poles jump into situations seemingly thoughtlessly. The Polish society thus developed a crisis mentality, which, coupled with the understandable hostility to authority and aversion to laws, virtually precludes the establishment of conditions for survival at a level that would yield comfort, security, and emotional satisfaction. Poland is the prime example of anarchy as a methodology of survival.

The single great positive achievement of Poland's rebellions was the development and enrichment of the Polish language, despite centuries of foreign domination and despite sustained efforts to eradicate it. This fact alone indicates that the nature of the Polish resistance was structurally and intentionally quite different from resistance movements proliferating in other nations.

Most resistance movements start with usually well-defined political-ideological positions and politicize the culture to further their own interests. The Polish resistance based itself on a culture in which language was the centerpiece and inculturated the political ideologies it employed in its action program. For example, socialism, which started off by being international, was changed in Poland into a national liberation ideology, in the Soviet Union into a faith, and in China into a ritual. The role of socialism in Poland's resistance will be elaborated on later, but it should be noted now that the term *national socialism*, meaning national liberation and social justice, was coined by Bronislaw Limanowski around 1863. In a sustained debate that lasted about thirty years, the Polish socialist theoreticians achieved a fundamental restructuring of socialist theory that made it adaptable to the needs of the so-called emerging nations of our times. The result was to stipulate that national independence be the prime requisite of a socialist revolution.

Without denying that there is a continuous process of interpenetration between the cultural and the political, and that there is a feedback mechanism linking the two phenomena of social life, in Poland, Polish culture was the dominant element.

The only area occasionally open to Poland's rebels for a massive effort benefiting the nation was culture—the intangibles of a nation's history, i.e., collective memory, intellect, creativity, religious faith, and language. Poland's intangibles were never subjugated.

The basic expression of the vitality and maturity of a nation's culture is its language. Never in its entire history of nonexistence as a state did the Polish language become submerged or secondary in importance. Whereas the Czechs, for example, had to recreate their lost language and Frantisek Palacky, the first Czech historian, had to write the history of his nation in German, Poland always had a vivacious language suitable for creativity, one that gained acclaim throughout Europe.

The primary emphasis in Poland was on the cultural or the intangibles. For the past two centuries, therefore, Poland was the battlefield between the proud, always free, always vital intangibles and the concrete reality in which Poland had to live. This battlefield, when looked at through a more subtle lens, is the consciousness of every Pole, regardless of the social stratum to which he or she may belong. The concrete, for example, was the Prussian/German occupation of Poland; the intangibles were the Polish language, poetry, theater, folk songs, and peasant costumes. Bismarck, the architect of the German Empire, understood that the concrete cannot withstand the long-range siege by the intangibles. He caused, therefore, a law to be passed forbidding a Prussian to marry a Polish woman, because culture was transmitted by the woman. Putting her baby to sleep, the mother would sing a Polish lullabye—and thereby create a base for the survival of Poland's culture. The Iron Chancellor, however, did permit a Polish man to marry a German woman because, for the identical reason, the child would grow up German. This admittedly racist reasoning emphasizes the fact that women play a far more significant role in a resistance based on culture than in a resistance based on an ideology. No resistance movement owes more to women than the Polish defense of their intangibles.

Women provided the shelter for conspiratorial activity. For example, in Warsaw in 1880, there was a boarding school for "high-born ladies." The Polish women teachers kept the revolutionary literature, and sometimes even their authors, in their rooms because the Russian rulers of Warsaw would hardly suspect that a school for the "high-born" would serve as a nerve center for revolutionary activities.

In most cases, women assumed the organizational continuity of resistance groups, especially when the men had to flee or were arrested. The women continued their work until the organization could be reconstituted. Women were the activists. They participated in strikes and demonstrations and acted as fighting partisans. The first modern woman poet leading a partisan group in 1863 was Emilia Plater, who was eventually executed by the Russian authorities.

The culture of Poland was and is its lifeblood; the Polish resistance movement evolved from being the "shield of Christendom" to becoming the defender of the Polish Catholic culture. In Poland the two cannot be separated, despite the fact that Polish culture was clearly secular and attracted and included hundreds of thousands of non-Catholics.

The Catholicism of the resistance was not the Catholicism of the Roman Curia, or the papacy, or the high clergy. Today, when the countries of South America are clamoring for social justice, the lower clergy, nuns, and religious orders are in the forefront of that struggle, while the Roman Curia and the prelates more frequently than not side with the oppressors. This phenomenon, so headline-making in our times, was not an uncommon occurrence in Polish Catholicism.

The open, tolerant Polish Catholicism of the fifteenth and sixteenth centuries was destroyed by the Jesuits, yet the foundations of Catholicism, laid down in earlier ages, and the devotion of a number of great theologians and church leaders kept this other stream of Catholicism alive—but just barely. Some among the lower clergy and a few bishops were truly dedicated to ministering to the needs of "their flock." The overwhelming majority of the clergy, however, gave its loyalty to those in power and to those who could fill their pockets.

It is the usual historical experience that power either destroys ethics or forces then underground. The Catholic power in Poland forced ethical Catholicism underground, and during the period from 1918 to 1939, Poland's Catholic church was in the very forefront of all that was despicable, racist, and antisocial. This is, however, part of the larger tragedy of the Catholic church in our century, a tragedy recognized by Pope John XXIII, who once again set the Church of Rome in the direction of Catholic humanism. And this task is being continued by the "Polish pope," John Paul II.

It should be emphasized, however, that despite the indefensible position of the church as an institution during the Nazi occupation of Poland, an essential Catholic humanism did survive. Cardinal Sapieha of Krakow saved hundreds of Jews; as did the Ursulan Sisters, who gave shelter to Jewish children; as did many parish priests, who helped in any way they could in full knowledge that if they were caught they would be executed.

Despite the overwhelming Catholicism of Poland's culture, its secular strands were also vigorous. Its sources were in the secular thought that began to burgeon in Europe in the fourteenth century. And it was Copernicus who, in the sixteenth century, successfully challenged the theologians by proving that not the earth but the sun is the center of our universe. Subsequently, the European Enlightenment and the emergence of freemasonry gave a powerful impetus to Poland's secular thought. The masons were traditionally organized into lodges; Lodge Grand Est and the Illuminati, a group of masons, had and continue to have a powerful influence on Poland's political thought. It is a little-known fact that the masons of the nineteenth century created the conditions for the emergence of Poland's socialism, financed it, and nursed it to its maturity. Although the Polish masons never denied their Catholicism, they were freethinkers, liberal, and very supportive of the arts and sciences.

Yet Polish Catholicism, with all of its drawbacks and its brilliant flashes of ethical strength, is the constant of Poland's culture and the core around which it grew into its multifaceted, flawed maturity.

This Catholicism, which generally operated on the principle of rendering unto Caesar what is Caesar's regardless of who that Caesar might be, and rendering unto God what is God's no matter who says what that should be and how it is to be collected, hindered the work of the resistance. Thus, a dialectical relationship developed between the resistance movement and Catholicism. They influenced each other, they shared values, but they generally respected each other's independent polarities. In social terms, these polarities are represented on one side by the multitude of Polish peasants who accept the dictates of the church without question and at times with blind obedience, and on the other by the intelligentsia, the main force of the resistance. The intelligentisia genuflects obediently on Sunday, but does what it has to the rest of the week. Only since the ascendency of Pope John Paul II has the Polish intelligentsia begun to take its faith more seriously. That is because its church is beginning to take Poland seriously. This is a very novel phenomenon.

The Polish intelligentsia is not a homogenous group. Its membership originated in all of the ethnic groups inhabiting the multinational territories of the Polish Kingdom. The largest single component of the intelligentsia, however, consisted of the descendants of the gentry class, identified by the Polish label *szlachta*. It needs to be noted that the *szlachta* cannot be compared either to the English gentry or to western European aristocracy. The closest comparison can be made with the Spanish *hidalgo*, with whom the *szlachta* shared an exaggerated notion of honor, a very formal devotion to Catholicism, an aversion to work, a distaste for the trades, and an abhorence to any form of manual labor. During the first half of the nineteenth century, economically the *szlachta* were peasants with social aspirations and a coat of arms of some sort.

In fact, the Polish intelligentsia was stimulated into being by bright young people who wanted to escape the pretentious obscurantism of their monotonous, melancholy existence fed by fabricated dreams of past glory. The reality of a smelly peasant hut with a cavalry sword hanging on a wall as a memento of a forebear's participation in the siege of Muscovy, the defeat of the Swedes, or the defense of Vienna was not enough to sustain the imagination and fulfill the ambitions of a young man who saw a new world emerging all around him.

The ethnic Polish members of the intelligentsia became intellectuals engagé because they rejected the slovenliness of the *szlachta*, with its swashbuckling tales used as a rationalization for a reckless life in a cocoon of indolence.

It was the tragic political and social history of Poland that became the causal factor for a transformation of a small but significant number of Poles into an intelligentsia.

As the influence of that small group grew, as its economic well-being improved and its social standing rose, the number of sons and daughters of the *szlachta* who began to emulate the intelligentsia also increased. Consequently, toward the end of the nineteenth century and during the first decades of the twentieth century, more and more descendants of the *szlachta* infiltrated the ranks of the intelligentsia without really becoming members of it. Most of the newcomers acquired eclectic knowledge, modes of behavior, and mannerisms that gave them the outward appearance of being part of the intelligentsia. They frequented the coffee houses and restaurants of the intelligentsia and made sure to develop ties of friendship. They also managed marginally to be of service to the real intelligentsia. The numbers of the pseudointelligentsia grew so fast that in time it appeared that the intelligentsia of Poland was a continuation of the noble *szlachta* tradition.

This is one example of legends of convenience invented by social losers. After 1918, when Poland became independent, the descendants of the *szlachta* who got into power proved themselves to be incapable and inept at ruling a state. In order, however, to maintain their social and political prestige, they reified the legend of their ancestors' contributions by imposing on schoolchildren and grownups with a mediocre education a view of Poland's history that revealed the "*szlachta*'s grandeur" and made their descendants the guardians of it in Poland's moment of independence.

This use of a legend, which was neither accepted nor generally supported by either the intelligentsia or the professionals (most of whom also came from gentry families), served the convenience of ambitious leaders who wanted Poland to become a power on the Nazi model. People such as Roman Dmowski, the leader of the National Democrats who demanded racial purity even before that became a Nazi slogan, and Adam Koc, who in the mid-1930s unleashed a propaganda offensive of pure Polishness, pure Catholicism, and unabashed anti-Semitism, availed themselves of this legend of Poland's history. It is to the credit of Poland that neither Dmowski nor Koc ever became its leaders. But the work they did not only damaged the cause of Poland in the eyes of many liberal and democratic Westerners, but also damaged the historical perceptions of Poland's largely uneducated masses, who swallowed uncritically the propaganda line of the "mighty Poland," the "pure Aryan Poland."

The intelligentsia was and is a cohesive group of freedom fighters who consciously, actively, and persistently oppose, through the use of their talents and the power of their intellect, any form of oppression. Although members of the intelligentsia created in the past and continue to create today various ideologies, if they become uncritical slaves of these ideologies they cease to be an intelligentsia. They become ideologues, propagandists, apologists. Having given up their critical perceptions, they are no longer thinkers, because a thinker by definition cannot accept any form of repression. Nonthinkers cannot be members of the intelligentsia—they may wear imperial clothes, but they are not emperors. Unfortunately, the term *intelligentsia* has become an umbrella concept that includes the best and brightest as well as the worst and most nefarious.

The other most important ethnic group comprising the Polish intelligentsia descended from assimilated Polish Jews who lived in Polish territory since the fourteenth century, from Jews who migrated into Poland from Prussia late in the eighteenth century, and from Jews who converted to Protestantism. The Jews who came to Poland from Russia late in the nineteenth century were also an intelligentsia, but this was not a "Polish intelligentsia." It was at times affiliated with it, and shared a lot of its values, but it was primarily interested in the fate of the Jews and of Russia. This Jewish intelligentsia emerged as a very significant factor in eastern European history. The two intelligentsias supported each other, were allied in common struggles, and frequently defended and sheltered each other's members. The two groups maintained social and personal ties until the early decades of our century.

The Jewish intelligentsia of eastern Europe, of Russian and Lithuanian origin, universalized itself after a Russian Revolution of 1917 through assimilation and emigration. Most of its members perished. Some survived and moved to Israel, where the intelligentsia is declining for the same reasons the Polish intelligentsia of the 1930s declined: it serves uncritically a virulent nationalism.

The emotional bond that gave Polish intellectuals the cohesiveness of a group deserving a common identity was patriotism. In an occupied country, patriotism is an official crime. Poland was occupied, thus forcing many of the intellectuals who wanted to continue to function as patriots to escape the tightly woven ring of the Russian, German, and Austrian police forces and their ubiquitous spies. In order to express their love for their fatherland and to actively fight against its occupiers, many members of the Polish intelligentsia joined the armies of the enemies of their enemies. Toward the end of the eighteenth century, the greatest foes of the powers that occupied Poland were the French and their unfortunate symbol of "liberty, fraternity, and equality"—Napoleon. The young Poles flocked to France and Napoleon's army. The Polish intelligentsia, wearing the splendid uniforms of the Imperial Army, became French in culture, life-style, and political knowledge. The great anomaly of the Polish intelligentsia was, and to a degree continues to be, the fact that many of its members gained their status in emigration, and there is a lot of justification in the claim that the "roots" of the Polish intelligentsia are in France.

The social origins of the Polish intelligentsia—its peregrinations, heroism, and romanticism—are a fascinating story but do not suffice as an explanation of its towering influence in the history of that country. After all in 1945 there were less than two thousand people in

Poland with higher academic degrees and the intelligentsia as a group was close to total annihilation by the Germans and the Soviets. Yet today its ranks have been replenished and augmented by sons and daughters of peasants, workers, and professionals. But their behavior, values, and mode of expression are not visibly or in content different from those who preceded them. There is an undeniable continuity of the history of that group. The basic explanation for this phenomenon, without references to the mystique of blood or race, is that, like the intelligentsia of the nineteenth century, the contemporary Polish intelligentsia was also born of resistance directed against very similar oppressors.

Resistance is activated and maintained by rebellious perceptions of conditions prevailing in a society. These perceptions are created and communicated by artists, writers, academicians, musicians, poets, and journalists. It matters little whether they bring out the "actual truth" or the "deeper truth" of "the truth" that is either implicit in any situation or hidden by the concreteness of that situation. Instead, what matters is the implementation of the social good whose absence caused this rebellious perception to emerge.

Thus, the Polish intelligentsia, motivated by patriotism and a total commitment to freedom from oppression, began to produce poetry, theatrical plays, learned treatises, political manifestos and proclamations, and superb journalism. They did it in the nineteenth century under the Russians, Germans, and Austrians; they did it in the twentieth century under the Nazis and the Soviets; and they are doing it now under a communist regime, which in their rebellious perception has no national roots.

The unity of the highly diversified Polish intelligentsia is its creativity. The only unity of creativity is creativity itself. The images drawn by it, the techniques it employs, and the themes it chooses are as varied as is the imagination that spurs the creativity. Creativity has to contain a universal ethic. Unethical creativity is a contradiction in terms.

Poland's intelligentsia in all of its manifold expressions is preciously aware, as was its great Russian counterpart, of the universal ethic that is contained by the universality of humanity itself. Ethics such as humanism are indivisible and always fundamentally theological, even if their essential expression is always secular. In the case of Poland it makes no sense to talk about humanism without a theological component, regardless of the personal, conscious intention of the artist or writer.

THE REALITY

The Copernican revolution of 1543, as the heliocentric theory of our universe is referred to, is one of the milestones by which historians measure the beginning of modernity. By then the Polish Kingdom was already known as the Confederation of the Kingdom of Poland and the Grand Duchy of Lithuania. The confederation came as a result of the 1386 marriage of Queen Jadwiga of Poland to Grand Duke Wladyslaw Jagiello of Lithuania. This matrimonial union provided Poland with its strongest royal dynasty—the Jagiellonian kings, who ruled the Commonwealth* until 1572.

The rule of the Jagiellonians, despite the many wars, is referred to as the golden age of Polish history. Thus it could have been expected that the Polish Kingdom, having reached the gates of modernity in equal or better shape than France or Germany or even England, could perform well in the race with the other great powers.

In terms of territory, Poland was the largest kingdom in Europe. It had social stability, a generally competent administration, sagacious and usually prudent kings, and a well-defined succession procedure. Poland's industry was on a par with all of continental industry, and the Polish peasants were relatively free compared to those of France and Germany. Poland's agricultural production was abundant and Poland was among Europe's leading exporters. The cultural life of the kingdom was exciting and comparatively unencumbered by the heavy hand of Vatican-imposed strictures and barren religious debates. Poland was in the mainstream of Europe's intellectual efforts and was a significant contributor.

There were fissures in Poland's society that could be called "nationality problems." The Federated Kingdom consisted of, in addition to the ethnic Polish population, Prussians, Lithuanians, Livonians, By-

---

*Hereafter Poland will be identified either as the Polish Kingdom, or the Federated Kingdom, or the Commonwealth, since all three designations are equally valid.

elorussians, and a large, amorphous group of people known as Ukrainians. On its southern border, the Polish Kingdom included at one time or another Slovaks, Valachians, and Moldavians (now known as Rumanians). Although there are no population statistics available for the fifteenth and sixteenth centuries, it is quite possible that the Poles were in fact a minority in their own kingdom.

It is, however, an undisputable fact that Poland's culture dominated the Federated Kingdom, which reached from the Baltic Sea in the north to the Black Sea in the southeast and from about the Dniester to the Oder rivers in the east and the west respectively. It is characteristic of Poland's culture that it was and remains rigid and incapable of either assimilating or accommodating other cultures. The culture of Poland knows how to dominate but not how to accommodate. There are two plausible explanations for this phenomenon: first, Poland's nationalistic, messianic Catholicism; second, the Polish government used and continues to use its culture as a means for dominating and controlling its own people and the nationalities living within its borders. The political cohesiveness of the multinational kingdom was based on using Poles in all responsible leadership positions. These administrators frequently had neither sympathy nor an understanding of the people for whom they were responsible; neither did they respect these people's cultures, primitive though they may have appeared to be.

Polish was, next to Latin, the official language. At universities and all the way down to local schools two subjects were taught: Catholicism and Polishness—and frequently it was difficult to distinguish between them.

A dominant culture that cannot integrate even a weak native culture causes that culture to become a focus of resistance, a resistance that quickly moves from purely cultural-artistic expressions to political action. A specific example is that of the Ukrainians. The label "Ukraine" was given to the land occupied by a diversity of peoples living beyond the borders of the principality of Muscovy (later the Russian Empire) and outside the borders of the Ottoman Empire but vaguely within the boundaries of the Polish Kingdom. The culture of these people, who moved into that sparsely populated land because they loved their freedom, was a mixture of Greek Orthodoxy, Ottoman styles, Polish mannerisms, and a memory of a proud heritage left to them by the Byzantine Empire. Their language sounded like a mixture of Polish and Russian, but they wrote wih the Cyrillic alphabet—a legacy of their conversion to Greek Orthodoxy by the Byzantine church.

The dominant Polish culture and the Roman Catholicism of Poland refused to accept the vitality of the Ukrainian culture, even when some of the Ukrainians became Uniates, that is, Greek Orthodox who accepted the primacy of the pope of Rome. From about the fifteenth century on, the Polish leadership and the large Polish landowners attempted to curb the Ukrainian culture, control it, and if possible eradicate it—even in such great centers of Ukrainian faith and culture as the ancient city of Kiev, the cultural capital of the Ukraine.

The consequences of this policy were predictable. The Ukrainians resisted, and at a crucial stage of the ongoing, endemic struggle between Poland and the principality of Muscovy, the Ukrainians joined the latter, not simply because it was Greek Orthodox, but because it fought Poland. The Russian Empire grew into a European power by being able to assimilate to a degree the Ukrainians by promising to respect their culture. The promise was never kept, but at the time it had the desired effect.

It should be noted that, when Poland had a moment of independence in the years from 1918 to 1939, the Polish government resumed this policy of cultural domination and ruthlessly proceeded to move against the Ukrainians who happened to live within the boundaries of the republic. The Ukrainians responded as they had three centuries earlier—they butchered Poles at every opportunity during the Nazi occupation of that part of Poland.

The custom of using only Poles in top administrative posts in the capital and the provinces had the effect of creating powerful satrapies, which obeyed the central authority of the king only if that king was powerful and victorious in battle. The kings, on the other hand, began to include non-Polish magnates (landowners) and competent officers within the Polish elite hoping to buy their loyalty with which to counterbalance the questionable support of the "real Poles." That was, for example, how the Radziwils prospered.* The "converted" Poles, of course, like most converts, were initially more zealous in Polonizing their provinces than the Polish administrators.

The accepted method of rewarding successful commanders in victorious wars was to give them land. Poland's unwarranted and unnecessary expansion eastward, at the expense of a nearly total neglect of the kingdom's western borders, created landed magnates who could and did challenge the king's authority, repress the local peasants, and assume all the trappings of the arrogance of power, includ-

---

*The Radziwil family belonged to the Lithuanian aristocracy, which became thoroughly Polonized and passed for the aristocracy in Poland.

ing the conduct of foreign affairs, to suit their own seemingly insatiable appetites. They also quickly learned that, if they acted in concert, they could render all central authority impotent.

What occurred in Poland was the opposite of the events that transformed France and England into powerful kingdoms, whereby the kings, helped by loyal crown councils, broke the independence of dukes and barons long accustomed to ruling their provinces with a free hand. In Poland, the magnates and their cohorts—sycophants and dependents—helped destroy a flourishing kingdom. Within less than a century (the seventeenth), Poland lost its position of equality with the other great states on the road to modernization and industrialization. It became a bloated giant without muscle or direction.

No single cause, however, can bring a kingdom to its knees so quickly. There was a confluence of events that contributed to Poland's descent from dominance to submission, from independence to centuries of occupation.

The overriding events that shaped the destiny of Europe, and thus of Poland, were the discovery of America and the breakdown of the unity of Christendom. The discovery of America and the general expansion of the concept "world" caused a shift in the trade routes from the Mediterranean and the Black Sea to the ports of western Europe. Poland, which was astride the arterial highways for the north-south trade of Europe, found itself in the backwaters of mercantile and industrial development, where it has remained.

Since people make history, history flows toward the centers of vitality. Poland ceased to be a center, but the Polish people could not see that and, if they saw it, refused to accept it as fact. This is not unusual. The identical phenomenon is now facing Western civilization, whose leaders refuse to accept the fact that history is denying them supremacy. In the defense of that supremacy, the artless political hacks, who persist in believing they still have it, are willing to destroy the world.

When these periodic shifts of the epicenters of history occur, they are reflected in the structures of the universalisms that evolved when they were in fact the epicenters. The shocks caused by these shifts span centuries and bury more people than the most powerful earthquakes.

In Europe, the shift of the center of civilization from the Mediterranean to the shores of the Atlantic broke up Catholic unity, or more precisely the unity of the value structures identified as Roman Catholicism.

This breakup of Catholic unity, accompanied as it was by the emergence of a militant Prussia and a powerful England caused the Vatican to charge the Hapsburg Empire to be the executor of the policies of intolerance. The Roman Curia created a prototype "moral majority." The Jesuits, who descended upon Poland like a black tidal wave, were "the soldiers of Christ" executing the orders of the Vatican.* Since the last decades of the sixteenth century, they have fostered obscurantism and intolerance. They curtailed the freedom of the universities and destroyed the humanistic Catholicism that had flourished in Poland. By siding with the magnates and the *szlachta*, the Jesuits created all possible obstacles to the formation of a middle class. The Jesuits also played leading roles in formulating policies and bear the brunt of the responsibility for massive, pernicious anti-Semitism. They laid the foundations for its continuous growth. They taught the lower clergy, who in turn were ready to support any measure aimed at the "murderers of Christ." They supported any repressive policy dictated by the Vatican and never in the history of their institution—until Pope John XXIII—did they protest any repressive measures that were not officially condemned by the Vatican. The Vatican officially condemned only Soviet Russia.

The underlying, internal political cause for the collapse of the Polish Kingdom showed the world a tragedy whose implications are only now receiving their due attention and are at the brink of being understood. The tragedy is that democracy, or even an honest attempt at democracy, can provide a rudimentary political system only if the process of socialization and the methods of wealth distribution stimulate the masses of people of perform the basic acts of political responsibility required for the functioning of that system. In the absence of an equalizing wealth-distribution system, and with the corresponding absence of a political value structure conducive to democratization, democracy remains an empty theory and the language of democracy becomes the tool of demagogues, tyrants, and robbers in costumes of officialdom.

This fact became obvious when the orderly transfer of political power within the Polish Kingdom broke down, and with it the methods of sharing wealth eroded. After the death of the last of the dynastic kings in Poland in the middle of the sixteenth century, the position of Polish king became elective. Upon the death of a king, all the electors of Poland, meaning all eligible voters, would gather in a Coronation Congress and elect a new king. In Poland, any landowner

---

* Obviously this kind of generalisation is not applicable to all individual members of the Jesuit order, only to the order itself.

with some miniscule claim to gentry origins was deemed to be eligible to vote. Thus, as was noted in the previous chapter, the Polish Kingdom had about eight hundred thousand voters and statistically qualified as a democracy. These statistics were transformed into a legend that Poland was a "gentry democracy." In fact, the electors were a rabble-rousing, ignorant, drunken mass who used the Coronation Congresses as one huge party time, with the alcohol and the entertainment provided by the magnates and the various pretenders to the throne who would eventually tell them how to vote. There is no record as to how many of that motley crowd ever did really vote—or knew who they were voting for. In addition to this already unruly procedure, the Congress operated under a law of unanimity. This meant that, if any one of the electors present were to object to a law or a provision that was to be signed by the new king, the measure would be defeated. This law carried the noble classification of "liberum veto" (the objection of a free man freely expressed, presumably after a soul- and consciousness-searing reflection). Yet any of the drunkards stumbling about the grounds of the Congress could be, and usually was, paid by one of the magnates who did not like a given candidate for the position of king to cast his "liberum veto."

The Polish kings were in fact "presidents for life." In order to be elected, the various pretenders to the Polish throne would compete with each other in the scope of concessions they would grant the magnates and the gentry. The competition was so fierce that no pretender could really establish the foundations for a strong centralized authority and still hope to be elected. The results were inevitable. Poland did not have the kind of effective government needed to govern a state in the process of transition from an overwhelmingly agrarian to a mixed merchant-industrial economy of the kind that formed the backbone of other European states. Thus, towns declined, industry stagnated, taxes were not collected, the currency was debased, and the armed forces sank into ineptitude. The combination of all of these factors precluded the emergence of a healthy, energetic, native Polish bourgeoisie. Eventually, both trade and industry fell into foreign hands.

Moreover, every elected king had his own notion of grandeur, which he brought with him from the royal court in which he was brought up. Thus, when in 1572 the Poles elected Sigismund III of the Swedish royal family Vasa, known in Poland as "the Jesuit king," he began to dream of uniting Poland with Sweden—a Catholic kingdom with a Protestant kingdom, which he probably hoped to convert. The consequence of that political nightmare was to embroil Poland in a series of wars with Sweden that hastened the devastation of Poland, but gave rise to a magnificent legend.

One of the few smidgens of Polish territory that was not conquered by the Swedes was the cloister of Jasna Gora and the area around it, which includes the town of Czestochowa. The cloister was well fortified and like all cloisters had a chapel decorated with a painting of the Virgin Mary. Since the Virgin Mary was the Queen of Poland, the valiant defenders of the cloister used to carry the painting along the parapets of the fortress, which was besieged by the Swedes. The Virgin Mary was the last hope for victory. In the course of battle and various fires, smoke blackened the image of the Virgin and She became known as the "Black Virgin of Czestochowa."

The Swedish armies, whose supply lines were overextended and whose troops were tired from decades of fighting, sustained a defeat in Czestochowa and as suddenly as they inundated Poland they also left. The facts are not important. The people believed that the Black Madonna of Czestochowa miraculously saved Poland. She became the most revered and holy of the symbols of Poland's patriotism. To this day no political system governing Poland can even attempt to erode the power of that legend and no Polish resistance movement can hope to gain popularity without invoking Her image.

The dreary succession of mediocrities occupying the Polish throne and the descent of Poland into anarchy was occasionally interrupted by attempts of intelligent kings such as Jan III Sobieski and Stanislaw August Poniatowski, the last king of Poland, who, though ridiculed for his love affair with Catherine the Great, did lay the foundations for the Constitution of the third of May. He was helped in his endeavors by the great families of Poland—the Zamoyskis and the Czartoryskis—as well, of course, as his own, the Poniatowskis. Stanislaw August abdicated the throne of Poland on November 25, 1795, and not until November 11, 1918, was Poland to have her own ruler again.

Except for the biblical towns of Sodom and Gomorrah, there are at least ten just men to be found in every historical period of every nation. Poland had more than its share of dedicated humanists, realists, and fundamentally just people. They analyzed, diagnosed, counseled, acted, and failed. Yet in politics failure is not synonymous with a lack of success; neither is disaster totally devoid of positive effects.

The fact that Poland's kings were elected from among the ruling houses of Europe and brought with them their own artists, architects, writers, and "people of culture" meant that those among the Polish magnates and burgeoning intellectuals who were so inclined could be exposed to the culture—both political and artistic—of Europe's most advanced societies. Thus the forces of Europe's Enlightenment engulfed Poland with an astonishing rapidity, partially explained by the fact that French became the lingua franca of educated, aristocratic Europe and of Poland. Simultaneously, the Jesuits lost their great power and their monopolistic hold on Poland's educational and cultural life.

The revival of Poland's culture and the foundation for Poland's resistance in the long ordeal of subjugation was laid down by the Commission for National Education in 1773. This commission was the first European protoministry of education. Its work was financed by the proceeds from the sale of properties held by the Jesuit order. The primary object of the commission's work was to secularize education, save the Polish language, and reverse the all-encompassing illiteracy. The commission also wanted to introduce studies that were needed in a state desirous of improving its level of economic productivity.

The commission could not save Poland's independence, but it created a center, a hearth. It attracted a group of people who knew what was needed, who knew each other, and who helped form this uniquely diverse yet cohesive group, which was later to be identified as the Polish intelligentsia.

As part of the ambiance created by the commission and as a direct consequence of Europe's Enlightenment and of the French Revolution, Poland's political thought woke from the lethargy induced by the slovenly anarchy of centuries past. Statesmen, theoreticians, and thinkers representing all the sound elements of Poland's political, professional, and intellectual elite joined in a massive debate, which resulted in a dramatic acceptance of Poland's famous Constitution of the third of May, 1791. It was passed by a Congress whose procedures voided the "liberum veto."

The Constitution envisaged Poland as a liberal constitutional monarchy. It laid down the principles of democracy under the rule of law. Although this basic document had its flaws, it would have served with the same distinction as the United States Constitution, whose philosophical assumptions were shared by the framers of the Polish document. Unfortunately, the Constitution remained a magnificent silent document. Poland ceased to be independent before the Constitution could have the chance to start the work of rebuilding the nation on a new model.

The loss of national independence to the Russians, Prussians, and Austrians caused thousands of Poles to emigrate to revolutionary France, and their numbers were continuously swelled by refugees who actively opposed the repression of their fatherland. This emigration was qualitatively, sociologically, different from the massive emigration of Polish peasants to northern France, Belgium, and the United States. The overwhelming number of those Poles who settled in Paris, or Switzerland, were representative of the intellectual groups and the enlightened gentry. The other, much more numerous, emigration was a function of the poverty and hunger that were so much a part of the daily existence of the majority of Poles.

Most of the political history of Poland throughout the nineteenth and the early twentieth century is based on comprehending the fact that the theories for saving Poland dreamed up by the emigrés seldom, if ever, corresponded to the needs and expectations of the Poles who stayed at home.

How people live under occupation—the horrors, the outrages to human dignity—need not be retold in our century. Many Poles experienced all of them; but that does not mean that the majority of Poles suffered. Many of the magnates were welcomed at the courts of the kings and emperors whose troops occupied Poland. Many other Poles made brilliant political and professional careers in the service of the occupiers, and quite a few amassed great fortunes. Among them there were many who had no use for an independent Poland, especially among those who lived under the more tolerant Austrian occupation.

In most accounts of Poland's history it has become fashionable and commonplace to refer to Polish nationalism, patriotism, and the Poles' readiness to sacrifice their lives for their beloved fatherland. All of this is true for a relatively small group of Poles.

The Polish peasants did not care who ruled Poland as long as they were secure in the ownership of their land. In fact, in most of Poland's resistance movements the majority of the peasants either did not participate or sided with the occupying powers. The last really effective peasant participation in an insurrecton occurred in 1794 under the leadership of Kosciuszko, who promised them land. The church never cried out against injustices perpetrated by the occupiers and it actually sided with the occupiers. Thus the peasant population and other devout Polish Catholics saw no moral imperative to act. (Certainly there were quite a few courageous priests who fought and protested and helped the resisters but their total number was insignificant in comparison to the total number of clergy in Poland—over ten thousand.)

Poland's great nationalism was primarily the product of the emigrés, among whom the intellectuals and artists played the leading role. Poland's drive for independence was nurtured in emigration, financed from it, and truly supported within Poland mainly by artists, all of Poland's major poets, some artisans, and eventually part of the proletariat.

The awkward historical truth is that the Polish people did not win their independence but inherited it from a unique historical drama in which the occupiers of Poland killed each other. Austria and Germany lost World War I (1918), and Russia became the Soviet Union, which under the leadership of Lenin proclaimed the right of each nation to self-determination.* Lenin's pronouncement found its echo in Wilson's famous Fourteen Points. In the United States president's direct reference to Lenin's nationality policy, stated in testimony to the Senate Foreign Relations Committee, one could find the main reason for Wilson's determined support for Poland's independence.

Thus, at the conclusion of World War I, sometime in November 1918 a suddenly independent Poland was ruled by a "Regency Council," which debated whether to offer the crown of Poland to one of the Hapsburgs. The council really did not know what to do because, as one of its august members said, "Gentlemen, independence exploded among us; what do we do with it?" Eventually, under the pressure of the intelligentsia and the well-organized Polish Socialist party, assisted by various military groups generally referred to as the Legionnaires, Poland emerged as a democratic republic—with every intention of making democracy work. The Poles elected their first president, who was promptly assassinated by a fanatic Polish nationalist.

An emerging nation is not a collection of dreary statistics showing low productivity, unemployment, ignorance, and a lack of well-defined social and political priorities. An emerging nation is primarily a group of people in search of a new value structure that would help them overcome those aspects of the past that kept them in a state of "underdevelopment." That was precisely the case in Poland. Although it was also economically an emerging nation, it was primarily a nation in search of a new consciousness, of a new national ethic, of a new understanding of what it meant to be a Pole. This type

---

* As in many other instances, Lenin took credit for the theoretical works of others. The Russian revolutionary postulate for Poland's independence was actually promulgated by the Menshevik faction of the Russian Social-Democracy. Lenin, in fact, was planning a Soviet government that was to rule an "independent" Soviet Poland.

of a search can be conducted only under close to ideal economic and political conditions, and since those are very rarely present, the search usually ends by abandoning the notion of democracy, installing a strong man as leader, and hoping that he will create the conditions under which the dialogue can continue. A strong man does not have time for dialogue. He is motivated by pragmatism, which in some instances dictates tolerance and mandates an educational process in the art of being a good citizen, but in other instances decrees just the opposite manner of governing. Poland's strong man wanted to be the father of a democratic republic, but forces beyond his control made him into the builder of a militaristic state. The debate on national values eventually degenerated into nationalistic jingoism, which glamorized the values of the "gentry democracy," of power posturing, of insolence, and of intolerance.

As a result, Poland participated with Nazi Germany in the final dismemberment of Czechoslovakia in 1938 and, in view of the obvious acceptance of Hitler by the Western powers, especially France, Poland also fundamentally altered its foreign policy to being pro-German. Within one year, however, Poland became the object of Hitler's propaganda and was the first nation to oppose Hitlerism with her limited arms. By fall 1939 Poland ceased to exist as an independent country. The other two emerging nations' military strong men—Hitler and Stalin—while hating each other, decided that the dismemberment of Poland was worthy of a joint venture. The Poles fought valiantly, and when they lost, they did what they were best at—resisting. The essence of resistance in action is to break the laws of the occupiers; the anarchic past of the Poles stood them in good stead. Anarchism again became equal to patriotism. But the fact that, during the short span of independence, the Poles did not develop a new value structure divided even the resistance forces. The socialists, communists, and social democrats generally formed the minority wing of the resistance, and the nationalists the majority element. In Poland one wing of the resistance killed members of the other, the nationalists committing the vilest of crimes.** They shot other patriots. Eventually they too were shot, but that was the consequence of one more of the cards of irony history dealt to Poland, or more precisely, one more card of irony the Poles drew from the deck.

May 8, 1945, was liberation day for millions all over Europe. The Third Reich surrendered unconditionally. But for Poland and its

---

** This ultra-nationalist group, known as the NSZ (National Armed Forces), was composed of all the pre-1939 fascist organizations in Poland. In 1944 the National Armed Forces split in two. One group joined the Home Army (AK) while the other elected to retreat to Germany with the German army.

people it was the beginning of a new march underground, which was completed in 1948 when Stalinism took over the government of Poland and reduced that country to a total dependency on the Soviet Union. Yet the Poles, or rather the new Polish intelligentsia that was being formed to replace those the Nazis and the Soviets had eliminated, began a debate on a "national value structure." This discourse had to go on covertly because Polish secret police agents totally loyal (for good pay and good food) to the Polish United Workers party—the official name of the ruling Communist party—were all over the country. The debate was an agonizing reappraisal of Poland's history, of the values that brought Poland to the brink of annihilation, not only as a country but as a people.

The new intelligentsia had to reject three cherished legends: the notion of the "gentry democracy," the delusion of being a power, and the illusion that the Western democracies really cared about the fate of Poland. The intellectuals, most of whom were about twenty years old and had survived the war either as resistance fighters or as kids with "street smarts" who knew how to evade cops and break laws without getting caught, included in their budding rebellious perceptions a great respect for the realities of Poland's position.

They opted for a program of a gradual decrease from subserviency to the dictates of the Kremlin and simultaneously began to form a "Polish road to socialism." Their molelike work paid off in 1956 when they were strong enough to oppose the Soviet regime, which at that time was internally weakened by the "de-Stalinization" campaign. The intellectuals who were in the forefront of the events in Poland now identified as the "Spring in October" (because the events took place in October), pushed only as far as they knew their forces could reach. The "Spring in October" was mostly a discourse; there was a minimum of violence. The basic tenets of Soviet socialism were respected, i.e., the dictatorship of the party, but they were modified in the name of Poland's nationalism. This nationalism was defined in terms of the needs of the workers, peasants, and intellectuals. It was a liberalization program for the benefit of strengthening a classless society.

The thunder and lightning of Poland's history came from the church and especially from one intransigent Polish patriot, the prince primate of Poland, Stefan Cardinal Wyszynski (who died in 1980). He was the enemy the Soviets feared most. He commanded the legions of Poland's peasants. Wyszynski did attack verbally, but he and the Polish episcopate were also realists opting for small gains, such as more Catholic schools, more new churches, more freedom for the clergy. In 1956 there were no clear victors and no real losers. The outward appearance of being solid members of the Soviet bloc countries was respected.

The consequence of 1956 was the continuation of the discourse on the Polish road to socialism and what it was supposed to mean. But the economy continued to be mismanaged; the ministers and directors responsible for industry and commerce were party hacks equal in ineptitude to those whom the "Spring in October" chased out. To defend themselves these officials had to find a scapegoat. They did. The Communist party of Poland, whose genealogy contains a great number of Jews, unleashed a wave of anti-Semitism in 1968.

The Jews who survived Hitler, the Jews who sacrificed their all, who were epigones of the Communist leadership decimated by Stalin in the great purge trials of 1938, were being accused of being agents of something called international Zionism, of capitalism, of the CIA, etc., ad nauseam. The government-sponsored anti-Semitic campaign found strong echoes among the survivors of pre-1939 Poland, but found no, or only infinitesimal, support among the intelligentsia, most of whose members really did not know what a Jew looked like.

The anti-Semitic campaign of 1968 ended in the collapse of the government that started it. It seems the elimination of a few thousand Jews through exile did not change the economic mismanagement. The discourse continued, then opened again in 1970, and is now culminating in the confrontation between the independent labor union Solidarity and the Polish government, which represents the Communist party.

For the first time in Poland's history since the promulgation of the Constitution of the third of May, Poland has a front of national unity. The Roman Catholic clergy, now acting under orders of a Polish pope, has learned that it has to be involved ethically and morally, yet realistically, in the political and economic existence of its most ardent parishioners. The clergy, from the very top of the hierarchy to the lowliest parish priest, has decided to play the role of counselor, guide, and peacemaker speaking the language of humanism.

The leadership of the majority of the Solidarity membership is fully aware of the political realities with which they have to exist, yet they are unable to control those among them who are still motivated by the romantic anarchism of Poland's past. There are still many Poles within Solidarity and outside of it who think and truly believe that their nation is capable of producing miracles simply because they wish them to happen. In combination they will eventually shatter this very tenuous attempt at cooperation between Solidarity, the government, and the church. In order to avert that inevitable tragedy, John Paul II announced that in the spring of 1982 he will visit Poland again. He hopes that this will restrain the "maximalists" of the current movement for democratization. Unfortunately, the pope—as a Pole and as a pope—believes in miracles. Solidarity will lose, but the Polish nation will gain a new sense of the meaning of being Polish and thus will have won a significant victory, whose fruits will become visible the next time the Poles move again into open resistance. That there will be a next time is beyond any doubt.

This currently emerging front of national unity did not spring up from barren soil; nothing in history ever does. Its antecedents are among the young men and disproportionately large number of young women of the late nineteenth century. They starved and studied; they were imprisoned and wrote revolutionary tracts; they were spied upon, molested, denounced; yet they published the most successful underground press. They had few allies and no money, but they procured arms and made themselves heard. They died when they decided that dying was the only way to prove that Poland remains alive and precious.

It was among those Poles that the great debate on the relationship between national independence and social justice first emerged to grow into the most pressing and potentially explosive question of our time. To put the problem in its most extreme formulation one has to find the answer to the question: Should a nation fight for independence knowing that it will be ruled by its own ruthless tyrant, or a collection of mafia-type thugs, or should the people of the nation first struggle for social justice and create a consensus on their national value structure, and having made significant progress in that direction, fight for independence? The answer to the question is frequently in the hands of the foreign powers whose brutality forces the people's choice, and the thugs win. They are either Soviet-supported thugs as in Ethiopia, or American-supported thugs as in Pakistan and El Salvador.

Poland's intellectuals, on the other hand, tried to come up with a creative synthesis, to which they gave the name national socialism, a name that was made unusable by the mire of blood in which Hitler covered Europe under the banner of a perverted national socialism.

The Poles of 1980, under the name Solidarity, are trying to restate that synthesis to fit this century and create a model for the next millennium. Their own pope defined it in two encyclicals for all the world to read and ponder; but the current brutality of history does not augur well for that latest attempt. No matter what the outcome, it will not go without a strong reaction within those very countries that see solutions only in terms of dictatorships rationalized by revolutionary slogans.

No panoramic view of Poland's history can be complete without facing the reality of "Polish Anti-Semitism." It is the Achilles heel of history that its tale has to be told within the structures of logic and grammar. The rationality inherent in language precludes developing a lasting and deeper understanding of the irrational forces that dominate recorded history most of the time. There is no logical explanation for the Ku Klux Klan, for the genocide of the American Indians, for the massive killings of the Armenians and the Kurds, for the horrors of the concentration camps in Germany, the Soviet Union, Cambodia, or wherever else they may now abound. The sufferings of the victims can be recorded, but only marginally understood. Moreover, the abundant historical literature of horror, through its very obscenity, has caused an ill-concealed voyeurism without providing an explanation. The horror story is told either in terms of its perpetrators, who usually see nothing wrong in what they are doing, or in terms of the victims, who as victims are blameless and whose suffering remains essentially incommunicable.

Yet there is a relationship between the perpetrator and the victim that goes beyond the acts performed by the former on the latter. Jacobo Timerman, the Argentinian publisher who was imprisoned and tortured for eighteen months by the military regime and was freed in 1979 because of international pressure, is quoted in an interview as saying that "anti-Semitism is the inability of the Jew to answer the anti-Semite." There is a responsibility for the horror that the parties involved shared, and nowhere in Western history is that relationship clearer than in the history of Poland.

Prior to describing a series of events and phenomena that are commonly identified as "Polish anti-Semitism," the concept of anti-Semitism itself has to be broken down into its many levels of meanings and modes of expression to be properly understood. It can never really be comprehended, because only rational events are subject to rational understanding.

The common denominator of all anti-Semitism since the fall of the Western Roman Empire is to be found in the policies condoned by the Catholic church and the social perceptions it inculcated throughout its domain—and that included the Protestant variants as well. Specifically, in Poland there is a record of a communication from the pope to the first king of Poland, Mieszko I, admonishing him not to be too friendly to a Jew. Apparently, Mieszko befriended a learned Jewish trader who happened to arrive in Poland from the Arab kingdom. Poland was converted to Christianity in 966, and the correspondence with the king took place around 977. But this letter had no visible impact on the actions of Polish kings until the seventeenth century.

There were Polish Jews who were completely assimilated, considered themselves Poles, participated in all Polish resistance movements, contributed heavily to Polish culture, supported Polish causes, and helped the Polish economy. Then there were Polish Catholics who were actually converts from Judaism, but whose Jewish ancestry was always whispered about. They were not Jews until it became convenient to declare them to be Jews. In addition, there were Prussian Jews who massively migrated to Poland in the last decades of the eighteenth century. Most of them became converts and Polish patriots, industrialists, bankers, and professionals. Their daughters married Poles and thus became Polonized completely because they had Polish names. But the male descendants carried their basically German names and thus were either considered to be German, which was bad enough, or German Jews, which was even worse. Then came the massive migration into Poland of Russian and Lithuanian Jews. They were entirely foreign and their influx was of such importance that it must be discussed separately. These "Litvaks," as the other Polish Jews referred to them, were not popular even among the Polish Jews. Thus in some instances, there was a Polish anti-Semitism directed by Polish Jews against non-Polish Jews.

All these distinctions, however, were completely erased in Poland in the years between 1919 and 1939, and more precisely between 1935 and 1939. Up until 1935, while there were some pogroms against the Jews, anti-Semitism was not an official policy. After 1935, it was.

It has previously been noted that the Polish Kingdom was, until the beginning of the seventeenth century, tolerant toward the Jews; it actually invited them and gave them areas in cities where they could live according to their laws. It was also noted that the Polish Kingdom was a federation of many nations; therefore, "Polish anti-Semitism" refers to anti-Jewish activities occurring within the ethnically Polish lands. The first organized pogrom occurred within Poland proper in 1881, when it was known as the Congress Kingdom, bereft of any Polish law and order—these were in the hands of the Imperial Russian police and army.

It was the policy of the Russian Empire to encourage the migration of millions of Russian Jews who lived in the "Pale of Settlement" (an area on the western borders of the empire assigned to Jews as their place of residence, except for the wealthy merchants who could live in other areas) into Poland. The Russian Jews transplanted into Poland had no point of identification with Polish history, did not speak Polish, and had their own distinct dress, language, and culture. They were strangers sent in by an occupying power for the purpose of increasing the occupying power's control over the Polish population.

The Polish population was overwhelmingly ignorant and associated its bad luck with strangers. In the case of the Jews, the strangers were "the murderers of Christ."

The historical experiences and religious strictures of eastern European and Middle Eastern Jews (some of whose descendants migrated to Russia via the Ottoman Empire) taught them to live in tight, distinct communities, maintaining their own culture, education, laws, and law enforcement. In many instances, this segregation came as a consequence of requests made by the elders of the Jewish community. Such, for example, was the case of the Jews who migrated from Spain and western Europe to Poland in the fourteenth century. They were welcomed by King Casimir the Great and were asked what they wanted to make them feel comfortable. They requested a sector of the city where they could live according to their religion and laws. Their request was granted and that was how the first ghetto in Poland came into being.

This fact, incidentally, is one minor reason why many of the Jews under the Hitler occupation accepted the notion of living in a ghetto, an area in which they could prosper and where, if they obeyed the laws of the conqueror, they could expect to survive. It is also a minor explanation why in the United States Jews have a tendency to freely create their own "ghettos." Historical memories do not die; neither do the ethnic ties of Italians, Irish, and Germans; but their ties seldom survive one or two generations.

The Russian Jews who began to migrate in massive numbers into the Congress Kingdom after 1863 were literate in an overwhelmingly illiterate society. They knew more and that knowledge gave them power that could be expressed and eventually became evident in economic and political terms.

The influx of Jews occurred when Poland had a very feeble middle class, virtually no merchant class, and very little industry. Poland's industry and trade were in the hands of various foreigners—just like Imperial Russian trade and industry. Thus there was a vacuum which the Jews could fill without actually harming the Polish population. The Jews, alongside the Germans, contributed to the rapid industrialization and urbanization of the Congress Kingdom that occurred in the last four decades of the nineteenth century. The Jews could fill this vacuum because they traveled and had trading networks that extended through many provinces of Imperial Russia and central Europe. Their trading generated cash in a land where most of the population lived basically in a barter economy with a minimal cash flow, and the cash was used to build factories.

The industrialization of the Congress Kingdom occurred at a time when agricultural prices were collapsing all over Europe and Russia. America was emerging as the major grain supplier for the European market. This, of course, created unbearable conditions in the countryside and was responsible for the migration of illiterate, unqualified peasants into towns where they swelled the ranks of the unemployed or the unskilled laborers. The need for industrial development in the Russian Empire was so great that anyone moving into industry had an opportunity to profit, and for reasons mentioned above labor was abundant and very cheap.

The Congress Kingdom, due to its proximity to the highly industrialized German Empire, became the most productive and developed province of the Russian Empire. Those Jews who went into industry, like the Poles who did, became wealthy and thus employers of Polish (and Jewish) workers. As capitalists, they exploited on a par with their non-Jewish competitors. But because they were Jews—some in name only—their exploitation was perceived by the Poles as being somehow more pernicious than the exploitation by non-Jewish industrialists. Ironically—and that is a matter of record—some Jewish industrialists, conscious of the fact that they were Jewish in a non-Jewish land, paid higher wages than other industrialists.

The growth of industry requires capital. The mercantile activities of the Jews provided capital and access to European capital markets. Some of the money not needed by the Jewish industrialists was loaned out and trickled down to the peasants in the form of loans. This normal economic phenomenon was perceived as a Jewish monopoly of financial control—although many non-Jews followed the same practice.

The prowess of expanding trade and industrialization provides a powerful impetus to higher education, especially professional education. Jews traditionally respected educaton above all other achievements, and since neither the Russian nor the Russified Polish universities offered the level of education that was needed, many of the wealthier Jewish families sent their children to Germany and to

Austria to earn their doctorates. Jews seldom sent their children to France because fin-de-siècle France was the hotbed of European anti-Semitism of that time. Thus in all respects the educational and economic gap between the Jewish minority and the non-Jewish majority grew.

Viewing the industrialization of Poland in the context of the areas of Poland under German and Austrian occupation, the uneven rate of that industrialization becomes evident. The most highly developed was the western part of Poland, which was ruled by the German Empire. The Jewish population, although socially segregated, prospered economically. The least industrialized and thus the poorest part of Poland were the lands of Galicia under Austrian occupation. Although the rule of the Hapsburgs was least repressive toward the Poles, as compared to Germany and Russia, the Poles and the Jews suffered the oppression of poverty. The Jews, however, as small merchants, traders, and owners of some industry, were economically a little better off than the overwhelming majority of peasants.

The peasants of Galicia were Poles in the western part of the province and Ukrainians in the eastern part. Anti-Semitism in the rural areas, especially those inhabited by the Ukrainians, was most frequently expressed through pogroms.

The economic picture of the Congress Kingdom was drastically different, because in the context of the Russian rate of industrialization, the Congress Kingdom was by far the most advanced province of the Russian Empire. The main factors accounting for this phenomenon were the proximity of Germany, whose industrialists were willing to invest in Poland, the better manufacturing base that existed in the Congress Kingdom by comparison to what was available in Russia proper, and the possibility the Congress Kingdom offered for the exploitation of the Russian market. Pots and pans manufactured in Poland were sold on the markets bordering Mongolia.

The Jews, as merchants, manufacturers, traders, but above all as literate workers, contributed and benefited more proportionately than the rest of the population. Moreover, since the industrialization of the Congress Kingdom primarily benefited foreign financiers, some of whom were Jewish, and since the goods produced in Poland did not primarily serve the needs of the Polish people, the entire process benefited the Poles only marginally.

This caused tension and discontent among the Poles, a discontent mostly directed against the Russian authorities, but cleverly deflected by Russian administrators against the Jews, who, the Russians claimed, took all the wealth. Russian authorities instigated most of the pogroms, especially those that occurred in smaller industrial centers.

Thus, in the popular perception, the Jews in the Congress Kingdom, like the few surviving Jews of People's Poland, were perceived as filling the needs of the foreign masters of the Polish nation.

Of course, the Jews were not responsible for the way they were perceived; yet they are responsible for reinforcing certain perceptions, e.g., that Jews are smarter, as was maintained by many Jews, including the noted historian Isaiah Berlin. Did the Jews have to show a marked preference for dealing mostly with Jews? Did the Jews use anti-Semitism as a rationalization for their very own marked defensive patterns?

Although all the above "objective factors" help explain why anti-Semitism was so forcefully expressed in Poland, they do not explain the mind set, the value structure, that produced and propagandized the concept of anti-Semitism to the point where it was internalized by the majority of the Poles. The essence of Polish anti-Semitism is to be found in the intangible fields of philosophy, political theory, and especially socialist thought.

Many Polish intellectuals who matured in France and returned to Poland became ardent followers of positivist philosophy and the Spencerian variant of that philosophy, which advocated the theory of the survival of the fittest, i.e., social Darwinism. The Polish positivists saw a method of saving Polishness without actually creating an independent Polish state. The positivists argued that "science is power" and that, if the Polish middle classes could be educated and the Polish peasants brought out from their state of ignorance, Poland would prosper. The positivists avoided direct political action and confrontation. They argued for programs that would push Poles into trades, manufacturing, banking, and the professions. The positivists never advocated anti-Semitism, yet by stimulating the emergence of a Polish middle class, they set up a condition conducive to fighting those who already were in it and who had the positions the Poles desired. It did not take long for the economic struggle to become a national struggle in which the weaker of the "enemies" were the Jews.

The Polonizing of the middle class occurred at a time when a wave of particularly vicious nationalism had swept Imperial Russia and touched Poland. The Russian ultranationalist group identified as "the Black Hundreds" declared war against all that was foreign in their land. They fought with the weapons of barbarism and brute force. The Polish answer to Russian nationalism was the creation of the Polish National Democratic party, whose members also began to hate all that was not truly Polish, meaning Roman Catholic. The Jewish answer to this nationalism was the creation of the Zionist party, which demanded a Jewish homeland—but did not specify at the onset where that homeland was to be located. The mind set and the value structures animating the Black Hundreds of Russia and the National Democrats were very similar, although they sprang from different historical experiences. The value structure of the original Zionists is comprehensible only in the context of the other great political explosion that rocked eastern Europe: Marxist socialism.

In the last two decades of the nineteenth century, a very limited geographic area of eastern Europe—roughly within a hundred-mile radius of Wilno (now the capital of Lithuania)—became the cauldron in which twentieth-century socialism assumed its final form. In very short order the Polish Socialist party was the first to become a major conspiratorial socialist party known as the PPS. Shortly thereafter, the Russian Social Democrat party emerged as an organized entity, followed by the "Bund"—the Jewish Socialist party—and among them all grew Zionism, which demanded a homeland but followed an essentially socialist vision of social justice.

Zionism was socialism wrapped in a nationalistic flag—a fact to which the early twentieth-century kibbutzim are a lasting testimonial. The kibbutz would not hire workers because it did not want to build its economy on any form of exploitation.

The socialists were neither anti-Semitic nor against national freedom. The membership within some of the parties overlapped and the enemies were Imperial Russia—the prison of nations—and the virulent capitalism that dominated Europe. The parties were staffed and led by brilliant intellectuals whose internal debates showed remarkable sophistication and a great depth of philosophical and historical knowledge. The debates remained largely unresolved and eventually splintered the socialist movements into fractions that persist to this day.

One of the themes of these dialogues that contributed most to the fracturing of eastern and, subsequently, western European socialism was the nationality question. The PPS was the party that forced—at the Second Congress of the Second International, held in London in 1894—the acceptance of national independence as the first demand of a socialist program aimed at people living under foreign domination. The nationalism of the PPS was, however, entirely different from the chauvinistic policies advocated by the National Democratic party of Poland.

History abounds in coincidences; but this eastern European confluence of clashing ideologies and political programs has a quality of uniqueness because from it sprang the minimal nobility of our century and also its overwhelming monstrosity.

Although socialism had its roots in the French Revolution, received its first theoretical framework in the France of the 1830s, and was codified into a tight political-action program by Marx and Engels in Germany, Belgium, and England, it matured in eastern Europe. The basic reason for that was to be found in the high degree of totalitarian repression pervading the Russian Empire. Its workers were, in fact, the most advanced class among the oppressed, and the intelligentsia (Polish, Russian, and Jewish) was generally in opposition to the czarist regime. Among the workers, the most literate and thus the easiest to educate and propagandize were the Jewish workers. Among the intelligentsia, the Jews were also one of the most radical elements because they were more oppressed and because they were also rebelling against the theocratic absolutism prevailing in Orthodox Jewish communities and rabbinical seminaries. These factors were responsible for the overwhelming number of Jews among socialist theoreticians, organizers, and leading party members.

This phenomenon provided Poland's National Democratic party with two of its most powerful arguments against the Jews. As socialists, the Jews advocated and supported the slogan "Proletarians of the World Unite," which meant that Polish workers ought to fight side by side with Russian workers against the czarist capitalist regime. The National Democrats twisted that argument to mean that Poland's independence was of little importance to the Jewish-dominated socialist movement. Second, Pope Pius IX, in his "Syllabus of Errors" (1864), equated socialism with the forces of the anti-Christ and threatened any Catholic who joined a socialist movement with excommunication. In 1894, Pope Leo X published the "Rerum Novarum" encyclical, which substantially softened the stand on socialism; but the Polish clergy and the National Democrats maintained the policy embodied in the "Syllabus of Errors," and consequently the Jews were not only the murderers of Christ but also the exponents of the forces of the anti-Christ. This argument alone helped the National Democrats to place the Jews among the enemies of Poland's Catholic culture—thus of Polish nationalism.

Simultaneously, the work of the positivists bore fruit and a real Polish middle class began to emerge. It had to compete with the Jewish middle class and, not having the experience, reputation, or family connections, it frequently failed. The National Democrats, and subsequently other protofascist Polish parties, took advantage of this economic happenstance and accused Jews of using unethical practices to gain advantages and of being exponents in Poland of international finance, which exploited Poland for their own benefit.

In consequence, the Jews were under attack for either being socialist internationalists or capitalist internationalists. Regardless of which camp they supposedly belonged to, they were enemies of Poland. Anti-Semitism was equated by the National Democrats with patriotism and pure Polishness.

Yet powerful as that force was, it would have been seriously and probably successfully challenged by the Polish Socialist party, which had the allegiance of most workers and had strong alliances with other liberal Polish parties.

The outbreak of the Russian Revolution of 1917–18, however, tipped the scale in favor of the National Democrats and their ideology. Although the National Democrats did not gain control of Poland's politics until after 1935, for reasons explained below, they did create the atmosphere of a permanent Polish anti-Semitism.

The Russian Revolution perceived itself as being the first of a series of revolutions that would ultimately create a socialist Europe. There were in fact communist revolutions in parts of Poland, Hungary, Austria, and Bavaria in southern Germany. In all of them Jews played significant roles. All of them were crushed.

This attempt to export the Russian Revolution and the response of Western capitalist countries destroyed the flexible structure of political, social, and economic socialist thought, which had begun to radiate throughout Europe and the United States. Socialism, however, became Leninism, then Stalinism, and all other forms of social democracy were condemned. The political Left was ossified into a set of dogmatic precepts and was ordered to stop doing what it did best— fight for human rights. It was told to stop thinking critically and creatively and stop fighting for social justice. The enforcer of this rigidity was the Comintern—the arm of Soviet foreign policy—and the "godfather," Joseph Stalin.

Without socialist opposition, the forces of anti-Semitism in Poland, and in Europe in general, could only be opposed by the liberals. And they were rapidly losing ground because of the economic deterioration of Europe following World War I and their own basic inability to deal with mass movements that acted outside the law. A very similar situation is confronting the epigones of liberalism in our contemporary world. Liberalism works through institutions whose character it tries to change by changing the fundamental laws that created them.

The masses are too impatient to wait for the elegant solutions proposed by liberals. Thus the liberal parties of Europe were powerless to stop the wave of anti-Semitism. Poland's anti-Semitism was a part of that wave, neither more nor less despicable than the French, British, or American variants of that aberration.

In 1918, Germany and Austria-Hungary surrendered to the Allies. Russia, now known as the Soviet Union, withdrew from the war. Thus, all three occupiers of Poland disappeared as powers capable of maintaining their hegemony over Poland. In November 1918, Poland became independent.

The new state inherited nationality problems (Germans, Ukrainians, and Jews lived within the borders of the new state, as well as Lithuanians, Byelorussians, and Slovaks), unresolved peasant demands for land, an empty treasury, a virtually destroyed industrial base, and a nationwide confusion that demanded the emergence of a strong man. He did emerge and his name was Jozef Pilsudski. He happened to be a socialist (PPS) and he had an overwhelming instinct for decency. He was free of anti-Semitic prejudices and had the trust of the majority of the workers and peasants, even though he said, "At the station marked independence I leave the train of socialism." He understood that the masses of conflicting ideologies ranging from Soviet-dominated communism to a hysterical nationalism, compounded by the Polish economic mess and the lack of competent administrators, precluded democratic solutions. He became the reluctant strong man, the dictator, and is today regarded as the father of the country.

A strong man at the helm of an emerging nation need not spell the doom of democracy. He may be the stabilizer that makes democracy possible. For this he needs international peace, enlightened economic partners among the rich nations of the world, and at home he must have the services of the intelligentsia. Pilsudski had an adequate power base within Poland, but he was not really supported by the rich nations. He was prevented in 1934 from attacking Hitler's Germany by the opposition of both Great Britain and France and thus had to turn toward a policy of accommodation. This move, coupled with Pilsudski's death in 1935, precluded the creation in Poland of a base for a representative government.

After Pilsudski's death, Poland was ruled by the most inept military junta of modern time, whose sole lever of power was the jingoism provided by the National Democrats, who openly espoused a Hitlerian anti-Jewish policy.

After the death of Pilsudski, the National Democrats and the National Radical Camp (ONR) could now freely accuse the Jews of being part of the communist international, whose objective was the destruction of Poland, and of international capitalism, which never really wanted an independent Poland.

In the absence of a cohesive Jewish policy (either in Poland or in any other part of the world), Poland became the second major power in Europe to institutionalize anti-Semitism. Poland passed laws directed against Jews in professions, against the number of Jews allowed in universities, and against the "ritual killing of animals" (meaning kosher meat, which could only be produced in very limited quantities). The church applauded it all, and the Western democracies were silent.

In 1938, Poland joined Nazi Germany in the dismemberment of Czechoslovakia, the only democracy in Central Europe at that time. Polish youth, along with members of the National Democratic party and the ONR, paraded wearing swastika arm bands and the Jewish communities did little but argued among themselves. The rich believed in the protective power of their money and fought the poor, who believed that the solution lay in a change of policy toward the Soviet Union. The rich were capitalists first and Jews second; the poor were socialists who happened to be Jews. This division between the rich Jews and the poorer Jews survived into the ghettos.

In August 1939, Hitler and Stalin signed the nonaggression pact, which included a secret clause providing for the division of Poland between them. In September, Poland fought valiantly and lost. The Germans took the western and central part of Poland; the Russians took the eastern part.

No one doubts that the Poles fought the Germans and resisted them through the long years of occupation, but that resistance was not strong enough to overcome the anti-Semitism endemic to so many Poles. Even under the occupation, the rural clergy did little to mitigate anti-Semitism or to quietly offer shelter to Jews. There are, of course, noble exceptions to that statement.

The Jews who were active in the resistance, and there were more of them than the current literature attests to, had to fight four enemies: the Nazis; the ultra-nationalist units of the Polish Home Army which the Polish government in exile in London could not restrain; Polish city hoodlums; and wealthy Polish Jews who believed they could buy their way to survival.

Everyone is or ought to be familiar with the Nazi atrocities. But few know that the Polish Home Army would kill Jewish partisans when they found them hiding in the same forests that gave shelter to the Home Army. Little is said about Polish city hoodlums who, for a cigarette, would turn in a Jew they spotted walking through the street to the Gestapo or their Lithuanian/Ukrainian henchmen.* And nearly nothing has been said about the wealthy Jews who lived in luxury in the ghetto, protected by its very walls from persecution or exposure by Polish hoodlums, while Jewish children starved to death and Jewish resistance fighters were refused shelter and money needed to purchase arms, and thus were condemned by their own to die, before the Gestapo could get to them.

No one wants to emphasize the fact that the Jewish uprising in the ghetto was started by a small band of Jewish socialists, who alone were among the minority of Jews who made the decision to die on their own terms. Jewish capitalists hated Jewish socialists and even the danger of extermination by Hitler did not dissolve these animosities. Certainly, once the uprising started within the ghetto, all the Jews had to join in, and in their death they became brethren.

The only allies the Jewish resistance groups found were among the Polish People's Guard (communist and former PPS leftists) and Red Army partisans. It also should be remembered that General Anders, the commanding general of the Polish Army in London, said words to the effect that "at least Hitler solved the Jewish problem for us," the "us" referring to the Poles. Anders said this in 1945—after the discovery of the crematoria.

But Poland's bloody history does not end in 1945. Between 1945 and 1948, the Polish Home Army, which wore the eagle with the crown on its military caps, fired at the Polish People's Guard, which wore the eagle without the crown. It does not matter who fired first; they were killing each other. The Ukrainians were killing anyone they could kill, and both Home Army and Ukrainians killed Jews. This lasted until 1948, when Stalin took over and installed a communist regime in Poland. Polish communists, among whom there were many Jews, took a horrible revenge on the Polish Home Army and on some of the leading nationalists. It does not matter if they did it on orders from Stalin. It matters that they did it. This action kept the embers of anti-Semitism alive and were fanned into their last open flame in 1968. The Jews were the scapegoats for Poland's economic failures. In 1968, the "Jewish Question" was in fact solved. In the supreme irony of history, now all Poles have become "Jews." Everyone talks about their rights, but no one will do anything to help them secure these rights.

---

*Many of these hoodlums were executed by the Home Army which, in this case, followed the directives from London.

POLAND IN THE PRESENT

If civilised countries want to return to Druid
hanging Rites in the Sacred Grove or to drink blood
with Aztecs and feed their Gods with blood of human
sacrifice, let them see what they actually eat
and drink. Let them see what is on the end of
that long newspaper spoon.

———William Burroughs,
*The Naked Lunch**

Since the end of World War II, Polish political history has been among the most obscene examples of the human condition, and Poland's economic history has been an outstanding example of the grotesque.

According to the Yugoslav politician and dissident writer Milovan Djilas's *Conversations with Stalin,* the Allies determined long before the end of World War II that Poland would be in the Russian sphere of influence. Once this decision was reached, no one with any knowledge of Stalin's modus operandi could for an instant believe that after the defeat of Hitler Poland would be allowed to be an independent state. It was important, however, for the Western partners of the Alliance, and especially for the United States, to be able to insist on a scenario that would make it appear that Poland was independent and that the Polish people were given the opportunity to determine their own fate. Consequently, it was agreed upon at the summit conference in Yalta (February 1945) that there would be free elections in Poland. Even Stalin accepted that proposal, because it would not enhance the stature of the Soviet Union, which fought against Hitler's domination of the world, to just march into Poland and take over. Thus, the

---

* Quoted from Peter Michelson, *The Aesthetics of Pornography* (New York: Herder and Herder, 1971), p. 74.

comedy of a struggle for a communist Poland waged by Polish workers and peasants against the "reactionary forces" was carefully staged. Between 1945 and 1948, the Polish Workers party (PPR), claiming to be nationalistic but pro-Soviet, slowly gained control over the levers of power from the inept Stanislaw Mikolajczyk and his associates who headed the London-based Polish Government in Exile. Mikolajczyk and a few of his closest collaborators returned to Poland in 1945. Theoretically, his power base was among the Polish peasants, whom he represented in the Polish Parliament prior to 1939. His actual power was supposed to be the Polish Home Army, which was under the command of the Government in Exile, thus pro-Western and definitely anti-Soviet. The Home Army, however, was not allowed to return, armed, to Poland, and therefore could not play a significant role in opposing the Stalinist takeover. Those who returned, especially if they were officers, were, with a few exceptions, liquidated. Most of the enlisted men were allowed to return to their farms but found themselves under constant surveillance and were, moreover, discriminated against.

Mikolajczyk's power was completely eroded when the PPR, jointly with the PPS (Polish Socialist party), passed the "Small Constitution" in 1947, which decreed the expropriation of land owned privately or by the church to be immediately distributed among the peasants. The size of the allotments varied according to the quality of soil and the geographic location of the land.

According to an agreement ratified by the Allies during the Potsdam Conference (July 1945), Poland received most of East Prussia, Silesia, Pomerania, and other German lands lying on the eastern banks of the Oder and Neisse rivers. Poland lost all its pre-1939 eastern provinces, which were incorporated into the Soviet Union. Polish peasants displaced from those areas were relocated in the "western land" and were eligible to receive about one hundred acres of land and monetary subsidies from the government to help them cover their initial expenses.

It is a historical axiom that once a peasant gets his land his political ambitions are satiated and he will remain loyal to the government that gave it to him—providing he can get a good price for his product. The PPR and the PPS took credit for the land reform and in November 1947 Mikoljaczyk and his advisers fled Poland. At that particular time the leading worker parties were popular and the Poles enjoyed four basic freedoms: the freedom to worship, the freedom of movement, the freedom to choose their own jobs, and the freedom to criticize the government privately. There were also no cultural restrictions.

The reason for this "gentle" approach to the complete takeover by Stalinist forces operating within Poland was the popularity of some of the nationalist leaders of the PPR and the immense historical popularity of the PPS. By 1948, however, the Stalinists felt strong enough to carry out a "revolution" in Poland that was backed only by Soviet bayonets. They forced a merger of the PPR with the PPS and created the United Polish Workers party (PUWP) which ruled Poland from 1948 until 1981. It started off under the complete control of loyal Stalinists and it ended totally discredited by General Wojciech Jaruzelski, the current military leader of Poland.

The three decades of rule by the PUWP is one full of murder, mass arrests, abrogation of personal freedom, denial of privacy and basic human dignity, and the falsification of Poland's history to the point of the absurd. The very crudeness of the approach used by the Polish Stalinists was bound to reawaken the instinctual Polish resistance and a yearning for the ethos of Polish history. Fortunately for the Poles, some of the documents of Poland's past did survive the methodical German destruction of Polish literary and historical works and monuments. Despite the Nazi liquidation of most of the intelligentsia, despite the book burnings and the Soviet attempts to duplicate the same efforts in territories under their control, enough Poles were left alive to protect the embers of a fire that a new generation could fan into a strong flame.

But their task took place in a completely altered social setting. The German occupation left Poland a classless society, rendered so not by some revolutionary design but by a deliberate policy to turn Poles into robots for the German economy. Moreover, of the 3.5 million Jews who contributed so much to the fine and performing arts, to poetry, literature, journalism, and a superb humor, perhaps as many as three hundred thousand living shadows remained. Renegades of Judaism, outcasts of Jewish culture, did occupy the highest positions in the land during the Stalinist period. This unfortunate truth kept Poland's anti-Semitism alive. Many Poles saw such Stalinists as Berman and Rozanski simply as Jews destroying Poland; they did not see them as nonhumans whose parents happened to have been Jews. The Stalinists of Jewish origin were as venomous in their hatred of the Jews as they were of all who dared resist them or dared to question their right to rule.

The Poles survived the war but many were decimated; the economic base of the country was destroyed, the means of transportation was rendered useless and major cities like Warsaw and Gdansk were in ruins. The greatest devastation, however, was psychological. An example would be the forest people who survived by pillaging, murdering, conspiring, and terrorizing. They did it for a good cause, "for our freedom and yours," but they were hardly the base on which an orderly society could be built.

The majority of the Poles were quiet. They behaved according to the laws of the occupiers, be they Soviet or Nazi. They were not collaborators, but for them survival was the prime goal and they were able to adapt just like their parents were able to during World War I. Many had great difficulties, but most of them managed.

The survivors in most of Poland's cities were members of the lower middle class. They brought with them into the post-war period their irrational values: anti-Semitism, a fundamental hatred of the Russians, and an acrimonious Polish nationalism. They still believed that the West would recognize the valor of Poland and somehow miraculously come to the aid of their fatherland.

The workers—men and women—on the other hand, did have the self-image of a proletariat and were the one group that wanted to rebuild a socialist Poland. But for them socialism had nothing in common with Leninism-Stalinism. The PPS version of socialism meant worker ownership of the means of production, decency in the administration, tolerance in social relations, and towering above it all, patriotism as the emotional energizer. No task was too difficult for them to undertake. They performed the miracle of the restoration of Warsaw from a heap of three-foot-high rubble and a few grotesquely burnt-out shells of buildings into a thriving, beautiful city. They, their teen-age children, and the teen-age children of the middle classes, were the rebuilders. None of them were prepared to accept the heavy hand of Stalinism that took Poland by the throat and came close the choking the life out of the nation.

Despite the hardships of Stalinism, the workers of Poland made two decisions: one was to rebuild Poland, the other to educate their children no matter what the cost is. The second decision was the more important. The ranks of the Polish intelligentsia were decimated. There is statistical evidence that in 1945 there were about one thousand people with doctoral degrees left in Poland. Therefore, schools and universities, books and teachers, child care and food for the young were top priority. And even when the Stalinists took over, and all schools on all levels were forced to teach a falsified Polish history and they force-fed Polish youth with love for Stalin and reverence for Lenin and the October Revolution (1917), the fact remained that children were being taught and the stories told by their parents and the clandestine schools that continued to function despite the vigilance of the Stalinist secret police, which surpassed the Gestapo in efficiency and equaled it in brutality, made the young into critically thinking individuals. Also, news of the West was not cut off until 1948, and even then it kept seeping through with the help of government officials who opposed Stalinism, and sometimes through other clandestine means which became one of the arts that flourished in Poland.

By far the greatest single social group in Poland were the peasants. Some among them resisted Stalinism; many became rich by comparison to their standard of living prior to 1939. But when the peasants received land and were allowed to sell some of their products in the "free market," they became nonpolitical in all spheres except one— the church.

Under these circumstances (in the absence of a gentry)—a void left by the holocaust and an elite consisting of Soviet-trained, Kremlin-loyal communists—the entire rich ethos of Poland's history had but one repository common to all Poles—the Polish Catholic church.

When the Poles' national existence was threatened, the church moved and moved very energetically. It became the focus of opposition to Sovietism. Two cardinals of Eastern Europe, Mindszenty of Hungary and Wyszynski of Poland, were responsible for being the guardians of the ethos of Polish and Hungarian nations, whose histories show many parallels.

Yet the church, as the guardian of the ethos of a nation, is naturally prone to defend the religious element in it and to disregard its strong and vital secular component.

The Polish Catholic church under the leadership of the very strong-willed and obstinate Wyszynski, who insisted on being identified as the "prince primate" or the "primus" of Poland—titles left over from the period when Poland elected its kings and the cardinal—ruled during the interregnum. He operated on one principle: to be a Pole meant to be a Catholic.

As the primus, Wyszynski disposed of the only well-staffed organization operating in Poland, which was only marginally damaged by the Nazis, who saw the church as a more or less docile institution capable of keeping social and political tranquility in the Polish countryside. Thus in 1945 the church as an institution was the only functioning religious and political entity whose continuity of action spanned the period from before the war (1939) to its end in 1945. The Soviet/Polish government was well aware of the power of the church and moved against it. The Catholic church of Poland became the "silent church"—but it was silent only in the official political arena.

The peasants kept going to church, and when that was not possible the church went underground. Priests kept performing their required rituals in homes, in small gatherings, under the open sky, and they kept on talking about Poland to those of the young who otherwise would have never known about Poland. But the church presented an image of Poland that fits its needs, i.e., creating and recruiting good Catholics. The persecuted clergy did a magnificent job. They laid the foundations for the most vigorous religious education, which now produces more priests, seminarians, and members of religious orders than most of the countries of the West.

The secular part of the ethos of Poland's history was kept alive by the epigones of the PPS and by the fact that, given the capabilities of modern communication technology, it was impossible to keep Polish people isolated from the West. The BBC broadcasts penetrated Poland; so did some of the broadcasts of Radio Free Europe and the Voice of America. Books published in the West found their way into Poland; works by young Polish writers were circulated in manuscript form. There was a network that kept some of the Poles in touch with the major intellectual and political developments in the West. Among these was the rebirth in the West of humanism—which also was an important element of the ethos of Poland's history.

The negative aspects of that ethos was maintained by a former Polish fascist Boleslaw Piasecki, who sold his services to the Stalinists and was accepted by them because he promised that he could create a Polish national church that would become a countervailing force to the Roman Catholic church. He was allowed to establish an organization known as Pax, which had the right to operate outside the economic and political controls of the party and the government. Pax was given the exclusive right to deal in religious objects: crucifixes, pictures of Christ and the Virgin Mary, crosses, rosaries, etc. Since nearly all Polish homes either have these objects or want more of them, giving Pax the monopoly was one way of undercutting the economic base of the Catholic church. Pax was also granted the right to deal in gold, maintain bank accounts in Western countries (a right denied Poles), and most important, Pax had its own publishing house, run on a profit basis. All of these activities made it possible for Pax to remunerate faithful party members by giving them money to travel in the West or to live very luxuriously in Poland. Pax also became a haven for the surviving gentry and the exponents of all the negative qualities of Poland's historical ethos—anti-Semitism among them. The Pax publishing house did, however, bring out books dealing with Poland's past in terms other than the official party line.

In a country starved for reading material, with writers whom years of occupation and Stalinism deprived of any opportunity to find an audience for their creativity, Pax became an important outlet. Valuable works of literature did come out under its imprimatur. Pax succeeded in its secondary mission of generating extra income for the party leaders and had a limited success in helping to enrich Polish literature; but it failed completely in its primary function of combating the influence of the Polish Catholic church. Recently, Pax seems to have been dissolved, but for nearly thirty-two years under Piasecki it was the most nefarious influence in Poland, entirely staffed by Poles who still believed in the glorious Poland of the prepartition days.

The period of Poland's isolation from the West, together with the fact that her new and growing intelligentsia had a strong reality principle, had the beneficial effect of making Poland's creative forces look inward to find an ethos that was neither hard-line Wyszynski nor gloriously nationalistic. In this search for the real Poland and for an ethos based on reality and an honest, deeply felt love for the country, the intelligentsia was accidentally helped by the official endorsement of the "materialist concept of history" by the party. This endorsement had practical consequences in the form of grants and huge funds for research in the area of the "material culture" of Poland's past, i.e., archeological digs, linguistic studies, studies of folk art and music. The sum of all these studies turned the attention of many writers, artists, and historians to those who manufactured this material culture, that is, the peasants. It was an amazing discovery that the peasants had both a functional and a decorative art based entirely on the usual materials available to them—wood and knives, paint and cloth. The peasants had a representational and a devotional art. For many Poles the discovery of the so-called primitive art had the impact of a revelation. The peasant had an aesthetic that was disdained by the gentry, but which was discovered and cherished by Poland's people.

Another important impact on building a new ethos came from archeology and the study of linguistics. The Poles discovered that as Slavs, as isolated tribes, they had had a tremendous history and a very vital culture before 966 when Christianity arrived in Poland. There was a Polish culture—genuine, rich, independent, and not dominated by the church. This did not turn the Poles against the church, but made them curious of the history of their church not only in Poland but in other parts of Europe. The government encouraged that interest because the history of the church as a political, secular institution is as inspiring, or uninspiring, as the histories of all institutions that connive to become rich and powerful. Polish historians and philosophers became very interested in the movements of the Waldesians, the Brethren, and other similar social movements that opposed the practices of the Roman court. From there it was a short step to the study of the Renaissance in Poland and to becoming very proud of something that was essentially Polish—humanism. This strain of a deep social conscience was never broken, but it was always driven underground by the Catholic church, the occupying powers, and by the rare native Polish governments.

The post–World War II intelligentsia determinedly studied this humanism and discovered that the roots of Polish socialism had an aspect that had seldom been referred to in the years between 1919 and 1939 and had never been referred to during the Stalinist period. This aspect was an ethical socialism, a socialist nationalism based on tolerance, democratic procedures, and an absence of repression, although its goals were entirely in keeping with those identified by Marx—a classless society devoid of all aspects of exploitation.

The government encouraged the Polish intelligentsia to hold up a mirror to the past that was supposed to discredit the church, the gentry tradition, and the slavishly pro-Western orientation of the Poles. The educational policy of the government was more successful than it had expected. The intelligentsia discovered and propagated genuine reasons for being proud to be Polish. It wove a tapestry of Polish history, which included all the elements of Poland's traditions but allowed those that were good to shine in all their glory and those that were evil to reflect the enormity of their evil.

It needs to be remembered, however, that the Poles were poor and in desperate need of all sorts of consumer goods. These had to come from the West and Poles began to imitate Western styles. Snobbism was involved in it, but most of it was dictated by necessity. Those who especially aped Western materialism were the privileged children of the Communist ruling class.

In 1953 Stalin's empire began to crack. There was a bloody workers' revolt in East Germany. It was brutally crushed by Soviet armor. On March 5 of the same year Stalin died. What was perceived by the West as a monolith revealed itself to be a great diversity of people and ideologies whose leaders showed a superficial conformity to Soviet ideological orthodoxy, a real fear of Soviet power, and a penchant for ruling by Soviet methods.

But without Stalin's commanding personality to keep the status quo in his empire, the fissures became cracks and the cracks developed into two revolutions—a very bloody one in Hungary, and a sophisticated one in Poland. These both occurred in 1956. In both countries the liberal elements gained control of the party apparatus. Although the Soviets crushed the Hungarian rebellion, they installed Janos Kadar, who was reviled by the West and by Hungarian emigrés, but who turned out to be the most liberal of rulers and apparently the most successful. Hungary enjoys the highest standard of living of any country in the Warsaw Pact. Part of the reason is that Hungary, unlike Poland, borders the West (Austria) directly, and shares its southern frontier with Yugoslavia, whose late leader, Tito, broke with Stalin in 1948. The proximity of these two countries gave Hungary a greater freedom of action than was available to Poland in the years between 1956 and 1980. It has to be emphasized over and over again that Poland is surrounded on all sides by Soviet armor.

The geographic location of Poland contributed to the self-imposed restraints of the leaders of the Polish "Spring in October," the 1956 revolution. The impetus, the organizational framework, the leadership of the revolt of 1956 came from Poland's young intelligentsia, from within the party itself, many of whose members were disgusted with the leadership's subserviency to the Kremlin and the excesses of the Polish secret police, which in Poland operates as a separate army under the Ministry of Interior. Moreover, the Poles were quite aware that Polish goods, both manufactured and foodstuff, were exported to the Soviet Union under very disadvantageous conditions.

The reformist program proposed by the 1956 group was the nationalization of Poland's road to socialism—a slogan meaning a decrease of Soviet control over the Polish economy and over Poland's cultural life. Although the workers supported the October events and comprised the massive political muscle of the revolt, the primary beneficiaries were the "liberals" within the party, the intelligentsia, the artists, and to a certain extent the city dwellers. The peasants remained generally neutral. The big winner was Wyszynski's church, which gained the right to build new churches, increase the circulation of its newspapers, open seminaries, gain support for the clergy, and put an end to religious persecution.

The Soviets, although not quite willing to give in, were themselves shook up by the revelations of Stalin's crimes, which were made public by Nikita Khrushchev, the first secretary of the Communist party of the Soviet Union (CPSU). The face-saving formula for the Soviets was provided by their then close ally China, whose leader, Mao Tse-Tung, said, "Let a thousand flowers bloom"—meaning, let each nation find its own road to socialism. Mao's pronouncement coincided with the advocacy of policentrism by the leader of the Italian Communist party, Palmiro Toglliatti. Policentrism was a code word meaning that Moscow does not have the monopoly on a "faith" called Marxism-Leninism. In 1957 a Unity Congress of Socialist Parties was held in Warsaw and the astute foreign minister of China, Chou En-Lai, helped hammer out an agreement that "sanctified" the "Spring in October."

If there was one important consequence of the events of 1956, it would have to be the flow into Poland of scientific, technological, cultural, and intellectual information from the West. The isolation of Poland, which had lasted virtually without meaningful interruptions since 1939, was finally broken. The Poles found that many nations that had been as destroyed by World War II as Poland was had somehow managed to achieve a better standard of living than was attainable for the average Pole. They saw that capitalism was neither collapsing nor completely degenerate, neither were the workers more exploited by capitalism than they were by Sovietism. As a matter of record, by blaming all economic hardship on the war that ended in 1945 and on the animosity of the world against the Soviet Union, Sovietism exploited the workers by paying them starvation wages in the name of building socialism and providing for the defense of the first proletarian state in the world.

The new Polish leadership under Wladyslaw Gomulka, a nationalist communist who has been jailed by the Stalinists and liberated by the events of 1956, was tremendously impressed by the phenomenal Western productivity. Gomulka began to move cautiously in the direction of increasing productivity that would benefit all Poles. His mistake was to try to achieve these ends without changing the Soviet model of national economics; he wanted to have everything centralized and every activity a priori planned and approved by the party.

His concepts were seriously challenged from the beginning by the intellectuals who concentrated their attention on the new (for them) achievements of American sociology and on the philosophical questions of all systems raised by secular French existentialists.

American sociology devised what was then the most sophisticated method of public-opinion polling and of analyzing the answers. According to the basic tenets of Marxism, scientifically obtained data could not be disregarded by anyone who considered himself a Marxist. Both hard or social science, if valid, had to be incorporated to "enrich Marxism." Under this doctrine of "enriching Marxism," Poland's world-renowned sociologists such as Stefan Ossowski, Maria

Ossowska, Jozef Chalasinski, and Jan Szczepanski, began to question Marxist-Leninist assumptions concerning the classlessness of Polish society and the bureaucratization of the daily life of the average Pole, and eventually they were at the point of questioning whether the United Polish Workers party was in fact the vanguard party representing the interests of the proletariat. They and their young assistants started preparing and circulating opinion questionnaires.

Most of the opinion polls conducted by American-trained Polish sociologists in the late 1950s and the early 1960s were immediately suppressed by the government; evidently the government did not want an enrichment of Marxism. The fact that this was done gave credence to widespread rumors that neither the party nor the government fared well in Poland's public opinion.

The major responsibility for training Poland's sociologists belongs to the Ford Foundation and the Fulbright Fellowship program administered by the Institute for International Education. The Polish government did not want to lose the funding made available by these two institutions and allowed Polish sociologists to continue to study in the United States; but as soon as they returned home the government put them to work on less politically sensitive problems, such as how to stimulate productivity, what kind of consumer goods the Poles needed most, what the direction of higher education should be.

In the meantime Gomulka, despite the good advice he received from Oscar Lange, the leading socialist economist and a former professor at the University of Chicago, refused to decentralize the economy or to allow Poland to borrow the capital it needed to modernize and expand its industrial base. He was a firm advocate of the pay-as-you-go policy.

Unfortunately for him, the industrial world entered its expansionist-inflationary stage; prices began to rise and Poland, which needed food and raw materials from the West, was again beset by shortages that could only be overcome by raising the price of food sold within Poland and by allowing a moderate inflation. Gomulka wanted to raise prices but hold down wages. He was promptly thrown out of office by irate workers and their wives, who protested that their earnings did not suffice to buy the necessities of life. In addition to this purely economic problem, Gomulka was caught by the impact of the Arab-Israeli war of 1967 and had to follow the harsh anti-Israeli policy dictated by the Kremlin. In 1967, when Israel defeated the combined Arab armies in six days, many Polish intellectuals held celebrations because for them the Israeli victory meant the defeat of a Soviet-sponsored conflict. The only other time Poles placed candles in their windows was when John F. Kennedy was assassinated.

While the sociologists were muzzled, and the economists went unheeded, the creative powers of the nation enjoyed an unheard of (in Eastern European countries) freedom, in the period from 1956 to about 1968. Polish films by Andrzej Wajda and Roman Polanski received international acclaim. Jerzy Kosinski's novels sold hundreds of thousands of copies. Polish graphic arts and animated films won prestigious awards. In short, the Western world was treated to a spectacle of the productivity of an intelligentsia no one knew existed. Moreover, this intelligentsia dealt with universal problems not in the context of doctrinaire Marxism but humanism, the deep sense of which grew out of a closing of the gap that had previously existed between the ethos and the reality of Polish history.

It is most important at this point to emphasize that there is no such theoretical construct as "socialist humanism." Marx meant socialism to be humanist and the label "socialist humanism" is redundant. It makes about as much sense as to say that butter is butter—what the French call *la verité de la pallisse*—the truth of the obvious. The label was useful in making a distinction between Sovietism and socialism/communism; but the concept humanism does not need a qualifier. It has been in existence ever since the Old Testament stated that man was made in the image of God. Humanism can be either theological or secular, but in either version it is just humanism—a system fit for people to live within, not survive under. The term "socialist humanism" is an admission of the failures of the former and the impotence of the latter, an impotence, however, that is transitory. Solidarity marks its renaissance.

In 1970 Gomulka was ousted and replaced by Edward Gierek. The Polish people expected that Gierek, who was educated in Belgium, would westernize Poland's industry and life-style. Ironically for him, he delivered both but based them on an antiquated economic and administrative model. He refused to, or was forced to refuse to, decentralize industry and place it on a profit-making basis the way Janus Kadar of Hungary had. Instead of doing that, he created colossal administrative units—superagencies—which were responsible for the operation of entire segments of industry, i.e., chemical, petrochemical, maritime and foreign trade, etc. These superagencies frequently planned their production without coordination with each other. Each of the agencies wanted to look good and paid scant attention another superagency. If any one failed, it would do so on its own. This created anomalies that can best be illustrated by a humorous incident.

A retail shoe store received a shipment of only size-nine men's shoes. The reason for this unusual event—even for Poland's consumer economy—was that the packaging industry was under a different administration and delivered to the shoe factory boxes that would only fit size-nine shoes. Situations like this ranged from the trivial to the catastrophic, and consequently Poland's industry lost billions of credit dollars Gierek had negotiated for industry.

The other contributing factor was Gierek's mania for designing gigantic projects that would rival anything in the West. This was especially evident in the petrochemical industry. He based his calculations on the supply of low-priced crude oil from the Soviet Union, which was being delivered to Poland through the "friendship pipeline" from the Baku oil fields, and on medium-priced Saudi light crude and some Libyan crude oil. When the crude oil prices jumped, Gierek's dream turned into a nightmare, with an uncontainable ripple effect. Higher crude oil prices forced all prices up. While building up the petrochemical industry, Gierek increased Poland's automobile and machinery production and even entered into the high-technology computer field. He believed that Poland could produce quality goods cheaper than the West and find a ready market in the Third World countries. Evidently, his grandiose plans were judged economically sound because Western banks gave Poland huge loans. Although these banks charged high interest rates, they did consider the loans to be within the range of risk banks were willing to assume. The world economy, however, was changing too rapidly for a centrally administered economy to respond quickly enough to meet emergencies, and the superagencies did not want to scrap projects they knew would not work because that would have diminished their positions.

The basic fallacy of Gierek's plan was its overadministration, the exclusion of all workers who knew what was going on from all planning activities and even from most of the benefits that should have been theirs from whatever small successes there were. The beneficiaries were top administrators, their families, and their cronies. They received huge salary increases and other prerogatives deemed proportionate to their responsibilities, and what they did not get officially they accepted as gratuities from foreign suppliers and buyers. Top-level graft became the modus operandi.

Yet the peasant economy was expected to deliver food at near the 1960s prices. The situation turned so bad that in 1976 Gierek tried to do the same thing Gomulka had done—increase the prices of consumer goods without increasing the base earnings of peasants and workers. There were strikes. Gierek relented; he rolled back some prices and granted salary increases. But the requirements of the foreign debt service, combined with a decrease in exports, poor harvests, floods, an ever-increasing administrative disarray, and graft, meant that workers and peasants, although they had more money, could buy less than in pre-Gierek days. The government even resorted to the creation of special luxury stores in addition to the already existing dollar stores where Poles with dollars could buy Polish ham, which was not available to workers whose salary was paid in zlotys.

Under this messy condition the intelligentsia fared better than the workers and peasants. Travel restrictions were eased; their standard of living improved. It needs to be noted, however, that the ranks of the intelligentsia were bloated by an influx of children of high party officials, wealthy administrators, and well-off professionals. Children of peasants and workers were routed into professional-technical schools regardless of their intrinsic talents and their own desires.

The new Polish upper class resumed the airs of the gentry and even invented ancestry in the gentry. It was not unusual to find eighteenth-century cavalry sabers in homes that were sumptuous even by Western standards. Members of the upper class had summer homes (one even had a hunting lodge in Kenya), dollar accounts, and foreign cars. In the perverted sense of the word, People's Poland, ostensibly ruled by the proletariat, in the 1970s had three *aristocracies:* administrative, intellectual, and peasant. The peasant aristocracy consisted of these who lived by making special food deliveries to the other two aristocracies. Numerically, this group may have amounted to about two percent of Poland's population of more than thirty million.

The workers and the low-level bureaucrats, in order to exist, were forced into petty thievery, which was generally condoned by the big thieves at the top. Those who did not have the opportunity to steal subsisted by doing extra work in the private sector as maids, drivers, car mechanics, and tailors. The old people and those who were forced to live on retirement pay, whose levels were fixed in the 1960s, hired themselves out as "in-line standers"—they would stand in line for products in short supply at a rate of about ten cents per hour and when their turn came they'd buy the product for their employer. This kind of an economy was bound to collapse the instant the government could no longer afford to subsidize the cost of food and housing, which was the only way workers marginally survived on their take-home pay. In terms of purchasing power, the average Polish worker with a family of four earned $150 to $200 per month. Even that figure is misleading because there never was enough price-controlled food to buy and workers had to supplement this by making purchases on the free market, where the prices were close to double those charged in official stores. Thus, the workers' real income was even lower.

Paralleling the changes occurring in Poland were the changes that were taking place within the Catholic church in general and the Polish church specifically. It could be said that both institutions were running on tracks, but the trains moved in opposite directions. The government train ran away from its socialist obligations into economic illusions that matched the political illusions of pre-1939 Poland, while the church moved toward a broader understanding of its responsibility for Poland.

The events of 1956 made it possible for the church to reenter the arena of public dialogue. Although Cardinal Wyszynski perceived it as his primary duty to rebuild the basis of power of the church as an institution—build more churches to serve the increasing population, build more schools to teach children (religious education), which, in turn, required more priests and nuns and thus made it necessary for the government to allocate more money and resources to the churches—most of the income of the church came from its parishioners. Gomulka and Wyszynski did not get along and Wyszynski frequently had to steer a deliberate confrontation policy with Gomulka. The primate of Poland was conservative in his views of the role of the church in society, and if he was a supporter of Pope John XXIII's (1958–63) social policies, he was a lukewarm one at best. Cardinal Stefan Wyszynski demanded church rights in the name of Poland's traditional Christianity and in the name of Poland's traditional nationalism. He would not seek a policy of active accommodation with Gomulka or even with the subsequent Gierek regime. As long as his clergy was not intimidated, but allowed to study and travel to Rome to complete their education, Wyszynski tended to keep out of the internal administrative affairs of Poland. He was a permanent critic of communism, not because it was an evident social failure, but primarily because it was atheistic. Moreover, Wyszynski still looked to the West to help Poland in the struggle against the Russians, whom he hated with a hatred reminiscent of that of Poland's nineteenth-century resistance movements. Valid as his actions may have been, Stefan Cardinal Wyszynski could not comprehend the changes occurring in the ethos of his country and in the mission of the church. When the wartime babies were reaching maturity and the postwar babies were reaching their late teens, most of the Poles became Sunday and Christmas Catholics and, except for the older generation, were not really interested in the Church.

But outside of Poland, under the impetus given it by John XXIII and the Second Vatican Council, the Church of Rome began to use its vocal chords of social justice, which were rusty from centuries of silence. Wyszynski did not fit this mold and that is why John XXIII cast about for a more representative spokesman of the church in Poland and elevated an energetic man in his thirties to the position of archbishop of Krakow—Karol Wojtyla, a protegé of Austria's liberal Cardinal Francis Konig.

Wojtyla, without ever disagreeing with Wyszynski, who had after all saved the Polish church, began moving the church into the position of social activism. He moved the church toward workers, toward cooperation with the government in those areas where the government's actions had positive consequences, and began to force the church of Poland to recognize the fact that at this time, in this century, the Soviet Union is the overriding reality of Poland's existence. Simultaneously, however, he began to exploit the obvious failures of the system both as a theory and practice of social change. He knew he had the peasants in his fold; he was determined to gain equal support among the workers and expected that when this happened the intellectuals would follow. His strategy was subtle and long range.

In the 1960s, Wojtyla, as a professor at the Catholic University of Lublin, began to hold seminars on the subject of "man." He looked at the human condition in a perspective other than that dictated by theology, but without neglecting it. He and his students examined the subject of exploitation in a broader context than just economics or systems. He asked about the meaning of the "dignity of the human person" and searched for the reasons for the erosion of that dignity. He linked exploitation to the failing dignity of the human person. His lectures were not anti-Marxist; they went beyond Marxism. The seminarians began to feel a concern with the workers and expressed this in nontheological language. Simultaneously, they heard an equally sharp critique of the materialism of the West, which was no different from the materialism of their own ruling elite.

Wojtyla was sounding an old-new theme in the ethos of Polish history—nationalistic to be sure, Catholic to the core, but intensely humanistic. It spoke of being Polish by being Christian and not of being Polish as simple, if heroic, defenders of a Christianity that may have been Christian in form only.

Wojtyla subtly but deliberately injected the Polish resistance movement with a universal ethic and began to attract the intellectual, atheistic critics of the government, which claimed to represent the proletariat.

In 1970, when many of Wojtyla's students were already parish priests and active among the poorer sections of cities, he made the most dramatic move toward the workers and laid down the clearest challenge to the regime. Karol Cardinal Wojtyla decided on building a church directly across from the Lenin Steel Work of Nowa Huta, a suburb of Krakow. The government refused to grant the permit. Wojtyla had expected that refusal.

Imagine the scene, in the middle of the twentieth century: a cardinal dressed in the full regalia of an officiating prince of the church holding mass in front of a simple wooden cross and behind a makeshift altar. He was there for the workers. He dared the government to move against him, like some apostle of Roman times. Wojtyla timed his masses to take place when shifts changed. He tied up traffic, raised havoc with production schedules, and showed everyone that the government could not move against a determined mass of people. As a remit, he was given the permission to build a church on the spot he chose.

The workers began to feel he was a new force behind them. The proletariat, for whom the high clergy of Poland showed only a perfunctory interest—and that included Wyszynski—suddenly saw a "prince of the church," a "lord cardinal," fighting in person to give them the choice to be Christians.

Catholicism became an active social force in Poland. The Communist party could not move resolutely against it because the party itself was in deep trouble. It had virtually no public support and when, out of desperation, it tried to raise food prices in 1976, it did not have the power to do so. It was the church that prevented 1976 from turning into the year of the great confrontation. It began its moderating and guiding role in internal Polish affairs. Wojtyla's subtle hand was in evidence. In 1978 Wojtyla became Pope John Paul II, but one could say he also became the king of Poland.

Where so many foreigners became rulers of Poland, Poland finally has her own king, who was also the emperor of Christendom—a modern emperor, a people's emperor. Although it was in the ornate halls of the Vatican that Wojtyla was ordained Pope John Paul II, it was on a balcony in Warsaw overlooking the palace of Poland's kings that John Paul II became the leader, the symbol of a people's hope—a people whose son he was. History is its own greatest dramatist.

The road from that visit to the emergence of Solidarity has been well traced by the media in recent times. Solidarity, in its approach, its symbolism, and its actions, is the fruit of the labor of Wojtyla and his students. Solidarity is the rebirth of a Polish Catholicism that is not a Catholicism of bigotry, the status quo, or sociopolitical neutrality. It is a Catholicism of activism "jointly with others" for social justice.

In terms of the ethos of Poland's history, this Catholicism is a return to the humanism characteristic of Poland in the fifteenth century, and it also contains a strand of that ethos that made Poland's King Jan Sobieski, who victoriously defended Vienna from the onslaught of the Turks, exclaim: "Veni, vidi, Deus vici"—"I came, I saw, God conquered" (a paraphrase of Julius Caesar's famous "Veni vidi vici").

In the Vienna of 1683, Sobieski's victory was visible. The enemy from the east retreated and Vienna was free. In the Poland of 1981, the resolution is very much in the balance. But the Poland of Solidarity cannot be erased from the annals of history; neither can it disappear as the challenger of Sovietism.

POLITICAL
THEORISTS
AND
SOCIAL
CRITICS

The theorists and critics discussed in this section have been included in an anthology of literary writings because they defined the major themes that surface in the greatest of Poland's writers. Even today, writers continue to debate across the ages with the validity of the observations made by the theorists and critics. The question raised by them as far back as the fifteenth century is: What is Poland? The continuity of Polish history can best be perceived in the context of this debate, because the reality of Poland's history is a series of total disruptions of all continuities save one—that of resistance.

Although we have selected excerpts from the writings of only three theorists, that does not mean that Poland did not have hundreds more. Those that followed used different languages, diverse idioms, and more modern-sounding labels; yet the essence of their message was the same.

Even before the discovery of America, Poland's social thinkers demanded equality before the law for all citizens of the kingdom. They asked for a just system of taxation, a separation of church and state, and a mechanism that would resolve international conflicts through negotiations instead of war. This is especially noteworthy because, at the same time, Machiavelli was advocating the use of power and deception if the "reason of state" demanded it. While Italian principalities, the papal states, and the great dynasties of Europe used murder, poison, terror, and ruthless wars as instruments of power, Poland's theorists advocated the use of reason, accommodation, and social justice. It went unheard by Europe and by those in power in Poland.

To bring the enormity of the request of equal justice under the law into its proper relief it has to be noted that there were five laws operating in the Polish Kingdom simultaneously and independently of each other. There were the crown laws, which generally defined the scope and authority of the king and of his central administration. The second set of laws, identified in Polish history as the "Magdeburg Law," was actually German law and was applicable to burghers and cities in general. The explanation for this phenomenon was the fact that most Polish burghers were either Germans or Poles of German descent. Their number was eventually augmented by Jews who came to Poland first from Germany and Prussia and later from Imperial Russia. The third set of laws was that which governed the Roman Catholic church and actually gave the church the position of a state within a state. Not unlike the laws of the church, were the laws of the gentry (*szlachta*). It was governed by its own judicial system and was actually free (after the seventeenth century) of any obligations to the crown. The last category of laws were those establishing the rights of the peasants. Most of these laws were traditional and up to the fifteenth or even sixteenth century were generally respected. The Polish peasant was free and could be compared to the modern American farmer. Thereafter, however, he quickly lost his freedom and his land, and he became *glebe adscriptus*, "ascribed to the land." The peasant was simply an extension of the land he worked; he was not even allowed to leave without permission of the owner. Most of his rights were trampled into nothingness by church and gentry.

Contemporary Poland has a uniform code of laws based on the code Napoleon gave her, but the problem of equality under the law is far from resolved.

Although Polish schoolchildren are taught that they are now living in a classless society and that they are equal under the law, they, their teachers, and their elders know that there are three laws operating in People's Poland. One set of laws is applicable to those Poles who directly serve their Soviet masters. They are in fact above the law. The second set of laws are operative for those who are solid members of the party, the Polish United Workers party, that is. The third set of laws is valid for the rest of the citizenry. If these general laws are broken by members of the other two groups, they are simply not enforced. Thus, one of the main demands of the independent labor union Solidarity is at least a reasonable approximation of the principle of equality under the law.

A full implementation of this principle has not been achieved anywhere in the world (except for some primitive tribes), but there are a few countries—very few indeed—in which this principle is at least taken seriously.

The other point worthy of emphasis is that the Polish theorists and critics cited in the anthology argued against the ruthless exploitation of Poland by the papacy, yet they did not advocate that Poland, like northern Germany or Prussia of the fifteenth century for example, should become Protestant.

The Polish Kingdom not only poured millions from its national treasury to support the extravagances of the papal court, but on instigation by the Vatican, it fought wars that were detrimental to its national interest, for example, most of the wars fought against the Turks and Muscovy. As far as Poland's national interests were concerned, it did not matter if Poland won or lost any of these wars. In either event, it drained Poland's physical, economic, and human resources and placed its soldiers in areas where they had no reason to be and where they could not be protected because of their distance from Poland proper.

Contemporary Poland is experiencing the substitution of the Kremlin for Rome. The modus operandi is identical. For decades Poland's industrial production had to follow the dictates of the Soviet politbureau, and Polish products had to be sold wherever the Soviets desired, at a price the Soviets established.

Polish soldiers were mobilized and used for intervention in Czechoslovakia in 1968, and now as members of the Warsaw Pact Polish soldiers may be used to fight against countries with whom they have no quarrel and who in fact have been their allies. They may even be ordered to fight their own countrymen. That is, however, the point at which the ethos of Poland's history will prevail: the mass of Polish soldiers will disobey.

In truth, Rome did give the Poles the substance of faith, just as the Soviets are giving some subsistence for bodies, i.e., food; but until now neither Rome nor the Kremlin considered Poland's existence as a nation of any importance. Neither does any other power on earth. Poland exists in the rhetoric of its allies, the hearts of its people, and the very being of John Paul II, the vicar of Christ on earth.

Jan Ostrorog (1436–1503)

Ostrorog was the governor of the state* of Poznan. From about 1500, he wrote about political conditions in Poland in which he argued for the independence of Poland from papal supremacy and against the constant intervention of Rome in the internal affairs of Poland.

He favored centralization of power in the hands of the king, equal taxation, and the urbanization of Poland; he opposed the guild system because it "exploited the gentry." The guilds were early forms of monopolies and opposed the "free enterprise" system favored by Ostrorog. The excerpt from his writings that follows emphasizes his critique of the Roman oppression of Poland.

Treaties on Improving the Republic
Concerning Donations

God ordered tithing. I do not deny that he gave this order to Aron [the high priest—Editor] and to the tribe of Levis who guarded religious laws. But he did not order the collection by extortion from the laity as this is happening now. . . . There was a time when the tithe was taken from the rich and not from the poor. Now, however, the poor landowners are making their donations to the wealthy and the fat who—in their pride—accept them.

What ever happened to the principle that stated "I want compassion and not sacrifices"? If someone wants to accept a donation when the donor wants to make it, this should happen not according to the will of the recipient but the capability of the giver.

Concerning the Election of Bishops

If bishops and all the clergy were in reality only spiritual leaders as they ought to be and if they behaved as I suggested they should

---

*I have used the concept "state" as it is used in the United States. The Polish word is wojewódstwo.

behave, I would fervently approve the principle that no secular power should intervene in the selection of the clergy. The king should concern himself with secular matters and the clergy with spiritual values that fall in their domain. Then, as it should be, these powers would be separated.

Since the laws governing the behavior of bishops and the clergy are, however, dispersed among many tomes, how is it possible to know them. How indeed—if there are no teachers to teach them and no students to learn them. . . . Therefore to avoid even greater evil it would be preferable if the king were to select the bishops because they would not only be learned but also decent . . . and they would not continue to feed hatreds of one class against another.

On Payments Made to the Pope

A painful and inhuman practice drains the Polish Kingdom, which in other ways is so free and equal. . . . Due to the . . . cunning of the Italians, we're duped to giving yearly huge sums of money to a court they call Roman. We are asked . . . to give in the name of our faith, but actually we are giving by being pressured to do so in the name of falsehoods and superstitions.

Every year we disperse from the treasury huge sums of money under the labels of "sacra" and "annaty." [The "sacra" were tributes paid to the bishop and the "annaty" were special taxes imposed on Poland to cover the cost of the war against the "infidels," who could be anyone the pope so designated. Usually, however, the term *infidel* was applied to the Turks, the Ottoman Empire.—Editor]

. . . The cunning Italians usurped for themselves this power of taxation, while we as a nation yawned and slumbered. It is well known that Germans [living in Poland—Editor] and Polish masters agreed to pay a special tax for a few years to cover the cost of the aggressors against the Christian faith. The Poles wanted to deter an attack from the brutal Turk.

. . . But one thing is certain: the "few years" are long past but this special tax continues to be paid, but now is used for purposes quite different than those they were supposed to serve. It is therefore necessary to cease this expression of imagined religiosity. The pope should not be a tyrant hiding under the mantle of faith. Just the opposite, he ought to be the kindly father as loving as the one whose deputy on earth the pope claims to be.

Translated by Alfred Bloch

Andrzej Frycz Modrzewski
(1503–1572)

Modrzewski was a political writer and moralist. He wrote exclusively in Latin and his works were well known in Europe. He was obviously a learned man and a humanist well acquainted with ancient literature, philosophy, theology, and the morés of his times. His most important work, *De Republica Emendanda*, was published in Basle, Switzerland. In it he makes Christian morality the basis for the lives of individuals, societies, and states. According to this work, all people should be equal before the laws, and the attachment of the peasant to the soil, submission of the peasant to the jurisdiction of the master, and so on, must be abolished.

Wars are an absolute evil that should be combatted. Only defensive wars are justified, but even those should be avoided by means of a proper foreign policy and arbitration of disputes.

Education, the main task of the state, should be public and paid for by the state. Modrzewski also suggested the establishment of supreme courts, supervisors of the poor (welfare), and guardians of public morals.

Improving the Republic

The purpose of laws is the promotion of honesty and of service for the common good. Laws must give equal recognition for services well done and mete out equal punishment for wrongdoing.

No freedom should be so highly valued that anyone defending it illegally could either avoid punishment or take advantage of inequality of punishment. True freedom depends on restraining evil designs and acts. True freedom is not an individualistic defense of that which someone is pleased to defend. . . .

If there has to be a differentiation in punishment then it should be based on restraining the evils that might be committed by leaders. Therefore, magnates, members of the gentry, and people occupying high government positions should be punished more severely than the poor, the peasants, and those who have no official position. . . .

Therefore, the first consideration of the lawgiver is to promulgate laws that promote honesty and the public good. That is what reason dictates.

[If laws do not promote honesty and do not serve the common good then] what is the good of a cure of the liver if it damages the stomach.
. . .

It happened that in one community two people got into a fight. One was a simple person; the other was a member of the gentry. Both were well off. The member of the gentry started the fight, but in consequence of the wounds he received, died. The simple man was apprehended, tried, and convicted to death by decapitation. The justification for the sentence was a statute according to which if a simple man kills or seriously injures a member of the gentry he has to be condemned to death. But—according to the same statute—if a member of the gentry commits the same crime, he is allowed to remain free on his land, is called in by the judge, and condemned to pay a monetary fine. . . .

This [example of differentiation in laws] creates two republics in which the citizens of either do not need each other, do not know each other, and the result of all this is that they share neither the water, the air, nor the sun.

. . . In a republic where such laws prevail one should not expect the results for which a people create a community. . . .

. . . Efforts should be exerted to avoid the necessity of war. All efforts should be exerted to maintain peace with neighbors and avoid giving them an excuse to become enemies. But if due to the actions of either side controversies do arise, then all efforts should be made to find a solution within the law, or to find a resolution of the conflict formulated by reasonable men acting in good faith.

Translated by Alfred Bloch

Stanislaw Staszic (1755–1826)

Staszic lived through the period when Polish patriots attempted to reform the kingdom by establishing the Commission for National Education and promulgating the Constitution of the third of May. Their efforts were thwarted by the magnates and Poland was partitioned. Staszic was by social origin a member of the middle class. He was very well educated and represents the Polish version of the Enlightenment and the tradition of the encyclopedists. The dominant influence on his writings was exerted by Jean Jacques Rousseau. Staszic, who wanted to reform the entire political structure of Poland, reserved his strongest advocacy for the rights of the peasants. He wanted land reform that would give them ownership of the land, release them of all forms of bondage, and grant them full equality under the law. Staszic is the prime example of what was later to become the Polish intelligentsia. He reflected the best in European culture and tried to adapt it to specific Polish conditions.

A Warning for Poland

The ruin of the Poles were the magnates. They broke all the respect for law, they refused to obey the government and they left laws unenforced. They are responsible for the fact that the Poles lost the concept of justice. They transformed law into an empty form, which was imposed only if it served the pride of the magnates or their greed and their ill will.

In this land in which laws became the instruments in the hands of scoundrels, the republic of citizens changed into a republic of plunderers, traitors, perjurers, and agents in the pay of foreign powers. The result of all this was that the one who had most weight [money] sits in the highest places.

. . . Who took the innocent gentry, which was so deeply and honestly committed to the well-being of the fatherland, and through deceit, bribes, turned them into slovenly drunkards—the magnates.

. . . Who sold the crown [of Poland]—the magnates. Who bought the crown—the magnates. . . . Who brought foreign armies into the country—the magnates. Who, through senseless policies, tore the proud and valorous cossacks from Poland and forced them to become Poland's enemies—the magnates.

. . . The magnates made two nations out of one country. . . .

The family that could muster the largest number of gentry followers assumed the leadership position. . . . The magnates controlled all elections. . . .

If any member of the *szlachta* had the courage to sustain a law, to defend the common good . . . he would be fortunate if he were not instantly hacked to pieces . . . that is how all was leveled by the ruling elite. Whosoever wanted to live in peace, enjoy his property, and be assured of justice would surrender to the magnates to be protected by their power.

Parents imbued innocent children with meanness. They taught them to be knaves, they broke their will and their self-confidence so necessary for a free man. Every day they showed the dishonest means through which they gained their unjustified wealth by serving their masters. The clergy in its teachings, the nuns from their pulpits, public teachers in their schools took advantage of every public occasion to laud the virtues, the citizenship, the justice of those who committed the greatest evils and crimes. A member of the gentry who received such an upbringing, and such an education had no will of his own. He did not feel his soul. . . .

. . . [the magnates] destroyed the national character. A member of the gentry from being courageous turned into one who fears everything . . . from being born to freedom to being ready to accept the heaviest serfdom. . . . The proof of that are the partitions. . . . Bereft of the knowledge of justice, the greatest injustice does not bring his blood to boil. . . . It is easy for him to bear false witness. The fame of the nation, the love of the fatherland does not move him to sacrifices. . . . He does not feel anymore that death is preferable to outrages of serfdom.

Landed Peasants Means Industrious Peasants

I have four-fifths of the Polish nation before my eyes. I see millions of beings, some of whom are half naked, others are covered with skins or rough cloth. All are dried thin, impoverished, . . . hairy, filthy. Their eyes are deeply sunk into their heads, they breathe laboriously.

Their faces are brutalized, dumb, stupid. They feel little, they think less; and that is their greatest luck.

It is difficult to discover in them a sensible soul. From the first sight of them they are more like animals than human beings. . . . Their food is bread made of the coarsest of flour, and during a quarter of a year it consists of greens. Their drink is water—or the inside-burning vodka. Their lodgings are holes—shacks above the ground to which no ray of the sun gains entrance. They are filled with stench and they smoke the good smoke that makes it difficult for the peasants to see their utter poverty . . . it chokes them day and night, it shortens their miserable lives—and mostly it kills babies. In this atmosphere of stench and smoke, the farmer, exhausted by his daily chores, sleeps on a rotting bed of misery. Next to him sleeps the small woman and on it stand the cow and the calf and the sow with the piglets. . . .

Noble Poles—those are the pleasures of the people upon whom the fate of your republic depends. These are the people who feed you.

These are the conditions of the peasant in Poland.

Translated by Alfred Bloch

THE
GENTRY

Henryk Sienkiewicz
(1846–1916)

Sienkiewicz was and remains the most brilliant of Poland's historical novelists. His works are comparable to those written by Sir Walter Scott. He was so well known in America that when President Daniel Coit Gilman of Johns Hopkins University participated in the quincentennial celebration of Jagiellonian University, held in Kracow in 1910, he said:

> America thanks Poland for three great names: Copernicus, to whom the whole world is indebted; Kosciuszko, who spilled his blood for American independence; and Sienkiewicz, whose name is a household word in thousands of American homes, and who introduced Poland to America.

A Pole sitting in the audience was so moved by this tribute that he shouted, "That's it. As long as Sienkiewicz lives Poland is not yet dead."* ("Poland is not yet dead" is a rough translation of the first line of the Polish national anthem.)

Sienkiewicz's fame in Poland is based on his trilogy *Fire and Sword, The Deluge,* and *The Little Knight*. His fame in America rests on some of his short stories that were published while he was in California (1876–79), and above all on *Quo Vadis*, a story that was made into a number of Hollywood films. Sienkiewicz was awarded the Nobel Prize for literature in 1905 and thus became one of the three Poles to be so honored. The other two were Wladyslaw Reymont in 1924 and Czeslaw Milosz in 1980.

Sienkiewicz's powerful novels were read by millions of Poles. Incidentally, when his books were first published in the last decades of the nineteenth century, they would have been too expensive for the average Pole to buy. A very wealthy Jewish industrialist, Hipolit Wawelberg, made a substantial contribution to cover the publishing costs and thus make the books cheaper and more accessible. His writings popularized and propagated the story of a powerful Poland led by a fearless gentry, which was not only the embodiment of Christianity but also its shield.

---

* The two quotations were taken from Sylvia E. Bowman, editor, *Henryk Sienkiewicz* (Boston: Twayne Publishers, 1968), p. 39.

Sienkiewicz was a patriot who made patriotism the supreme cultural and ethical value. His motto could have been the well-known slogan "My country right or wrong."

The excerpt from *Pan Michael* or, as it is known in this country *The Little Knight*, recalls events occurring during the endemic wars between the Commonwealth of Poland and the Ottoman Empire supported by Tartars and many marauding cossack bands. Noteworthy in this excerpt are the use of the titles "Pan" and "Knight," and the duality of standards applied on the one hand to the Poles and on the other to the Turks/Tartars.

The designation "Pan" in contemporary Poland is equivalent to the Anglo-Saxon "Mister," but Sienkiewicz uses it as a distinctive title implying a status above the ordinary citizen. The English equivalent would be "Your Worship." Sienkiewicz also uses the descriptive label "knight." By the mid-seventeenth century, when the story takes place, knighthood was a phenomenon of the past; yet Sienkiewicz uses it deliberately because knights, at least symbolically, represented honor, chivalry, honesty, compassion, and above all an unshakable commitment to Christianity. The author's entire thrust is to show that the gentry and the magnates were the glory of Poland.

The use of the historical novel to form national consciousness was emphasized by George Lukacs in his analysis of literature published in the United States under the title *Historical Novel*. Sienkiewicz typically reifies values he wanted modern Poles to believe and to live by.

Some readers and critics compared Sienkiewicz's trilogy to Homer's *Iliad*. It was an epic story whose heroes had the qualities of the demigods of ancient Greek mythology. But more sophisticated readers would agree with the assessment of Sienkiewicz by Witold Gombrowicz, a tireless foe of obsolete myth and meaningless conventions, who said:

> I am reading Sienkiewicz. What tormenting reading. We say "that is bad enough" and we continue to read. We exclaim "an intolerable soap opera" and we still read with enchantment. What a powerful genius—and there never was such a first-rate writer of the second-rate class. This is a second-rate Homer, a first-rate Dumas. . . . Sienkiewicz, this magician, this seducer, planted in our heads . . . Wolodyowski [Pan Michael] and the Great Hetman [Jan Sobieski, the king of Poland who rescued Vienna from the Turks—Editor] and corked them up. . . . If the history of literature adopted a criterion of the influence of art on people, Sienkiewicz, this demon, this catastrophy of our mind, this wrecker . . . should occupy the first place.*

Sienkiewicz did contribute to the creation of the ethos of Polish history. His world is powerful, magnificent, and fierce.

---

* From Mieczyslaw Giergielewicz, *Henryk Sienkiewicz* (Twayne Publishers, 1968), p. 164.

Pan Michael

Beyond every expectation, the Volodyovskis found guests at the fortalice [fortress]. Pan Bogush had come; he had determined to fix his residence at Hreptyoff for some months, so as to treat through Mellehovich with the Tartar captains Aleksandrovich, Moravski, Tvorovski, Krychinski, and others, either of the Lithuanian or Ukraine Tartars, who had gone to the service of the sultan. Pan Bogush was accompanied also by old Pan Novoveski and his daughter Eva, and by Pani Boski, a sedate person, with her daughter, Panna Zosia, who was young yet, and very beautiful. The sight of ladies in the wilderness and in wild Hreptyoff delighted, but still more astonished, the soldiers. The guests, too, were surprised at sight of the commandant and his wife; for the first, judging from his extended and terrible fame, they imagined to be some kind of giant, who by his very look would terrify people, his wife as a giantess with brows ever frowning and a rude voice. Meanwhile they saw before them a little soldier, with a kindly and friendly face, and also a tiny woman, rosy as a doll, who, in her broad trousers and with her saber, seemed more like a beautiful boy than a grown person. Nonetheless did the hosts receive their visitors with open arms. Basia kissed heartily, before presentation, the three women; when they told who they were, and whence they had come, she said:

"I should rejoice to bend the heavens for you, ladies, and for you, gentlemen. I am awfully glad to see you! It is well that no misfortune has met you on the road, for in our desert, you see, such a thing is not difficult; but this very day we have cut the ravagers to pieces."

Seeing then that Pani Boski was looking at her with increasing astonishment, she struck her saber, and added with great boastfulness, "Ah, but I was in the fight! Of course I was. That's the way with us! For God's sake, permit me, ladies, to go out and put on clothing proper to my sex, and wash my hands from blood a little; for I am coming from a terrible battle. Oh, if we hadn't cut down Azba today, perhaps you ladies would not have arrived without accident at Hreptyoff. I will return in a moment, and Michael will be at your service meanwhile."

She vanished through the door; and then the little knight, who had greeted Pan Novoveski already, pushed up to Pani Boski. "God has given me such a wife," said he to her, "that she is not only a loving companion in the house, but can be a valiant comrade in the field. Now, at her command I offer my services to your ladyship."

"May God bless her in everything," answered Pani Boski, "as He has blessed her in beauty! I am Antonia Boski; I have not come to exact services from your grace, but to beg on my knees for aid and rescue in misfortune. Zosia, kneel down here to before the knight; for if he cannot help us, no man can."

Pani Boski fell on her knees then, and the comely Zosia followed her example; both, shedding ardent tears, began to cry, "Save us, knight! Have pity on orphans!"

A crowd of officers, made curious, drew near on seeing the kneeling women, and especially because the sight of the comely Zosia attracted them; the little knight, greatly confused, raised Pani Boski, and seated her on a bench. "In God's name," asked he, "what are you doing? I should kneel first before a worthy woman. Tell, your ladyship, in what I can render assistance, and as God is in heaven, I will not delay."

"He will do what he promises; I, on my part, offer myself! Zagloba *sum!* it is enough for you to know that!" said the old warrior, moved by the tears of the women.

Then Pani Boski beckoned to Zosia; she took quickly from her bosom a letter, which she gave to the little knight. He looked at the letter and said, "From the hetman [cossack leader]!" Then he broke the seal and began to read:

Very Dear and Beloved Volodyovski!—I send from the road to you, through Pan Bogush, my sincere love and instructions, which Pan Bogush will communicate to you personally. I have barely recovered from fatigues in Yavorov, when immediately another affair comes up. This affair is very near my heart, because of the affection that I bear soldiers, whom if I forgot, the Lord God would forget me. Pan Boski, a cavalier of great honor and a dear comrade, was taken by the horde some years since, near Kamenyets. I have given shelter to his wife and daughter in Yavorov; but their hearts are weeping—one for a husband, the other for a father. I wrote through Pyotrovich to Pan Zlotnitski, our Resident in the Crimea, to look for Pan Boski everywhere. They found him, it seems; but the Tartars hid him afterward, therefore he could not be given up with other prisoners, and doubtless is rowing in a galley to this time. The women, despairing and hopeless, have ceased to importune me; but I, on returning recently, and seeing their unappeased sorrow, could not refrain from attempting some rescue. You are near the place, and have concluded, as I know, brotherhood with many murzas. I send the ladies to you, therefore, and do you give them aid. Pyotrovich will go soon to the Crimea. Give him letters to those murzas with whom you are in brotherhood. I cannot write to the vizir or the Khan, for they are not friendly to me; and besides, I fear that if I should write, they would consider Boski a very eminent person, and increase the ransom beyond measure. Commend the affair urgently to Pyotrovich, and command him not to return without Boski. Stir up all your brothers; though pagans, they observe plighted faith always, and must have great respect for you. Finally, do what you please; go to Rashkoff; promise three of the most considerable Tartars in exchange, if they return Boski alive. No one knows better than you all their methods, for, as I hear, you have ransomed relatives already. God bless you, and I will love you still more, for my heart will cease to bleed. I have heard of your management in Hreptyoff, that it is quiet there. I expected this. Only keep watch on Azba. Pan Bogush will tell you all about public affairs. For God's sake, listen carefully in the direction of Moldavia, for a great invasion will not miss us. Committing Pani Boski to your heart and efforts, I subscribe myself, etc.

Pani Boski wept without ceasing during the reading of the letter, and Zosia accompanied her, raising her blue eyes to heaven. Meanwhile, and before Pan Michael had finished, Basia ran in, dressed in woman's garments; and seeing tears in the eyes of the ladies, began to inquire with sympathy what the matter was. Therefore Pan Michael read the hetman's letter for her; and when she had listened to it carefully, she supported at once and with eagerness the prayers of the hetman and Pani Boski.

"The hetman has a golden heart," cried Basia, embracing her husband; "but we shall not show a worse one, Michael. Pani Boski will stay with us till her husband's return, and you will bring him in three months from the Crimea. In three or in two, is it not true?"

"Or tomorrow, or in an hour!" said Pan Michael, bantering. Here he turned to Pani Boski, "Decisions, as you see, are quick with my wife."

"May God bless her for that!" said Pani Boski. "Zosia, kiss the hand of the lady commandress."

But the lady commandress did not think of giving her hands to be kissed; she embraced Zosia again, for in some way they pleased each other at once. "Help us, gracious gentlemen," cried she. "Help us, and quickly!"

"Quickly, for her head is burning!" muttered Zagloba.

But Basia, shaking her yellow forelock, said, "Not my head, but the hearts of those gentlemen are burning from sorrow."

"No one will oppose your honest intention," said Pan Michael; "but first we must hear Pani Boski's story in detail."

"Zosia, tell everything as it was, for I cannot, from tears," said the matron.

Zosia dropped her eyes toward the floor, covering them entirely with the lids; then she became as red as a cherry, not knowing how to begin, and was greatly abashed at having to speak in such a numerous assembly.

But Basia came to her aid. "Zosia, and when did they take Pan Boski captive?"

"Five years ago, in 1667," said Zosia, with a thin voice, without raising the long lashes from her eyes. And she began in one breath to tell the story: "There were no raids to be heard of at that time, and papa's squadron was near Panyovtsi. Papa, with Pan Bulayovski, was looking after men who were herding cattle in the meadows, and the Tartars came then on the Wallachian road, and took papa, with Pan Bulayovski; but Pan Bulayovski returned two years ago, and papa has not returned."

Here two tears began to flow down Zosia's cheeks, so that Zagloba was moved at sight of them, and said, "Poor girl! Do not fear, child; papa will return, and will dance yet at your wedding."

"But did the hetman write to Pan Zlotnitski through Pyotrovich?" inquired Volodyovski.

"The hetman wrote about papa to the sword-bearer of Poznan," recited Zosia; "and the sword-bearer and Pan Pyotrovich found papa with Aga Murza Bey."

"In God's name! I know that Murza Bey. I was in brotherhood with his brother," said Volodyovski. "Would he not give up Pan Boski?"

"There was a command of the Khan to give up papa; but Murza Bey is severe, cruel. He hid papa, and told Pan Pyotrovich that he had sold him long before into Asia. But other captives told Pan Pyotrovich that that was not true, and that the murza only said that purposely, so that he might abuse papa longer; for he is the cruelest of all the Tartars toward prisoners. Perhaps papa was not in the Crimea then; for the murza has his own galleys, and needs men for rowing. But papa was not sold; all the prisoners said that the murza would rather kill a prisoner than sell him."

"Holy truth!" said Pan Mushalski. "They know that Murza Bey in the whole Crimea. He is a very rich Tartar, but wonderfully venomous against our people, for four brothers of his fell in campaigns against us."

"But has he never formed brotherhood among our people?" asked Pan Michael.

"It is doubtful!" answered the officers from every side.

"Tell me once what that brotherhood is," said Basia.

"You see," said Zagloba, "when negotiations are begun at the end of war, men from both armies visit one another and enter into friendship. It happens then that an officer inclines to himself a murza, and a murza an officer; then they vow to each other life-friendship, which they call brotherhood. The more famous a man is, as Michael, for instance, or I, or Pan Rushehyts, who holds command in Rashkoff now, the more is his brotherhood sought. It is clear that such a man will not conclude brotherhood with some common fellow, but will seek it only among the most renowned murzas. The custom is this,— they pour water on their sabers and swear mutual friendship; do you understand?"

"And how if it comes to war afterward?"

"They can fight in a general war, but if they meet alone, if they are attacking as skirmishers, they will greet each other, and depart in friendship. Also if one of them falls into captivity, the other is bound to alleviate it, and in the worst case to ransom him; indeed, there have been some who shared their property with brothers. When it is a question of friends or acquaintances or of finding someone, brothers go to brothers; and justice commands us to acknowledge that no people observe such oaths better than the Tartars. The word is the main thing with them, and such a friend you can trust certainly."

"But has Michael many such?"

"I have three powerful murzas," answered Volodyovski; "and one of them is from Lubni times. Once I begged him of Prince Yeremi. Aga Bey is his name; and even now, if he had to lay his head down for me, he would lay it down. The other two are equally reliable."

"Ah," said Basia, "I should like to conclude brotherhood with the Khan himself, and free all the prisoners."

"He would not be averse to that," said Zagloba; "but it is not known what reward he would ask of you."

"Permit me, gentlemen," said Pan Michael; "let us consider what we ought to do. Now listen; we have news from Kamenyets that in two weeks at the furthest Pyotrovich will be here with a numerous escort. He will go to the Crimea with ransom for a number of Armenian merchants from Kamenyets, who at the change of the Khan were plundered and taken captive. That happened to Seferovich, the brother of Pretor. All those people are very wealthy; they will not spare money, and Pyotrovich will go well provided. No danger threatens him; for, first, winter is near, and it is not the time for chambuls [military units of Turkish army], and, secondly, with him are going Naviragh, the delegate of the Patriarch of Echmiadzin, and the two Anardrats from Kaffa, who have a safe-conduct from the young Khan. I will give letters to Pyotrovich to the residents of the Commonwealth and to my brothers. Besides, it is known to you, gentlemen, that Pan Rushchyts, the commandant at Rashkoff, has relatives in the horde, who, taken captive in childhood, have become thoroughly Tartar, and have risen to dignities. All these will move earth and heaven, will try negotiations; in case of stubbornness on the part of the murza, they will rouse the Khan himself against him, or perhaps they will twist the murza's head somewhere in secret. I hope, therefore, that if, which God grant, Pan Boski is alive, I shall get him in a couple of months without fail, as the hetman commands, and my immediate superior here present" (at this Pan Michael bowed to his wife).

His immediate superior sprang to embrace the little knight the second time. Pani and Panna Boski clasped their hands, thanking God, who had permitted them to meet such kindly people. Both became notably cheerful, therefore.

"If the old Khan were alive," said Pan Nyenashinyets, "all would go more smoothly; for he was greatly devoted to us, and of the young one they say the opposite. In fact, those Armenian merchants for whom Pan Pyotrovich is to go, were imprisoned in Bagchesarai itself during the time of the young Khan, and probably at his command."

"There will be a change in the young, as there was in the old Khan, who, before he convinced himself of our honesty, was the most inveterate enemy of the Polish name," said Zagloba. "I know this best, for I was seven years under him in captivity. Let the sight of me give comfort to your ladyship," continued he, taking a seat near Pani Boski. "Seven years is no joke; and still I returned and crushed so many of those dog brothers that for each day of my captivity I sent at least two of them to hell; and for Sundays and holidays who knows if there will not be three or four? Ha!"

"Seven years!" repeated Pani Boski, with a sigh.

"May I die if I add a day! Seven years in the very palace of the Khan," confirmed Zagloba, blinking mysteriously. "And you must know that that young Khan is my—" Here he whispered something in the ear of Pani Boski, burst into a loud "Ha, ha, ha!" and began to stroke his knees with his palms; finally he slapped Pani Boski's knees, and said, "They were good times, were they not? In youth every man you met was an enemy, and every day a new prank, ha!"

The sedate matron became greatly confused, and pushed back somewhat from the jovial knight; the younger women dropped their eyes, divining easily that the pranks of which Pan Zagloba was talking must be something opposed to their native modesty, especially since the soldiers burst into loud laughter.

"It will be needful to send to Pan Rushchyts at once," said Basia, "so that Pan Pyotrovich may find the letters ready in Rashkoff."

"Hasten with the whole affair," added Pan Bogush, "while it is winter: for, first no chambuls come out, and roads are safe; secondly, in the spring God knows what may happen."

"Has the hetman news from Tsargrad?" inquired Volodyovski.

"He has; and of this we must talk apart. It is necessary to finish quickly with those captains. When will Mellehovich come back?—for much depends on him."

"He has only to destroy the rest of the ravagers, and afterward bury the dead. He ought to return today or tomorrow morning. I commanded him to bury only our men, not Azba's; for winter is at hand, and there is no danger of infection. Besides, the wolves will clear them away."

"The hetman asks," said Pan Bogush, "that Mellehovich should have no hindrance in his work; as often as he wishes to go to Rashkoff, let him go. The hetman asks, too, to trust him in everything, for he is certain of his devotion. He is a great soldier, and may do us much good."

"Let him go to Rashkoff and whithersoever he pleases," said the little knight. "Since we have destroyed Azba, I have no urgent need of him. No large band will appear not till the first grass."
"Is Azba cut to pieces then?" inquired Novoveski.

"So cut up that I do not know if twenty-five men escaped; and even those will be caught one by one, if Mellehovich has not caught them already."

"I am terribly glad of this," said Novoveski, "for now it will be possible to go to Rashkoff in safety." Here he turned to Basia: "We can take to Pan Rushchyts the letters which her grace, our benefactress, has mentioned."

"Thank you," answered Basia; "there are occasions here continually, for men are sent expressly."

"All the commands must maintain communication," said Pan Michael. "But are you going to Rashkoff, indeed, with this young beauty?"

"Oh, this is an ordinary puss, not a beauty, gracious benefactor," said Novoveski; "and I am going to Rashkoff, for my son, the rascal, is serving there under the banner of Pan Rushchyts. It is nearly ten years since he ran away from home, and knocks at my fatherly clemency only with letters."

"I guessed at once that you were Pan Adam's father, and I was about to inquire; but we were so taken up with sorrow for Pani Boski. I guessed it at once, for there is a resemblance in features. Well, then, he is your son?"

"So his late mother declared; and as she was a virtuous woman, I have no reason for doubt."

"I am doubly glad to have such a guest as you. For God's sake, but do not call your son a rascal; for he is a famous soldier, and a worthy cavalier, who brings the highest honor to your grace. Do you not know that, after Pan Rushchyts, he is the best partisan in the squadron? Do you not know that he is an eye in the head of the hetman? Independent commands are intrusted to him, and he has fulfilled every function with incomparable credit."

Pan Novoveski flushed from delight. "Gracious Colonel," said he, "more than once a father blames his child only to let someone deny what he says; and I think that 'tis impossible to please a parent's heart more than by such a denial. Reports have reached me already of Adam's good service; but I am really comforted now for the first time, when I hear these reports confirmed by such renowned lips. They say that he is not only a manful soldier, but steady—which is even a wonder to me, for he was always a whirlwind. The rogue had a love for war from youth upward; and the best proof of this is that he ran away from home as a boy. If I could have caught him at that time, I would not have spared him. But now I must spare him; if not, he would hide for ten other years, and it is dreary for me, an old man, without him."

"And has he not been home during so many years?"

"He has not; I forbade him. But I have had enough of it, and now I go to him, since he, being in service, cannot come to me. I intended to ask of you and my benefactress a refuge for this maiden while I went to Rashkoff alone; but since you say that it is safe everywhere, I will take her. She is curious, the magpie, to see the world. Let her look at it."

"And let people look at her," put in Zagloba.

"Ah, they would have nothing to see," said the young lady, out of whose dark eyes and mouth, fixed as if for a kiss, something quite different was speaking.

"An ordinary puss—nothing more than a puss!" said Pan Novoveski. "But if she sees a handsome officer, something may happen; therefore I chose to bring her with me rather than leave her, especially as it is dangerous for a girl at home alone. But if I go without her to Rashkoff, then let her grace give command to tie her with a cord, or she will play pranks."

"I was no better myself," said Basia.

"They gave her a distaff to spin," said Zagloba; "but she danced with it, since she had no one better to dance with. But you are a jovial man. Basia, I should like to have an encounter with Pan Novoveski, for I also am fond of amusement at times."

Meanwhile, before supper was served, the door opened, and Mellehovich entered. Pan Novoveski did not notice him at once, for he was talking with Zagloba; but Eva saw him, and a flame struck her face; then she grew pale suddenly.

"Pan Commandant," said Mellehovich to Pan Michael, "according to order, those men were caught."

"Well, where are they?"

"According to order, I had them hanged."

"Well done! And have your men returned?"

"A part remained to bury the bodies; the rest are with me."

At this moment Pan Novoveski raised his head, and great astonishment was reflected on his face. "In God's name, what do I see?" cried he. Then he rose, went straight to Mellehovich, and said, "Azya! And what art thou doing here, ruffian?"

He raised his hand to seize the Tartar by the collar; but in Mellehovich there was such an outburst in one moment as there is when a man throws a handful of powder into fire; he grew pale as a corpse, and seizing with iron grasp the hand of Novoveski, he said, "I do not know you! Who are you?" and pushed him so violently that Novoveski staggered to the middle of the room. For some time he could not utter a word from rage; but regaining breath, began to cry:

"Gracious Commandant, this is my man, and besides that, a runaway. He was in my house from childhood. The ruffian denies! He is my man! Eva, who is he? Tell."

"Azya," said Eva, trembling in all her body.

Mellehovich did not even look at her. With eyes fixed on Novoveski, and with quivering nostril, he looked at the old noble with unspeakable hatred, pressing with his hand the handle of his knife. At the same time his mustaches began to quiver from the movement of his nostrils, and from under those mustaches white teeth were gleaming, like those of an angry wild beast.

The officers stood in a circle; Basia sprang in between Mellehovich and Novoveski. "What does this mean?" asked she, frowning.

"Pan Commandant," said Novoveski, "this is my man, Azya by name, and a runaway. Serving in youthful years in the Crimea, I found him half-alive on the steppe, and I took him. He is a Tartar. He remained twelve years in my house, and was taught together with my son. When my son ran away, this one helped me in management until he wished to make love to Eva; seeing this, I had him flogged: he ran away after that. What is his name here?"

"Mellehovich."

"He has assumed that name. He is called Azya—nothing more. He says that he does not know me; but I know him, and so does Eva."

"Your grace's son has seen him many times," said Basia. "Why did not he know him?"

"My son might not know him; for when he ran away from home, both were fifteen years old, and this one remained six years with me afterward, during which time he changed considerably, grew, and got mustaches. But Eva knew him at once. Gracious hosts, you will lend belief more quickly to a citizen than to this accident from the Crimea!"

"Pan Mellehovich is an officer of the hetman," said Basia; "we have nothing to do with him."

"Permit me; I will ask him. Let the other side be heard," said the little knight.

But Pan Novoveski was furious. "*Pan* Mellehovich! What sort of a *Pan* is he? My serving lad, who has hidden himself under a strange name. Tomorrow I'll make my dog keeper of that *Pan;* the day after tomorrow I'll give command to beat that *Pan* with clubs. And the hetman himself cannot hinder me; for I am a noble, and I know my rights."

To this Pan Michael answered more sharply, and his mustaches quivered. "I am not only a noble, but a colonel, and I know my rights too. You can demand your man, by law, and have recourse to the jurisdiction of the hetman; but I command here, and no one else does."

Pan Novoveski moderated at once, remembering that he was talking not only to a commandant, but to his own son's superior, and besides the most noted knight in the Commonwealth. "Pan Colonel," said he, in a milder tone, "I will not take him against the will of your grace; but I bring forward my rights, and I beg you to believe me."

"Mellehovich, what do you say to this?" asked Volodyovski.

The Tartar fixed his eyes on the floor, and was silent.

"That your name is Azya we all know," added Pan Michael.

"There are other proofs to seek," said Novoveski. "If he is my man, he has fish tattooed in blue on his breast."

Hearing this, Pan Nyenashinyets opened his eyes widely and his mouth; then he seized himself by the head, and cried, "Azya, Tugai Beyovich!"

All eyes were turned on him; he trembled throughout his whole body, as if all his wounds were reopened, and he repeated, "That is my captive! That is Tugai Bey's son. As God lives, it is he."

But the young Tartar raised his head proudly, cast his wildcat glance on the assembly, and pulling open suddenly the clothes on his bosom, said, "Here are the fish tattooed in blue. I am the son of Tugai Bey!"

Translated by Jeremiah Curtin

Adam Mickiewicz
(1798–1855)

Mickiewicz is the poet laureate of Poland. Although he was born in Lithuania, his family was thoroughly assimilated into Poland's culture and had claims to gentry origin. Mickiewicz was the Tennyson of Poland. He was the bard whose creativity sprang from the melancholy and at times ferocious beauty of Poland's countryside.

He was, in common with other great poets, a "poet engagé." Like Byron and Shelley, Mickiewicz could not accept oppression in any form. Although Imperial Russia was Poland's jailer, in 1825 Mickiewicz allied himself with the first Russian revolutionary group that was aristocratic in origin: the "Decembrists." He became a close friend of Pushkin, the poet laureate of Russia.

Mickiewicz was forced to emigrate. He taught at the College de France. In his lectures on the history of Slavic literature, he never failed to place in proper perspective the tremendous contribution to literature by the Russians. Polish superpatriots criticized him for it. In 1848, Mickiewicz tried to organize a Polish Legion to help the Polish cause during the revolutions, which in that year shook up all of Europe except for England and Imperial Russia.

Finally, when Napoleon III joined in the Crimean War (1854–55), Mickiewicz went to Istanbul, the capital of Poland's historical enemy, the Turks, to recruit an army to free Poland. He died trying. In 1890, Mickiewicz's remains were transported to Poland and buried on the grounds of the Wawel Palace, the house of Poland's kings and the burial ground of Poland's heroes.

The excerpt that follows is taken from *Pan Tadeusz*, Mickiewicz's most important and most widely read epic poem. He shows us the beauty of the land, the hope there is to be found in nature, and the justice and harmony that could prevail among people of good will. His portrait of the gentry is vastly different from the one presented by Sienkiewicz. In the eyes of Mickiewicz, gentry, church, Jews, and peasants could live in harmony.

Mickiewicz is too idyllic and shares the notion prevailing in his time that somehow primitivism and closeness to nature could help create a truly democratic society. This belief was shared by the best among Poland's historians, Joachim Lelewel, and by the German historian Georg Ludwig

Maurer, who exerted a telling influence on at least one of his students—Karl Marx. The theme is explored by Marx in *Primitive Communism*.

The other important point made in this excerpt is voiced by a member of the lower clergy who admired Napoleon—the "most Christian of emperors"—and saw the salvation of Poland coming with the help of a heroic military figure, perhaps another Napoleon. Mickiewicz himself subscribed to this notion.

This search for a strong man, a messiah, who would save Poland is a recurrent theme in Mickiewicz's writings and symbolizes the poet's mystical notion of the "special nation"—Poland—which would carry "the word" to the rest of the world. He publicly shared the conviction with the Russian believers that they as Slavs would save the world. The Polish word for *Slavs* is *Slowianie*. The Polish word for *word* is *slowo*. Thus Slavs could mean the people who will receive the word.

Pan Tadeusz[*]

A vision in curl papers awakes Thaddeus—Belated discovery of a mistake—The tavern—The emissary—The skillful use of a snuff-box turns discussion into the proper channel—The jungle—The bear—Danger of Thaddeus and the Count—Three shots—The dispute of the Sagalas musket with the Sanguszko musket settled in favor of the single-barreled Horeszko carbine—Bigos—The Seneschal's tale of the duel of Dowejko and Domejko, interrupted by hunting the hare—End of the tale of Dowejko and Domejko.

Ye comrades of the Grand Dukes of Lithuania, trees of Bialowieza, Switez, Ponary, and Kuszelewo! Whose shade once fell upon the crowned heads of the dread Witenes and the great Mindowe, and of Giedymin, when on the height of Ponary, by the huntsmen's fire, he lay on a bear skin, listening to the song of the wise Lizdejko; and, lulled by the sight of the Wilia and the murmur of the Wilejko, he dreamed of the iron wolf;** and awakened, by the clear command of the gods, he built the city of Wilno, which sits among the forests as a wolf amid bison, wild boars, and bears. From this city of Wilno, as from the she-wolf of Rome, went forth Kiejstut and Olgierd and his sons, as mighty hunters as they were famous knights, in pursuit now of their enemies and now of wild beasts. A hunter's dream disclosed

---

*There are excellent poetic translations of *Pan Tadeusz*, but this prose excerpt is easier to read and fits the tone of the anthology.
**All the names refer to real or mythical heroes of Lithuanian early history prior to the union the Poland.

to us the secrets of the future, that Lithuania ever needs iron and wooded lands.

Ye forests! The last to come hunting among you was the last king who wore the cap of Witold, the last fortunate warrior of the Jagiellos, and the last huntsman among the rulers of Lithuania. Trees of my fatherland! If Heaven grants that I return to behold you, old friends, shall I find you still? Do ye still live? Ye, among whom I once crept as a child—does great Baublis still live, in whose bulk, hollowed by ages, as in a goodly house, twelve could sup at table? Does the grove of Mendog still bloom by the village church? And there in the Ukraine, does there still rise on the banks of the Ros, before the mansion of the Holowinskis, that linden tree so far-spreading that beneath its shade a hundred youths and a hundred maidens were wont to join as partners in the dance?

Monuments of our fathers! How many of you each year are destroyed by the axes of the merchants, or of the Muscovite government! These vandals leave no refuge either for the forest warblers or for the bards, to whom your shade was as dear as to the birds. Yet the linden of Czarnolas, responsive to the voice of Jan Kochanowski, inspired in him so many rimes! Yet that prattling oak still sings of so many marvels to the cossack bard!

How much do I owe to you, trees of my homeland! A wretched huntsman, fleeing from the mockery of my comrades, in exchange for the game that I missed how many fancies did I capture beneath your calm, when in the wild thicket, forgetful of the chase, I sat me down amid a clump of trees! Around me here the gray-bearded moss showed silver, streaked with the blue of dark, crushed berries; there heathery hillocks shone red, decked with cowberries as with rosaries of coral. All about was darkness: over me the branches hung like low, thick, green clouds; somewhere above the motionless vault the wind played with a wailing, roaring, howling, crashing thunder; a strange, deafening uproar! It seemed to me that there above my head rolled a hanging sea.

Below, the crumbling remains of cities meet the eye. Here an overthrown oak protrudes from the ground, like an immense ruin; on it seem to rest fragments of walls and columns; on this side are branching stumps, on that half-rotted beams, enclosed with a hedge of grass. Within the barricade it is terrible to look: there dwell the lords of the forest, wild boars, bears, and wolves; at the gate lie the half-gnawed bones of some unwary guests. Sometimes there rise up through the green of the grass, like two jets of water, a pair of stag's antlers; and a beast flits between the trees like a yellow streak, as when a sunbeam falls between the forest trees and dies.

And again there is quiet below. A woodpecker on a fir tree raps lightly and flies farther on and vanishes; it has hidden, but does not cease to tap with its beak, like a child when it has hidden and wishes to be sought for. Nearer sits a squirrel, holding a nut in its paws and gnawing it; its tail hangs over its eyes like the plume over a cuirassier's [a mounted, armored soldier] helmet: even though thus protected, it keeps glancing about; perceiving the guest, this dancer of the woods skips from tree to tree and flashes like lightning; finally it slips into an invisible opening of a stump, like a dryad returning to her native tree. Again all is quiet.

Now a branch shakes from the touch of someone's hand, and between the parted clusters of the service berries shines a face more fair than they. It is a maiden gathering berries or nuts; in a basket of simple bark she offers you freshly gathered cowberries, rosy as her lips. By her side walks a youth who bends down the branches of the hazel tree; the girl catches the nuts as they flash by her.

Now they have heard the peal of the horns and the baying of the hounds; they guess that a hunt is drawing near them; and between the dense mass of boughs, full of alarm, they vanish suddenly from the eye, like deities of the forest.

In Soplicowo there was a great commotion; but neither the barking of the dogs, nor the neighing of the horses and the creaking of the carts, nor the blare of the horns that gave the signal for the hunt could stir Thaddeus from his bed; falling fully dressed on his couch, he had slept like a marmot in its burrow. None of the young men thought of looking for him in the yard; everyone was occupied with his own affairs and was hurrying to his appointed place; they entirely forgot their sleeping comrade.

He was snoring. Through the heart-shaped opening that was cut in the shutter the sun poured into the darkened room like a fiery column, straight on the brow on the sleeping lad. He wanted to doze longer and twisted about, trying to avoid the light; suddenly he heard a knocking and awoke; cheerful was his awakening. He felt blithe as a bird and breathed freely and lightly; he felt himself happy and smiled to himself. Thinking of all that had happened to him the day before, he blushed and sighed, and his heart beat fast.

He looked at the window. Marvelous to say, in the sunlit aperture, within that heart, there shone two bright eyes, opened wide, as is wont to be the case when one gazes from daylight into darkness; he saw also a little hand, raised like a fan on the side toward the sun, to shield the gaze; the tiny fingers, turned toward the rosy light, reddened clear through, as if made of rubies; he beheld curious lips, slightly parted, and little teeth that shone like pearls among corals; and the face, though it was protected from the sun by a rosy palm, itself glowed all over like the rose.

Thaddeus was sleeping beneath the window; himself hidden in the shade, lying on his back, he wondered at the marvelous apparition, which was directly above him, almost touching his face. He did not know whether he was awake, or whether he was imagining one of those dear, bright childish faces that we remember to have seen in the dreams of our innocent years. The little face bent down: he beheld, trembling with fear and joy, alas! He beheld most clearly—he recalled and recognized now that short, bright golden hair done up in tiny curl papers white as snow, like silvery pods, which in the gleam of the sun shone like a crown on the image of a saint.

He started up, and the vision straightway vanished, frightened by the noise; he waited, but it did not return! He only heard again a thrice-repeated knocking and the words: "Get up, sir; it is time for hunting, you have overslept." He jumped from his couch, and with both hands pushed back the shutters, so that their hinges rattled, and flying open they knocked against the wall on either side. He rushed out and looked around, amazed and confused, but he saw nothing, nor did he perceive traces of any one. Not far from the window was the garden fence; on it the hop leaves and the flowery garlands were trembling; had some light hands touched them or had the wind stirred them? Thaddeus gazed long on them, but did not dare enter the enclosure; he only leaned on the fence, raised his eyes, and, with his finger pressed on his lips, bade himself be silent, in order not to break the stillness by a hasty word. Then he rapped his forehead, as though he were tapping for some ancient memories that had been lulled to sleep within him; finally, gnawing his fingers, he drew blood, and shouted at the top of his voice: "It serves me right, it does."

In the yard, where a few moments before there had been so many cries, now everything was desolate and silent as in a graveyard; all had gone afield. Thaddeus pricked up his ears, and put his hands to them like trumpets; he listened till the wind that blew from the forest brought to him the sound of horns and the shouts of the hunting throng.

Thaddeus's horse was waiting saddled in the stable. So, musket in hand, he vaulted upon it, and like a madman galloped toward the inns that stood near the forest chapel, where the beaters were to have gathered at early dawn.

The two taverns bent forward from either side of the road, threatening each other with their windows like enemies. The old one rightfully belonged to the owner of the castle; the new one Judge Soplica had built to spite the castle. In the former, as in his own inheritance, Gerwazy ruled supreme; in the latter Protazy occupied the highest place at the table.

The new tavern was not peculiar in its appearance. The old one was built according to an ancient model, which was invented by Tyrian carpenters, and later spread abroad over the world by the Jews; a style of architecture completely unknown to foreign builders: we inherit it from the Jews.

The tavern was in front like an ark, behind like a temple; the ark was Noah's genuine oblong chest, known today under the simple name of stable; in it there were various beasts, horses, cows, oxen, bearded goats; and above flocks of birds; and a pair each of various sorts of reptiles—and likewise insects. The rear portion, formed like a marvelous temple, reminded one by its appearance of that edifice of Solomon that Hiram's carpenters, the first skilled in the art of building, erected on Zion. The Jews imitate it to this day in their schools, and the design of the schools may be traced in their taverns and stables. The roof of lath and straw was peaked, turned up, and crooked as a Jew's torn cap. From the gable protruded the edges of a balcony, supported on a row of close-set wooden columns; the columns, which were a great architectural marvel, were solid, though half decayed, and were put up crooked, as in the tower of Pisa; they did not conform to Greek models, for they lacked bases and capitals. On the columns rested semicircular arches, also of wood, in imitation of Gothic art. Above were artistic ornaments, crooked as the arms of Sabbath candlesticks, executed not with the graver or chisel, but with skillful blows of the carpenter's hatchet; at their ends hung balls, somewhat resembling the buttons that the Jews hang on their foreheads when they pray, and which, in their own tongue, they call *cyces*. In a word, from a distance the tottering, crooked tavern was like a Jew, when he nods his head in prayer; the roof is his cap, the disordered thatch his beard, the smoky, dirty walls his black frock, and in front the carving juts out like the *cyces* on his brow.

In the center of the tavern was a partition like that in a Jewish school; one portion, divided into long and narrow rooms, was reserved exclusively for ladies and gentlemen who were traveling; the other formed one immense hall. Along each wall stretched a many-footed narrow, wooden table; by it were benches, which, though lower, were as like the table as children are like their father. On these benches around the room sat peasants, both men and women, and likewise some of the minor gentry, all in rows; only the steward sat by himself. After early mass they had come from the chapel to Jankiel's, since it was Sunday, to have a drink and to amuse themselves. By each a cup of grayish brandy was already frothing, the hostess was running about with the bottle, serving every one. In the center of the room stood the host, Jankiel, in a long gown that reached to the floor, and was fastened with silver clasps; one hand he had tucked into his black silk girdle, with the other he stroked in dignified fashion his gray beard. Casting his eye about, he issued orders, greeted the guests who came in, went up to those that were seated, and started conversation, reconciled persons quarreling, but served no one—he only walked to and fro. The Jew was old, and famed everywhere for his probity; for many years he had been keeping the tavern, and no one either of the peasants or of the gentry had ever made complaint against him to his landlord. Of what should they complain? He had good drinks to choose from; he kept his accounts strictly, but without any knavery; he did not forbid merriment, but would not endure drunkenness. He was a great lover of entertainments; at his tavern marriages and christenings were celebrated; every Sunday he had musicians come from the village, including a bass viol and bagpipes.

He was familiar with music and was himself famous for his musical talent; with the dulcimer, his national instrument, he had once wandered from estate to estate and amazed his hearers by his playing and his songs, for he sang well and with a trained voice. Though a Jew, he had a fairly good Polish pronunciation, and was particularly fond of the national songs, of which he had brought back a multitude from each trip over the Niemen, *kolomyjkas* from Halicz and *mazurkas* from Warsaw. A report, I do not know how well founded, was current throughout the district, that he was the first to bring from abroad and make popular in that time and place the song that is today famous all over the world, and which was first played in the Ausonian land to Italians by the trumpets of the Polish legions. The talent of song pays well in Lithuania; it gains people's affection and makes one famous and rich. Jankiel had made a fortune; sated with gain and glory, he had hung his sweet-toned dulcimer upon the wall, and settling down with his children in the tavern he had taken up liquor selling. Besides this he was the underrabbi in the neighboring town, and always a welcome guest in every quarter, and a household counselor: he had a good knowledge of the grain trade on the river barges; such knowledge is needful in a village. He had also the reputation of being a patriotic Pole.

He was the first to bring to an end the quarrels between the two taverns, which had often led even to bloodshed, by leasing them both. He was equally respected by the old partisans of the Horeszkos and by the servants of Judge Soplica. He alone knew how to keep an ascendancy over the terrible warden of the Horeszkos and the quarrelsome apparitor; in Jankiel's presence both Gerwazy, terrible of hand, and Protazy, terrible of tongue, stifled their ancient wrongs.

Gerwazy was not there; he had gone to join the beaters, not wishing that the count, young and inexperienced, should undertake alone so important and difficult an expedition. So he had gone with him for counsel, and likewise for defense.

Today Gerwazy's place, the farthest from the threshold, between two benches, in the very corner of the tavern (called *pokucie*), was occupied by the monk, Father Robak, the almsgatherer. Jankiel had seated him there; he evidently highly respected the Bernardine, for whenever he noticed that his glass was empty he immediately ran up and told them to pour out for him July mead. They said that the Bernardine and he had been acquainted when young, somewhere off in foreign lands. Robak often came by night to the tavern, and consulted secretly with the Jew about important matters; they said that the monk was smuggling goods, but this was a slander unworthy of belief.

Leaning on the table, Robak was discoursing in a low voice; a throng of gentry surrounded him and pricked up their ears, and bent down their noses to the monk's snuffbox. Each took a pinch, and the gentlemen sneezed like mortars.

"Reverendissime," said Skoluba with a sneeze, "that is fine tobacco, it goes way up to your topknot. Never since I have worn a nose"—here he stroked his long nose—"have I met its like"—here he sneezed a second time. "It is real Bernardine, doubtless made in Kowno, a city famous throughout the world for tobacco and mead. I was there in—"

"To the health of you all, my noble gentlemen!" Robak interrupted him. "As for the tobacco—hm—it comes from farther off than my friend Skoluba thinks; it comes from Jasna Gora, the Bright Mountain; the Paulist Brethren prepare such tobacco in the city of Czenstochowa, where stands the image, famed for so many miracles, of Our Lady the Virgin, Queen of the Crown of Poland: she is likewise still called Duchess of Lithuania! She still watches over her royal crown, but in the Duchy of Lithuania the schism is now established!"

"From Czenstochowa?" said Wilbik. "I confessed myself there when I went on a pilgrimage thirty years ago. Is it true that the

French are now visiting the city, and that they are going to tear down the church and seize the treasury—for this is all printed in the *Lithuanian Courier*?"

"No, it is not true," said the Bernardine. "His majesty the Emperor Napoleon is a most exemplary Catholic; the pope himself anointed him, and they live in harmony, and spread the faith among the French people, which has become a trifle corrupted. To be sure they have contributed much silver from Czenstochowa to the national treasury, for the fatherland, for Poland, as the Lord God himself bids; his altars are always the treasury of the fatherland. Why, in the Duchy of Warsaw we have a Polish army of a hundred thousand, perhaps soon there will be more. And who will pay that army? Will it be you Lithuanians? You are now giving your pennies only for the Muscovite coffers."

"The devil we are!" cried Wilbik; "they take them from us by force."

"Oh, my dear sir," a peasant spoke up humbly, bowing to the monk and scratching his head, "for the gentry it is only half bad, but they skin *us* like linden bark."

"You stupid son of Ham!" cried Skoluba. "It is easier for you; you peasants are as used to skinning as eels; but for us *men of birth*, us gentlemen accustomed to golden liberty! Ah, brothers! Why, in old times a gentleman on his garden patch—"

"Yes, yes," they all cried, "was a wojewoda's [governor of state] match."

"Today they even deny our gentle birth; they bid us hunt up papers and prove it by documents."

"That's nothing for such as you!" shouted Juraha. "Your precious ancestors were peasants who obtained nobility, but I am of princes' blood! To ask me for a patent, showing when I became a nobleman! Only God remembers that! Let the Muscovite go to the forest and ask the oak grove who gave it a patent to grow above all the shrubs!"

"Prince!" said Zagiel. "Go tell that to someone else! You will find no end of princes' coronets in this district."

"You have a cross in your coat of arms," shouted Podhajski; "that is a covert allusion to the fact that a baptized Jew was a member of your line."

"That is false!" interrupted Birbarz; "now I spring from the blood of Tartar counts, and yet my coat bears crosses above a ship."

"The white rose of five petals," cried Mickiewicz, "with a cap in a golden field: it is a princely coat; Stryjkowski writes frequently of it."

After this a mighty hubbub arose all over the room. The Bernardine had recourse to his snuffbox; he offered a pinch to each of the orators in turn, and the wrangling immediately subsided: each accepted for courtesy's sake, and sneezed several times. The Bernardine, taking advantage of the intermission, continued:

"Ah! This tobacco has made great men sneeze! Will you believe me that four times General Dombrowski has taken a pinch from this snuffbox?"

"Dombrowski!" they shouted.

"Yes, yes, he, the general. I was in the camp when he was recapturing Dantzic from the Germans. He had something to write; and, fearing that he might go to sleep, he took a pinch, sneezed, and twice patted me on the back. 'Father Robak,' he said, 'Father Bernardine, perhaps we shall see each other in Lithuania before the year is over. Tell the Lithuanians to receive me with Czenstochowa tobacco; I take none but that.'"

The monk's speech aroused such amazement and such joy that the whole noisy assembly was silent for a moment; then they repeated under their breath the words, "Tobacco from Poland? Czenstochowa? Dombrowski? From the Italian land?" until finally all at once, as if thought had fused with thought and word with word, as if a signal had been given, all began to sing with one voice "Dombrowski's march"!* All shouted together, all embraced one another; the peasant and the Tartar count, the prince's hat and the cross, the white rose, the griffin, and the ship; they forgot everything, even the Bernardine; they only sang and shouted: "Brandy, mead, wine!"

Father Robak listened to the song for a long time; finally he wanted to cut it short. So he took in both hands his snuffbox, broke up the melody with a sneeze, and, before they got together again, he hastened to speak thus:

"You praise my tobacco, my good friends; now see what is going on inside the snuffbox."

Here, wiping with his handkerchief the soiled base of the box, he showed them a little painted army, like a swarm of flies: in the middle sat a man on a charger, the size of a beetle, evidently the leader of the troop; he had made his horse rear, as though he wanted to leap into the skies; one hand he held on the bridle, the other up to his nose.

"Gaze," said Robak, "at that threatening form, and guess whose it is."

All looked with curiosity.

---

*Today this is the Polish national anthem.

"That is a great man, an emperor, but not of the Muscovites; their czars have never used tobacco."

"A great man," cried Cydzik, "and in a long gray coat? I thought that great men wore gold, for among the Muscovites any sort of a general, sir, fairly shines with gold, like a pike in saffron."

"Bah!" interrupted Rymsza; "why, in my youth I saw Kosciuszko, the chief of our nation: he was a great man, but he wore a Cracow peasant's coat, that is to say, a *czamara*."

"Much he wore a *czamara!*" retorted Wilbik. "They used to call it a *taratatka*."

"But the *taratatka* has fringe," shouted Mickiewicz, "and the other is entirely plain."

Thereupon there arose disputes over the various forms of the *taratatka* and the *czamara*.

The ingenious Robak, seeing that the conversation was thus becoming scattered, undertook again to gather it to a focus—to his snuffbox: he treated them, they sneezed and wished one another good health; he continued his speech:

"When the Emperor Napoleon in an engagement takes snuff time after time, it is a sure sign that he is winning the battle. For example, at Austerlitz: the French just stood beside their cannon, and on them charged a host of Muscovites. The emperor gazed and held his peace; whenever the French shot, the Muscovites were simply mowed down by regiments like grass. Regiment after regiment galloped on and fell from the saddle; whenever a regiment fell, the emperor took a pinch of snuff, until finally Alexander with his little brother Constantine and the German Emperor Francis fled from the field. So the emperor, seeing that the fight was over, gazed at them, laughed, and dusted his fingers. And now if any of you gentlemen who are present here ever serves in the army of the emperor, let him remember this."

"Ah! My dear monk!" cried Skoluba. "When will that be? Why, on every holiday set down in the calendar they prophesy to us that the French are coming. A man looks and looks until his eyes are weary, but the Muscovite keeps on holding us by the neck as he always has. I fear that before the sun rises the dew will ruin our eyes."

"Sir, it is womanish to complain," said the Bernardine, "and a Jewish trick to wait with folded hands until someone rides up to the tavern and knocks on the door. With Napoleon it is not so hard to beat the Muscovites; he has already three times thrashed the hide of the Swabians, he has trodden down the nasty Prussians, and has cast back the English straight across the sea: surely he will be equal to the Muscovites. But, my dear sir, do you know what will be the result?

The gentry of Lithuania will mount their steeds and seize their sabers, but not until there is no longer any enemy with whom to fight. Napoleon, after crushing everybody alone, will finally say: 'I can get along without you: who are you?' So it is not enough to await a guest, not enough even to invite him in; one needs to gather the servants and set up the tables; and before the banquet one must clean the house of dirt; clean the house, I repeat; clean the house, my boys!"

A silence followed, and then voices in the throng:

"How clean our house? What do you mean by that? We will do everything for you, we are ready for anything; only, my dear father, pray explain yourself more clearly."

The monk glanced out of the window, interrupting the conversation; he noticed something peculiar, and put his head out of the window. In a moment he said, rising:

"Today we have no time, later we will walk together more at length. Tomorrow I shall be in the district town on business, and on the way I will call on you gentlemen to gather alms."

"Then call at Niehrymow to spend the night," said the steward; "the ensign will be glad to see you, sir. An old Lithuanian proverb says: 'As lucky a man as an almsgatherer in Niehrymow.'"

"And be good enough to visit us," said Zubkowski. "You will get a half-piece of linen, a firkin of butter, a sheep or a cow. Remember these words, sir: 'A man is lucky if he has such fortune as a monk in Zubkow.'"

"And on us," said Skoluba; "and on us," added Terajewicz; "no Bernardine ever departed hungry from Pucewicze."

Thus all the gentry said good-bye to the monk with prayers and promises; he was already the other side of the door.

Through the window he had caught sight of Thaddeus flying along the highway, at full gallop, without his hat, with head bent forward, and with a pale, gloomy face, continually whipping and spurring on his horse. This sight greatly disturbed the Bernardine; so he hastened with quick steps after the young man, toward the great forest, which, as far as the eye could reach, showed black along the entire horizon.

Who has explored the deep abysses of the Lithuanian forests up to the very center, the kernel of the thicket? A fisherman is scarcely acquainted with the bottom of the sea close to the shore; a huntsman skirts around the bed of the Lithuanian forests; he knows them barely on the surface, their form and face, but the inner secrets of their heart are a mystery to him; only rumor or fable knows what goes on within them. For, when you have passed the woods and the dense, tangled thickets, in the depths you come upon a great rampart of stumps, logs, and roots, defended by a quagmire, a thousand streams, and a net of overgrown weeds and anthills, nests of wasps and hornets, and coils of serpents. If by some superhuman valor you surmount even these barriers, farther on you will meet with still greater danger. At each step they lie in wait for you, like the dens of wolves, little lakes, half overgrown with grass, so deep that men cannot find their bottom; in them it is very probable that devils dwell. The water of these wells is iridescent, spotted with a bloody rust, and from within continually rises a steam that breathes forth a nasty odor, from which the trees around lose their bark and leaves; bald, dwarfed, wormlike, and sick, hanging their branches knotted together with moss, and with humped trunks bearded with filthy fungi, they sit around the water, like a group of witches warming themselves around a kettle in which they are boiling a corpse.

Beyond these pools it is vain to try to penetrate even with the eye, to say nothing of one's steps, for there all is covered with a misty cloud that rises incessantly from quivering morasses. But finally behind this mist (so runs the common rumor) extends a very fair and fertile region, the main capital of the kingdom of beasts and plants. In it are gathered the seeds of all trees and herbs, from which their varieties spread abroad throughout the world; in it, as in Noah's ark, of all the kinds of beasts there is preserved at least one pair for breeding. In the very center, we are told, the ancient buffalo and the bison and the bear, the emperors of the forest, hold their court. Around them, on trees, nest the swift lynx and the greedy wolverene, as watchful ministers; but farther on, as subordinate, noble vassals, dwell wild boars, wolves, and horned elks. Above their heads are the falcons and wild eagles, who live from the lords' tables, as court parasites. These chief and patriarchal pairs of beasts, hidden in the kernel of the forest, invisible to the world, send their children beyond the confines of the wood as colonists, but themselves in their capital enjoy repose; they never perish by cut or by shot, but when old die by a natural death. They have likewise their graveyard, where, when near to death, the birds lay their feathers and the quadrupeds their fur. The bear, when with his blunted teeth he cannot chew his food; the decrepit stag, when he can scarcely move his legs; the venerable hare, when his blood already thickens in his veins; the raven, when he grows gray, and the falcon, when he grows blind; the eagle, when his old beak is bent into such a bow that it is shut forever and provides no nourishment for his throat; all go to the graveyard. Even a lesser beast, when wounded or sick, runs to die in the land of its fathers.

Hence in the accessible places, to which man resorts, there are never found the bones of dead animals. It is said that there in the capital the beasts lead a well-ordered life, for they govern themselves; not yet corrupted by human civilization, they know no rights of property, which embroil our world; they know neither duels nor the art of war. As their fathers lived in paradise, so their descendants live today, wild and tame alike, in love and harmony; never does one bite or butt another. Even if a man should enter there, though unarmed, he would pass in peace through the midst of the beasts; they would gaze on him with the same look of amazement with which on that last, sixth day of creation their first fathers, who dwelt in the Garden of Eden, gazed upon Adam, before they quarreled with him. Happily no man wanders into this enclosure, for Toil and Terror and Death forbid him access.

Only sometimes hounds, furious in pursuit, entering incautiously among these mossy swamps and pits, overwhelmed by the sight of the horrors within them, flee away, whining, with looks of terror; and long after, though petted by their master's hand, they still tremble at his feet, possessed by fright. These ancient hidden places of the forests, unknown to men, are called in hunter's language *jungles*.

Translated by George Repell Noyes

Andrzej Strug
(1873–1935)

Andrzej Strug is best known as the chronicler of Poland's underground struggle against the czars. His earliest literary efforts were dedicated to the "underground people" who were fighting for independence and social justice. As a youth, Strug himself joined the ranks of the underground, and he later became a prominent member of the Polish Socialist party (PPS)—as a soldier, journalist and creative writer.

Although he was one of the first to join the Legions of Pilsudski, after 1926 Strug broke with his former comrades and became a leading member of the opposition. In 1926, Pilsudski staged a coup d'état and Strug refused to be associated with this method of assuming power.

Representing the Left in Polish postwar literature, Strug attracted the younger generation of writers, which regarded him as their leader. His major novels, *The Underground People, Recollections of an Old Sympathizer,* and *Tomorrow,* which are as yet untranslated into English, bring into Polish fiction the underground people who, though related to Żeromski's "homeless people," live more dangerously. Strug's heroes are subject to brutal imprisonment, forced labor, and contemptuous treatment even at the hands of their own people. Strug creates the atmosphere of conspiratorial activities, and like Żeromski also emphasizes the "unknown soldier," the "little man." Through his fiction, Strug gives an accurate account of the important period in Poland's history immediately preceding World War I.

In the following excerpt from *The Underground People,* Strug bemoans the loss of a comrade but also immediately moves to the attack, the typical stance of a member of the underground. The work of a fallen comrade has to be and is picked up. The notion of the underground as a political force is novel. There were conspiracies, there always was terrorism, but the notion of an "underground," a notion of the existence of groups of people beyond the vision and comprehension of the authorities, was new. It implies that if a nation wants to it can go "underground." This concept of political action did not appear in European literature until the anti-Nazi resistance movement in western Europe, which was also called the "underground."

The Underground People

Everything took place as had been arranged. There were wreaths, there were crimson ribbons and a crowd of a thousand people. They sang "The Red Banner" over the grave, and there were encomiums to which the people listened. But the tributes went unfinished. The cossacks burst into the cemetery and the horses trampled the graves with their hooves. . . . A skirmish flared briefly and died and a score or two were arrested. . . .

The people are stirred; they have felt the wild wind sweeping through the foul air of their basements. Even after death you are useful.

My task is to chronicle your deeds and bring your unsung name into daylight. They'll stand at the type-form composing the words letter by letter . . . for the wide mourning box beneath the thin little lines of a cross. You must be honored . . . but how?

Let them, the people, know that you existed; and those who knew you, let them understand at last that it was you, you that they knew. No need for secrecy now. You shall have fame. Not a few will be roused, fired by your tale; not a few sustained in suffering. You shall have fame.

You took your leave at the worst moment. Was it fair? The task is still great; whom shall we put in your place? Unfair. . . . Orphans were left behind. In Wola [the worker's district of Warsaw] they ask whither you disappeared: "Did Walter get himself into trouble, or what? Why doesn't he come?"

He got himself into trouble, you folk of Wola, he won't be coming any more. . . .

You could have waited for today—not much, just a brief while of living.

I've a deep sadness for your sorrow, a deep sadness. . . .

Why did you hurry so? It was wrong of you. . . .

Listen, brother, listen well, the revolution's on its way, on its way and setting the earth atremble.

They're waking—even there below—waking powerfully, for they've been sleeping powerfully. Won't you believe it?

Listen! It's the truth, it's begun! New days are coming, days we've not seen before. The people look up differently, breathe differently, the enemy has a different fear.

We shall rise out of the earth now, rise with our treasures and reserves, begin to boast with our work. Tomorrow is not far, we'll live to see it.

Listen, brother, listen well. We'll rise from our underground and do a little fighting. Eye him to his eye, measure him, size him up.

Only you will not rise from the earth depths to see that shining day. Wouldn't it have been better to see it? Fill your eyes with the brightness? Swallow the free air?

One sultry evening in the underground you said: "To have to keep your eyes about you all your life, to have to hide, never let a sound escape you—a terrible thing, a shame. . . ."

We swam a long, hard way, lost strength, were sucked under; now we've made it, here's the bank, here, you can touch it . . . but you're at the bottom . . . how will it be on the bright bank without you?

Remember?

Student discussions, long papers, quarrels, taking sides, relations broken, renewed, groups, circles, plans, plans, plans, . . .

This fame of ours dragged through the streets of Warsaw, this pride of ours. . . .

Where, when was there ever a Napoleon more certain of ruling the world than we two, then?

The university threw us out, we said: We are destined for higher goals!

Locked up, behind bars, we said: Be brave, the eyes of the world are on us!

They set us free a few months later and we were ashamed to be free, it was a crime.

Into the world, the far world, we followed the rest of them.

Parisian years, the work, the fights, do you recall that noble pride of ours? Rue des Courcelles. Behind the barricades, two miserable starved dogs. The last of the borrowed sous had gone for the printing of polemical pamphlets.

London, merciless, terrifying, miserable, unendurable. Remember the misty autumn night we lay lifeless with hunger in the dark, unheated suburban room?

And that star-studded summer night thick with the odor of pine sap and pasture flowers, when we crept over the border and returned to the fatherland. . . .

The unuttered, unconfessed thought lay in each of us, to swear that never would we leave our land again. . . .

Now, after the years, it is hard to believe. How did we endure those days? The Testament is right: Faith lifts mountains and moves them from their place.

Days of hunger, cold and wandering . . . distrust, fear, envy. . . .

We did the work of ten, each of us did, and two of us ate for one. Our schemes tore like cobwebs in the wind and we patched them asking each of the other: Will anything come of it? Darkness, intrigue, betrayals, constant remorse engulfed us. It might have been worse. We were accustomed to fear.

We were lucky somehow. When inevitable disaster faced us we were saved by a miracle. We were astounded. You said: "It's clear that God is on our side."

Do you recall how we fled into that little shop to escape? In the Old City [a district of Warsaw]? No time to lose, and like that, instinctively. . . . The shopkeeper said nothing, we said nothing, not a word, there was no time; the police were there, hot on the scent. . . . Tell me, who told her, who taught her? . . . "Two of them ran by here toward Bugaj [a street in the Old City], I think. . . ." She slipped us out the back way through the gate, again without a word. . . . Is she still alive?

And that Jew at the gate. Remember him? "You gentlemen had better not go upstairs, the police are in the apartment." Who was he? How did he know us? Where did he come from?

We suffered it for the third, tenth, hundredth, thousandth time. Now our tribe has increased and even without us would endure.

Then why couldn't we have left together?

You died in a strange bed, they dressed you in a strange coat, strange boots for the coffin.

Listen, what did we ever possess of our own? Not a nook of our own, a moment, a secret of our own. Hardly a thought of such things. . . . Forever dragging ourselves about . . . but always . . . it was a dog's life.

You should have listened, you should have gone somewhere once in your life for a rest. You wouldn't listen to that.

You would have dragged on for another year or two. You would have seen something more, lived to see something—even if only a cleaner sun. And then it would have been easier for you. . . .

We prattled about it always: we would rest when they took us; in prison, in exile we would rest.

But there were moments of loneliness when a word tore out of us: "Let the devil send them for us already!"

To spite us they didn't come. . . . And so you fell, exhausted, like the end horse stumbling in the harness. Rest . . . rest. . . .

I'll write your tale with vibrant, palpable words. Something to be long remembered. Great, eternal fame for you, man of the underground, man without a name!
Let your name, unfurled, be the pride of thousands, a living signal, a goad, a call to battle.
Let them know you!

I have to work now. The copy is ready, waiting only for you. We'll print it up tomorrow. I'll spend the night at the type-form setting up your deeds. A single column was all they allotted you. Your life must fit into that, and your soul. It'll be bright for you in the mourning box and my tale will be short. I'll prepare it in the night, in the calm and safe night. This long night I'll spend with you alone, dead brother. . . . Setting type to type and reading the words off one by one.
Who knows? Perhaps out of the pain of memory, out of the sorrow of thought, perhaps out of the stillness of the night your shadow will rise and stand before me, quiet and sad, stand for a moment and nod and then drift away. . . .

Tomorrow the press will beat the pages off, one by one. The smithy will simmer with work. The quiet, skillful beating of the press, the rustle of papers and the heaps of newsprint rising hour by hour.
Your edition will go into the world by the usual routes. Throughout the Polish land the people will seize it and read it and shed a tear for you, a man's tear in which there is strength and an oath. It will spread through the world, passed from hand to hand, farther and farther until one day a crumpled, wrinkled scrap of it will fall somewhere sometime, borne by chance, blown by the wind, on an unknown road where an unknown man will find it and pick it up. . . .

Translated by Ludwik Krzyzanowski

Stefan Żeromski
(1864–1925)

Żeromski was a superb stylist and a great novelist. His subjects were always concerned with Poland, his heroes and characters were understandable only in the context of Poland's social history. He is an outstanding example of the Polish intelligentsia. He was a member of a resistance group; he did not finish high school because he had tuberculosis, but somehow managed to start veterinary studies. He never finished those and eventually, like many of his group, had to leave Poland and live in western Europe. He was inspired and driven by the Promethean dream of improving the lot of his fellow Poles. He was compared to Dostoyevsky. In style Zeromski was the superior novelist, but lacked the ability to universalize his subject, to elevate his characters the way Dostoyevsky did.

In the first selection, an excerpt from the *Dream of a Sword*, Żeromski subtly changes the ethos of Poland's history. No longer is Poland—its fate and its history—in the hands of the gentry; it is the responsibility of an anonymous everybody. It is a poignant story of a smuggler who transported forbidden news into Poland. He was shot by the czarist border guards. He was not the hero warrior who died sword in hand; he was a hero of "the word," the spirit, destined to receive his sword of knighthood only after death. But in Żeromski's symbolism, knighthood meant the possession of the highest values: freedom, dignity, and respect. In 1905, when the *Dream of a Sword* was written, these were attainable for a Pole only in death.

In the second selection, from *Forest Echoes*, Zeromski continues the critique of the gentry, who were supposedly so patriotic. He brings them down to the level of the ordinary people among whom some sell themselves for power and glory even at the price of killing a kinsman, while others are willing to die because they choose to, for the sake of an ideal, an ideal that in Poland was always the same—independence. In this selection, Zeromski also expresses his disgust with the obsequious world of pretty, corrupt officials who were always there, in Poland, to do the master's bidding.

Dream of a Sword

You went out into the darkest autumn night, where roared the gale and lashed the wind, while we, a nation of twenty millions, in our bedrooms, chambers, garrets, and subterranean kennels all slept the stony sleep of slaves. You went out stripped, lke a smuggler, to the waist. On your shoulders you bore the parts of a printing press. You were loaded with leaflets that announced the deliverance of our bodies and our souls. In your left hand you grasped a pole with which you groped in the dark for the sentry guarding the frontiers of our land, and in your right you held a revolver, ready to shoot. Thus you crossed the border streams. You came into our country bare and with bleeding feet. In that night independence was brought to this land of the poor in spirit, this night, too, was brought the declaration of the rights of the holy proletariat, which the greater power of the rich had trodden underfoot. You brought us then priceless scrolls of Polish law from the sunken graves of the emigrants. You brought us "a second string" torn from the lyre of the immortals. Having stepped on to your native soil you followed the groans of the people. Your signpost was the moaning of the working man. Those of whom the fatherland knew not, those by whose toil the world was fed, were found by you, lifted up, summoned and united into a comrades' camp of men who fight for freedom.

Who today will count the flaming brows that the frost of Siberia has chilled to steel? Whose understanding shall wade through the immensity of suffering that Polish socialism has borne in chains? Who shall measure the length of the road it has trodden out in the snows, across the frozen furrows and the swamps of exile? Its name and unstained honor are today decried by the Polish journalist, who lives by trampling on the fires of idea. Aping the torturer, he debases the chivalrous shade of the soldier to the level of the specter of the scoundrel who follows in his track and seizes the booty. Your steps, soldier, ring with a yearning echo in the recesses of the people's heart, as an echo resounds in the forest. As an echo in the dimness of the forest they die away. Yet you yourself are the people, and your blood seeps into the people. From the clotted puddles of blood, from those virgin recesses, are growing up wondrous legends such as Poland has not yet known. In people's souls are stirring dreams of the plume of fame.

For alone the Polish muse will not desert you, will not decry you, soldier! She alone will not take fright at your dreams and deeds. Even if your cause were lost, she will keep her faith in you. She will see and bear in mind your days and nights, your pains, efforts, toil, and death. She will lay your head, bashed by the butts of the soldiery, on a pillow of the most wondrous verse, that in years to come she will take from the splendor of our ancient tongue. With a cloak of dignity, woven of the most wondrous colors of her art, she will cover your naked body that knows no belt of gold or robe of red, when the people of Lodz dig it up from the common pit, to give it the only thing the people can give, a pinewood coffin.

Into your hands grown stiff, hands that are powerless only in death, she will lay her golden dream, the dream of so many generations of the young, the dream of a knightly sword.

Translated by M. A. Michael

Forest Echoes

General Rozlucki was sitting sternly on a folding stool. The stool (portable property of land surveyor Knopf) was placed right in the center of a rug taken down from the wall over my mother's bed. On the other side of the camp fire, on a tree stump solicitously covered with a blanket, sat the aforementioned land surveyor Knopf, wriggling and grimacing in his ankle-length raincoat as in a mobile tent. Close to him was assistant forester Gunkiewicz, stuck rather uncomfortably among the gnarled branches of a wind-felled tree, which the forest guard had brought along, holding on with infinite care to a tumbler of arrack [powerful alcoholic drink] to which two spoonfuls of tea had been added for appearance's sake. Community scribe Olszakowski and the old bailiff Gala, with a copper medal (for "suppressing the Polish rebellion") pinned to his Polish rust-colored peasant's greatcoat, sat side by side. My father, an old hunter, quite at home in the forest, was lounging on the ground. And I, the undersigned, who had just been honorably promoted from second to third grade, was all over the place.

General Rozlucki, retired, plenipotentiary of one of the most generously endowed beneficiaries, had just come to the farm my father had been renting for many years, to incorporate a large section of state forest in the estate, in accordance with an ukase [an order of the Imperial Russian authorities] on the exchange of land.

The cutting off of the triangle of forest land was almost completed.

Land surveyor Knopf, who had been "visiting" us for a week to everybody's dismay, had at last staked out the demarcation line, along which hired lumbermen had long been chopping down the trees of the old, dark forest. The plenipotentiary, who had also been staying with us for the last three days, was in a hurry to turn this additional land over to my father in the presence of the local authorities. The two teams of peasants cutting down the trees along the border line were approaching each other from opposite directions. It was expected that the transaction would be completed before sunset, but night had fallen and the work along the line was not quite finished. Nevertheless the general had decided to leave the next day. The officials, too, wished to be done with it. It was therefore agreed to work the night through till the morning, if need be.

A camp fire was lit at the edge of the forest. Supper was brought over from the manor two miles away, and we passed our time as best we could, waiting for the last few score fir trees to be chopped down.

Everybody was in fairly good humor. Good old Gunkiewicz, with the two last tufts of hair left on his temples, his scanty goatee tinted black with a cheap dye, had already imbibed at least nine tumblers of tea with arrack, asking anxiously every time I handed him another whether it would not be too much, ". . . for, I believe, this is my third. . . ." I kept assuring him, with the authoritative air of someone eminently well skilled in arithmetic (up to decimal fractions), that he was mistaken—whereupon he humbly submitted to my superior knowledge and accepted another tot of arrack.

Community scribe Olszakowski, versed in all things human, and particularly in county and community ways of making easy money (which had already made him "suffer" a term in the Kielce jail), an incontestable genius, who might easily have become minister of the interior or of foreign affairs, or who might even have filled both posts simultaneously, a notorious grafter, extortioner of peasants, exploiter of Jews, past master in circumventing the law and an all-round busybody—was drinking little in deference to the general present, and devoted more attention to the food. But being so omniscient he actually was not in the least impressed by the general and felt quite at ease to let his wit sparkle for the benefit of the little gathering.

Bailiff Gala was chewing and swallowing anything that was presented to him; he was not averse to drinking and mumbled cheerfully. Quite obviously he wholeheartedly enjoyed the government service in the woodland and he was quite satisfied with that day's activity.

Even Knopf, that walking gastritis (and enteritis), that shriveled-up neurasthenic, that creature who should eat nothing but certain easily digestible foods (nonacid and lean—foods such as no one had ever eaten, or seen, or even known by name in any remote village, and especially not in the Swietokrzyskie Mountains), that bore who could not sleep at night, who could not bear to hear cocks crowing, dogs barking, turkeys gobbling, geese gaggling, or even hens clucking—a veritable Egyptian plague to any sane and robust people working on the land in a country where everyone is so fond of dog kennels, where mongrels, hounds, pointers, dachshunds, well—"doggies" in general, of any breed and age, not only howl and bark all night long, but lounge on sofas and couches, where the cocks never stop crowing, and those who stop are at once put to death for being remiss—even Knopf, as I've said, was in fairly good humor that night.

He told us an acrimoniously witty anecdote about his astrolabe [an instrument used to observe the positions of celestial bodies] (which, according to evil tongues, he was in the habit of dressing up in his own galoshes, trousers and coat, to protect it from the rain). Although the point of his story was ruined by assistant forester Gunkiewicz bursting into laughter prematurely at a moment that wasn't funny at all, Knopf continued to smile—an event which was considered a real phenomenon within a radius of three counties, where it was talked about for several years.

The general, a fairly well-preserved old fogy, behaved with the appropriate dignity. During this improvised supper party he practically ignored the bailiff and the scribe, but tolerated their presence without a protest and did not object to their eating chicken and various cold roast meats with a hearty appetite, to their tossing down tumblers of homemade liquor with beer "for a chaser," nor even to their "warming up" with tea and arrack. To Gunkiewicz he addressed a gracious word every now and then, and with Knopf he talked. He himself ate slowly and sipped tea.

The general was a Pole and made a point of speaking Polish even in government offices. His pronunciation bore traces of a Russian accent, but that accent somehow fitted his tall figure, his thick jacket of a peculiar cut, his round cap with its red band and extraordinarily wide peak, his cloth spats and gray mustache curling upward.

The fire blazed, fed by the forest guard. The dry juniper burned, crackling merrily. From the forest across the evening dew came the thump-thump of falling axes. It resounded through the forests, through the vast Swietokrzyskie fir tree groves, deep into the damp, sleepy, silent wilderness. The echo of the blows sped from mountain to mountain, from grove to grove, toward a bleak distance, into the night, into the fog. Hounded, driven out, faraway voices trembled somewhere outside the world and called from the beyond. They returned frightened and mute from the distant marshes where no one dares walk, where it "spooks." From time to time one heard amidst the blows of falling axes the ominous creaking of a breaking tree, the rustling and crushing of its mass of boughs and branches, the hollow, formidable thunder of falling timber. The echo snatched up the sound and carried it into the dark, distant night, the sorrowful news growing faint and fainter, the heartbreaking message of that blow. The whole forest was breaking down, crumbling, with every tree roaring in testimony of a moment never to be forgotten, calling out of the depth of darkness with living voices.

Red and enormous, the moon emerged from the veils of the forest and went slowly on its way among the dark clouds. The group gathered round the fire fell silent. The air turned chilly. My mount (a gray, bony, half-retired farmstead mare whose mane and tail I had clipped on arriving for my vacation, and whom I tortured with the strap of an old saddle, and forced into perilous gallops) stood somewhere near the fire. One could see her fine head and shoulder blades, her pensioner's hoofs, and above all her eyes lost in meditation on the blazing fire and the people sitting round it. . . .

The general had put down his glass some time before and was sitting up straight with his chest stuck out and one of his legs gracefully stretched out sideways. At times, he turned his head toward the forest. He listened to the sound of the echoes and then turned his head back to its former position.

He turned to Gunkiewicz:

"Assistant Forester, how far is it from here to Suchedniow?" Gunkiewicz put down his tumbler and replied with the proper polite inclination of his camouflaged bald spot that it wouldn't be quite seven miles straight across the fields.

"You know the path round here, don't you?"

Gunkiewicz smiled proudly or condescendingly. He could not find a word vigorous enough to indicate the extent to which he was familiar with every nook round there; hadn't he been assistant forester there for twenty odd years!

"Yes . . ." muttered the general thoughtfully. "And do you know the one leading from Zagnansk to Wzdol? There used to be an inn near that path, right in the forest . . ."

"Zagozdzie—why, it's still there."

"A bumpy path full of roots went from there toward Suchedniow, and another, better one, toward Wzdol, toward Bodzentyn."

"That's right, General."

"You say that inn is still there?"

"So it is. A real thieves' kitchen. Horse traffickers from every corner of Poland meet under that roof."

"In front of that inn, across the road, on the other side, there was a sand hill. Big, yellow. . . . There were a few birch trees growing on that hill . . ."

"What a remarkable memory, General! Only one of those birches is still there. And what fine trees they were. That scoundrel of an innkeeper cut them down. One of the birches was left standing, and even that one simply because there's a cross leaning against it. This the blackguard daren't touch."

"What cross? How did a cross get there?" asked Rozlucki in an animated tone.

"Well, there is a cross, there . . ."

"But what's the reason for placing a cross at that spot, eh?"

"Well, that's the way with crosses, General. Some people put one up, others pass by and raise their hats, and it simply stays there. It's started rotting at the foot, but it's been secured with props on two sides."

"Who put it up?" insisted the general.

"To tell the truth," muttered Gunkiewicz with a shy smile, "to tell the truth, it's me who put up that cross. We've got plenty of wood hereabouts. I took a fine, firm, healthy pine. And our carpenter, who is among us now as our bailiff, fashioned it . . ."

"Oh, never mind . . . why mention it . . ."

"We dug the tree way deep into the sand, way deep . . ."

"But why precisely at that spot?"

"Because a man lies buried there under that hill, my General."

"A man's buried . . ." repeated the general. "And you had known that man, had you?"

"Well, certainly I knew him; in a forest district like mine one can hardly fail to know a man. . . . With miles and miles of woods all round. . . . Whoever gets into those woods doesn't bypass my house, or even my bed."

The general bowed his head and kept silent for a long spell. At last he took a silver cigarette case from his pocket and opened it, his hands rather unsteady.

"Well," he said with a cold grin, "do you know that the man buried there was my nephew?"

Land surveyor Knopf, who until then had been sitting motionless, staring into the fire with lips tightly pressed together and an expres-

sion of utter disgust on his face, suddenly gave the general a withering look:

"Rymwid?" he exclaimed.

The general turned toward him:

"Exactly, Rymwid. . . . You, too, seem to know something about
him . . ."

Knopf's lips twisted a number of times, as if he had just drunk
some pure lemon juice; he waved his hands in various directions,
blinking his white eyelids. Then, amid a series of hypocritical smiles
most insufferable to the eyes, he muttered:

"Well, yes . . . Rymwid . . . of course . . ."

"Rymwid!" repeated the general vehemently, with a sneer. "Lieutenant in my regiment—Rymwid! "The captain!" Well, he got his
due . . ."

"So he was your nephew?" Gunkiewicz asked fearfully, his eyes
fairly popping out of his head.

"My own brother's second son, John," said the general pensively.
"My brother died on the field of honor during the Sevastopol war,
before Malakoff Hill. Major-general, a man of the Nicholaian era.
Promoted for his conduct in the Hungarian campaign, awarded
medals, an estate in Penza. Dying on the battlefield, he asked me to
take care of his two sons. I gave him my word as a brother and a
soldier that I would make men out of them, that I would see to it that
they made their way in the world. And I kept my word. I did bring
them up. . . . The older one served in the Caucasus and died there of
cholera as staff captain. Peter, unmarried. The younger one, John,
served in my regiment after graduating from the cadet school. He
married young; she was a Polish girl, née Plaza; they had a baby son
when that vile Polish insurrection started. When that vile insurrection broke out, we got orders to transfer. I was lieutenant-colonel at
the time. We went to the Opoczno district."

The general lost himself in meditation. Knopf rolled himself a
meticulously even cigarette, pushed it carefully into his cigarette
holder and busied himself trying to find an ember to light it. The
general seemed to be waiting for the moment when the other would
at last have lit his cigarette, and when Knopf took his first puff, he
said:

"Well, then. That nephew of mine betrayed us. We had barely taken
up quarters when he ran away in the dark of the night to join the
gang. In the morning, Captain Shchukin reported what had happened: John was gone. A note was found on the table of the quarters
where we were living, in Sielpia, informing me, as the then com-

mander of three battalions, that 'faithful to his homeland' and such-like nonsense, he appealed to me, his superior and his uncle, to stain my honor as officer, break my oath and run away to the woods, to join the gang, as he had done. That's how it was, gentlemen."

Knopf was smoking his cigarette cautiously, slowly. He was blowing geometrically perfect smoke rings and following them with his eyes. Gunkiewicz no longer felt like having any tea. He sat there stunned, staring at the general.

"News reached me of our deserter being chief of staff of one of the gangs. All right, then, 'That's why he went there,' Captain Shchukin, under whom my nephew had served, told me. Service in the army is tough, hard, and thankless, but in the gang service is easy, light. There our lieutenant could be a captain without any great effort. 'If there's anything in those Polish armies that isn't hard to get,' he added, 'it's promotion.' "

Knopf had finished his cigarette; he laughed at Captain Shchukin's joke. The general continued:

"We were constantly on the march, in pursuit of one or other of the gangs. We'd barely get out of the Knoskie woods and reach Suchedniow woods, before they'd have run off deep into the woods toward Bodzentyn. We'd go back, and they'd be at our heels. There was one of their leaders in particular, a colonel or captain called 'Walter,' that fooled us more than the rest. He'd have lots of fires burning as in a camp, while he withdrew to a place quite a distance away, and spent the night without a fire. We arrive with a posse, and surround those camp fires as stealthily as possible, then we attack them at night and find—no one. He'd hear the fracas and come up on us like a brigand: shooting our soldiers, picking them out against the glaring ligh tof the fires, and running back into the woods again. He also made use of some peasants he had seduced: they would lead us at night to those dummy camps."

The village scribe shot an oblique glance at the bailiff and grinned wryly. The bailiff sat up very straight gazing fixedly at the general.

"That's what happened more than once in the Samsonow region . . ."

"Near Gozd . . ." chipped in Gunkiewicz.

"That's right, near Gozd, too."

"Near Klonow . . ." muttered Knopf.

"But the game did come to an end," said the general. "You can get away with a trick once, twice, maybe even three times, but it won't work forever. It so happened I was marching at the head of a few companies from Zagnansk to Wzdol—in fact, along that road to the inn. I spent the night at the inn and despatched Shchukin with one company to ferret out that man Walter. The rascal wouldn't come out to fight, instead he sits tight in the swamps between Klonow and Bukowa Gora for weeks, so we've got to look for him.

"I had barely fallen asleep that night, when my aide-de-camp, a young fellow, burst in to report 'heavy shooting in the woods!' I was immediately wide awake. The forest was roaring. . . . Just as we hear it roar now. . . . What a pity. . . . What a heartache. I despatched another company as reinforcement for Shchukin. It didn't take more than two hours, and they came marching back. A peasant has led them to the camp, that time to a real one. When they surrounded them and launched a bayonet attack, the majority fought their way out and fled into the forest; many were killed on the spot. Shchukin brought back one taken in hand-to-hand fighting; to put it briefly, it was none other than my nephew, Rymwid. I had received the irrevocable order from my brigadier-general to clear the forest up to Bodzentyn at any cost, including the power of life and death. There was no time to send the prisoners to prison in Kielce, and besides the forces at my disposal were rather limited. My officers were in a flurry and looked at me, his relative, with severe, questioning eyes.

"I immediately convened a court-martial, for we had to pursue the gang without any loss of time. I presided, with Captain Shchukin and Captain Fedotov on my right, and Lieutenant von Tauwetter and Sergeant Yevseyenko on my left. We went at once into session in the large room of that inn. A tallow candle was burning in the candlestick . . ."

The general spoke faster and faster, less and less distinctly, and using more and more Russian words, phrases, and even whole sentences. He moved to make himself comfortable on his stool and continued:

"They brought him in. Six soldiers, and he in the middle. Short, emaciated, black, ragged. Hair tousled. Barely recognizable. . . . I looked at him: Johnny, my brother's favorite son. . . . I had brought him up; used to hold him on my knees. . . . Stuck in some despicable rags. . . . His face, torn open right across by a bayonet thrust, all blue and swollen. As they brought him in, he stopped by the door, waiting. And you, judge, pass your sentence!

"First the usual formal question: who he is. He keeps silent. We all looked at him. A good comrade, beloved colleague, warm-hearted chap, outstanding officer. His face had become insolent, frozen into a sort of a grin which twisted that pleasant, kind and gentle face—as a blacksmith takes a piece of soft iron and twists it once and for all in the fire into a crooked hook.

"The soldiers who guarded him acted as witnesses. They testified that they had captured him in the forest fighting hand-to-hand; they testified that he was him all right, their own Lieutenant Rozlucki. A clear case, what else could there be? The vote. . . .

"At that moment, one of the judges on my right, Captain Shchukin, turned to me saying he wanted to ask the accused some more questions. All right, ask your questions. Shchukin rose from his seat, propped himself up on his fists as hard as he could, finally leaned over toward him across the table. The veins on his forehead were bulging; his face grew as dark as earth. He looked fixedly at the accused. We all wondered what else he was going to ask. Still the fellow couldn't utter a single word, for he was a hard man without much education. His nostrils were quivering, his brows knitted. At last he banged the table with his fist and shouted at the accused:

" 'Rozlucki, don't you dare stand before us with that insolent air! Don't you dare look at us in this fashion! Did you give your oath or didn't you? What did you do with your oath? Answer me! Did you swear allegiance—yes or no?'

" 'I did,' he said.

" 'You did!' Shchukin shouted again at the top of his voice, his fists pressed on the table. 'And how did you keep that sacred pledge? You deserted the ranks and went over to the enemy! Is that the truth or isn't it?'

" 'It's true.'

" 'In connivance with others who betrayed your sovereign you have ambushed and attacked his armed forces. You were a leader of the traitors, you gave them the most detrimental directives, you taught them where and how to attack. I have seen you with my own eyes today fighting the soldiers of your own company. I testify here that I have seen Private Denishchuk wounding you with his bayonet. Is this true or isn't it?'

" 'It is true.'

" 'If all this is true, don't you dare look at us—faithful, honest soldiers—with your air of a hero. You are standing here before a tribunal that stands for justice. Your own uncle will judge you. Look down and humble yourself, for you are a traitor and a villain.'

"To this he replied:

" 'I am standing before the tribunal of God. As for you, you may judge me according to your standards, if you wish.'

"Shchukin sat down.

"They voted: two votes—Shchukin's and von Tauwetter's—for punishment on the spot; two votes for sending him under escort to the prison at Kielce. It was up to me to tip the scale. And . . . I tipped it . . ." he said in a low voice, nodding.

"They were on the point of taking him out. Yevseyenko moved that he might have a last wish. I gave him the floor. He looked at me with those abysmal eyes, fixedly. We were all standing behind the table. He approached. He stared into my eyes, and I into his. Like the points of the guns . . . I remember his austere words:

" 'In the face of death, I order—and this is my irrevocable last will—that my little son, my six-year-old Peter, be brought up as a Pole, as I was myself. I order that he be told—even if this be against the conscience of his tutor—of everything his father did, up to the very end. I ordered him to work for his country and, if necessary, to die for it without batting an eyelid, without a sigh of regret, as I do. That's all.'

"He saluted us.

"They led him away.

"It was nearly daybreak. I went to the alcove where I should have slept that night. I opened the window. It was dawning. Morning. On the opposite side of the road six soldiers were speedily digging a pit in the sand. I withdrew to the far end of the alcove. It turned my face to the wall. My God! . . .

"When I went back to the window, it was bright daylight. I could see quite clearly. There he was, with twelve soldiers standing on guard, carbines at foot, sitting peacefully on the sand heap, his profile turned toward me. They had taken off his insurgent's jacket. He was in his shirt sleeves, and his shirt was torn on the chest. In his clenched hands, between his knees, he was holding a snapshot of his son, Peter. Head bent forward, hair falling over his forehead, lost in contemplation of the photo.

"Up from behind the corner of the inn marched the platoon of soldiers belonging to his own company. The platoon faced him. Von Tauwetter in command. The soldiers stood with their guns at the ready. They were still. A minute passed, then another, and a third. . . . I waited. I waited for von Tauwetter to give the command. Not a sound. Silence. He was unable to give the command. The other was still sitting with the eyes on his picture. I had the impression that he had died already, sitting there. For a fleeting moment, I felt relief. He was waiting. Then he raised his head, that seemed to weigh a thousand *puds*. He stood up on the heap of sand. His feet sank into the soft ground, so he readjusted his position once, and then a second time. He turned his head to look behind, brushed back the hair falling on his forehead and looked at the soldiers. Thank God, there it was again, that expression of disdain he had had when facing the court-martial. I watched it spreading slowly over his face, his forehead, his eyes. I felt elated to see it happen, just like that, proudly. . . . That he was a Rozlucki. . . . I sensed the terrible will power it took to pass through the stage of being an insensate corpse, to be transformed into something quite different.

"He called out in Russian:

" '*Zdarovo, rebiata!*' ['Hi, fellows!']

" '*Zdravia zhelayem vashemu blagorodiu!*' ['We wish you well, your honor!'] the soldiers shouted back, as one man.

"Yevseyenko was approaching to blindfold him. He stopped him with a mere glance. The sergeant went away. Then he pressed the little photograph to his heart and shut his eyes. His lips parted in a beautiful sublime smile. I closed my eyes too. I leaned against the wall with my chest. I waited, waited, waited. At last, . . . rat-t-t-t."

Land surveyor Knopf took off his cap murmuring to himself with parched lips. Gunkiewicz was digging with a stick in the ashes of the camp fire as if he wanted to bury the abundant tears of a drunkard rolling down his cheeks.

Silence fell. Echoes were calling one another from mountain to mountain.

Suddenly the village scribe turned to the general and asked:

"Will you permit me to ask a question, General? Where is that little son, Peter, now, who was then six years old?"

"And what business is it of yours where he is?" retorted the general rudely, in a harsh voice.

"I was just curious to know if the last will and order of that insurrectionist had been carried out."

"None of your business, and don't you ever dare ask me that question again!—D'you hear me?"

"I gathered that much right from the start," replied the scribe, looking the old general straight in the eyes with his roguish smile in impudent mockery. "I gathered that much right from the start; that last will of yours, my dear Captain Rymwid, must have given the devil a good and hearty laugh . . ."

Translated by Ilona Ralf Sues

BETWEEN THE GENTRY AND THE PEASANTS: VIGNETTES OF CITY LIFE

Until the mid-nineteenth century, Poland lagged far behind the rest of Europe in urbanization. It had few cities, but rather mostly drab, small provincial towns inhabited by shopkeepers, merchants, a few professionals, some students, administrators and their employees, and always a large or small army detachment and the ever-present police. Cities were service centers geared to supply an agrarian economy, distribution centers for movement of goods, and power centers for the rulers of Poland.

The larger cities such as Warsaw, Krakow, Poznan, Lwow, and Wilno compared favorably with other great European cities in the number of churches, cathedrals, and palaces; but still in all other respects they were very provincial. Their function was the same as those of the smaller cities, only the social and cultural setting was perhaps somewhat more appealing.

All of this changed when, with an inexplicable suddenness, industrialization descended on the Congress Kingdom, and on Poland in general. But it was in the Congress Kingdom, the province of Imperial Russia, where this industrialization produced its greatest ravages.

Within two or three decades following the 1860s, cities tripled and quadrupled in population. The old inhabitants were wrenched out of the somnolence of their drab existence to find themselves at the center of enormous industrial enterprises. The cities of Poland became targets of opportunity, where fortunes could be and were made. Textiles, machinery building, light industry, construction, railroad building—all mushroomed, fed by capital from Germany, Austria, and France. Most of the profits from this industrial miracle did not stay in Poland and the benefits to Poles, if any, were small in number and scope. Some merchants grew wealthy; some traders made fortunes; engineers could get good jobs; lawyers, doctors, and journalists came at a premium; artists found buyers for their art; and writers found an audience for their books. But for the masses, the rapidity of the industrialization brought an even worse misery than the one they were used to. Poor peasants who used to find a place to sleep in someone's stable or haystack rushed to the city hoping to make their fortune—and found nothing. Charles Dickens's masterful portrayal of London and the conditions of the working class would have to be exaggerated to an extreme to even come close to the conditions prevailing in a city like Warsaw toward the end of the nineteenth century and during the first decades of the twentieth. The official number of living quarters in Warsaw was reported to be about 250,000, but the population of the city hovered around one million. (Although the proportions today are somewhat better, there still are many more people living in Warsaw than there are living spaces for them.)

Poland's cities had two ghettoes. One section of the city was large in surface, luxurious, even elegant, and was reserved for the rich and the powerful. The other was smaller in area, filled to overflowing, and stinking from the smells of open sewers, cheap cooking, and perpetually decomposing clothes and bodies. The only thing the two ghettoes shared was the marketplace.

Within the ghettoes of the poor there were two distinct areas, one reserved for the starving Catholics and the other for the starving Jews. The dream they shared was to get out of the ghetto. When the road out of an inferno is narrow and barred, in the rush to save their humaneness people trample each other to death. This happened in Poland, and it happened more frequently to the Jews than to the Catholics, because the people who stood at the bars of the road leading to middle-class existence more readily accommodate a Catholic than a Jew. The Jew was forced to learn how to pole-vault over the bars. He learned well and for that he was despised. All of this has been described in so many novels, portrayed in so many films and poignant photographs that little is to be gained by repetition.

The Russian Revolution did not occur because Lenin planned it or Marx declared it as inevitable. The pogroms of Poland did not happen because suddenly some animallike instinctual hatred made the Poles butcher Jews. All of these horrors happen and will continue to happen when masses of people cannot stand the process of dehumanization one more instant. They happen when a people perceives that there is no further road down. How it happens depends on the action of those who will eventually profit from it.

On their surface, the following two stories—Maria Kuncewiczowa's "A Turban" and Eliza Orzeszkowa's "Powerful Samson"—deal with the repressions of anti-Semitism. In Poland it was better for a Jew to appear to be a Palestinian or an Arab than a Jew. In Poland,

the Jews needed a powerful Samson to help them. But Kuncewiczowa's and Orzeszkowa's Jews actually stand for all Poles, especially
poor city dwellers. Their motivation was to escape, escape at any
cost. But if you do not have "any cost" and still want to remain alive,
then escape as if through an illusion, a make-believe that just might
become a new reality.

Maria Kuncewiczowa
(1897–   )

A noted novelist well known to American and English readers through translations of her work, Kuncewiczowa is also a musician. She uses elements of music, as well as color, in her writing. Her novels include *The Stranger, The Keys, The Conspiracy of the Absent*, and *The Forester*. The following selection was taken from the short story collection *Two Moons*. Mrs. Kuncewiczowa now resides in the United States.

A Turban

The rain kept drizzling. A raw wind kept blowing from the river into the town, sniping at people. It was one of those annoying three-day summer rains with grayness so complete and the cold so ruthless and penetrating that it was difficult to recall the good weather breathing brightness and warmth some tens of hours earlier. Now it seemed like a dim vision in a narcotic dream.

Simon put on his windproof jacket and meandered out. When he arrived at the marketplace he found it quite deserted: only two porters were getting themselves officially wet while waiting for the bus near the well. The wife of the pharmacist, pulling at the sleeves of her sweater to cover the palms of her hands and peering out through the glass door of her store, watched a lonely hen strolling heroically on the slippery pavement. In contrast, homeless or idle townsfolk loitered or shifted from foot to foot in recesses, doorways, and under eaves. The rain was—for them—calamity or entertainment. It stripped the last bit of comfort from some. It sweetened extreme boredom for others. The homeless crouched and suffered, while the idle watched the eddying pools of water with the same dull interest with which they had watched spots of sunshine two days before.

Simon in his waterproof outfit waded aimlessly forward. Passing by the porters he looked around when he heard someone greeting him.

"How d'you do, sir. You seem to be headed for the telegraph office, sir. Is something wrong, God forbid?"

Moshek Ruchlingier shifted from foot to foot. His turned-up collar interfered with his beard, his hands were stuck in his pockets. He kept talking, his small beadlike eyes gleaming with anxiety. Behind the patience in his eyes lay suffering. It was obvious that at the moment he was cold and felt a stranger on this marketplace beside the Vistula.

Simon looked in turn at the other porter, Cackowski. This tall, slim man was leaning back against the railing of the well; his head, firmly placed on his stiff neck, was directed carelessly toward the clouds while drops of water fell down his cheeks and his chest from the visor of his porter's cap. Cackowski, however, was not showing any signs of discomfort and he was not trembling. Solidly poised in the mud, he gave the impression of a tree joyfully spreading out and up to receive friendly elements.

Simon shuddered. Suddenly he became keenly aware of how close his lot was to Moshek's: this shifting from foot to foot beside the unconquerable, strange trees. Despite his windproof jacket, he was cold and felt a tremor of horror go through him. Through this climate he saw the world. The ties binding his family to Jerusalem were nothing more than a biblical tradition. Who could tell if in Simon's system there was even one atom of Palestinian sunshine? But still these rainy August days were driving him on to the precipice of homelessness. And—oh shame! He felt no longing after the Orient. He longed to have the wet winds comb out his woolly curls and make them as straight as hemp, to have the cold chill and narrow his eyes. He longed after a more natural place for himself somewhere in a corner of the spacious Slavic fields.

He muttered something in reply to Moshek and then moved on. The absurdity of his own desires made every one of his thoughts disgusting. He recalled reluctantly his last telegram to his mother:

15 Zamenhof Street, Warsaw. Mrs. Chaja Goldman. First prize in landscape competition.

Much love, Simon.

Now his prize-winning painting appeared to him a horrible forgery. Those birch trees, marsh marigolds, and the shepherd! The creative work of Chaja Goldman's son, of 15 Zamenhof Street! Just at that moment there emerged from behind the corner of the tannery the head and then the trunk of the body of a brindled cow. The herd was returning from pasture. Simon turned his back. He could not stand looking at the boy who bore indifferently his shepherd's bliss over real meadows, a bliss denied to Jewish shepherds.

He turned into a side street. As he did so he had to force his way against the wind. He trudged along with difficulty, whistling, and deriding himself because of the clash between his body and his environment. His face was that of an Afro-Asian hydrid, wide-nosed, thick-lipped with a smile that seemed cut out with the blade of a sharp knife; his hands were swarthy, his figure heavyset—all these features seemed to anger Boreas himself. The young man blinked his stiff eyelashes and decided to return, especially since Jeremy had promised to come this noon for a friendly discussion on art.

Near the store a door suddenly squeaked, opening over the side-walk. A girl came down the steps of the shop and ran down the street. Her arm brushed Simon's side as she trudged across the muddy pavement. It was Madzia, the actress. He could see her profile and observe how carefully she skipped the mud by jumping on slim legs from one stone to another. He did not know her personally though he had often seen her about town. Heretofore he had not noticed any of the young girl's characteristics except that when she happened to be near him his heart would stop beating for a fraction of a second, and then it would thump. Still later, at night, he would dream heavy, enchanting, intoxicating dreams. Now at long last, despite the usual reaction in his chest, he could take a thorough look at her. Over her forehead the wind played with a streak of extremely fine and fair hair, while her eyes, pale as smoke, appeared to be without iris or frame. They were simply a gaze that expressed an aimless and a boundless sorrow. Her figure, or rather her lines, could not be easily distinguished, as they were all one with her fluid movements. But Madzia's nose was clearly bluish and her cheeks blue from the cold. Rather than walk she seemed to soar on the damp air, held in suspension by the secret of this rainy day whose essence was so completely entrusted to her.

Simon hurried home as quickly as he could. Jeremy was already there waiting for him. It goes without saying that there was no discussion on art. In his desire to know more about Madzia, Simon began a philosophical discussion in order to be able to talk about women with his older, usually reserved, colleague. Somehow Jeremy became interested in the discussion, which, in turn, was followed by light anecdotes, and before long Simon got out of him some stories about Madzia. They were all to her credit. She was an independent person. Her talents made up for a lack of natural beauty, and her love affairs were all well chosen and discreet. She had, however, one queer trait. Whenever she played the part of somebody's mistress at the playhouse she would spread dark makeup all over herself.

Simon began to dream about conquering Madzia. He had no idea, though, how to go about it. Above all he did not know how to cover up nor how to adorn his all too evident Jewishness.

The rainy weather was soon over and the visitors again returned to the beach. Since Simon had become aware of his love for the pale actress he was afraid to go there. He was tortured by the thought that even at this very moment Paul was sprawling on the sand beside Madzia, his heavy, white body close to her misty, snow-white flesh. He could see them rubbing cream on their arms and thighs, and then shading their eyes to estimate the strength of the sun, as though it were a healing lamp. Those children of the August rain and of the April snow! Now they are probably swimming, while lapwings cry something to them that only they understand. The splashing water murmurs some confidential secrets to them; then they dash back to the shore and wring out the water from their soft, fair hair. A couple of cold-blooded blonds! A couple in their native habitat. A couple not driven out of Paradise.

Simon walked about his rented room, flashing his nakedness in mirrors and laughing. What else but a laughing stock was this Jewish sample of a man on this flaxen river?

One morning Simon was looking through his suitcases in search of a blue tie. (Blue had a softening effect upon his features.) He could not find the tie but came across a richly embroidered silk scarf. It had come as a sample of still life with a case of grapefruit sent him by a friend from Tel Aviv. Simon passionately wrapped himself a turban over his curls. Now there at last was something for him, an attire of attires! He reached for the mirror. The bright head of a native of Yemen looked back at him. Angrily he bared his teeth—the head laughed a monstrous, ghostly laugh. Simon pushed the mirror away and, trembling with inspiration, jumped to the wardrobe, grabbed his linen working pants and put them on as fast as he could. With undiminished speed he put on a dirty, colored shirt. He rolled up the sleeves, pushed his turban acock, and stuck a pipe between his teeth. He now for all the world looked exactly like an Arabian porter. Once again he showed his teeth in a grin and with this Mohammedan smile he ran to the landing.

Old Shulim, the boatman, was instantly taken aback by the metamorphosis. Bashfully he turned his eyes away. Several girls who were already seated in the old skiff when Simon jumped in looked at each other in amazement and got out.

Around the island as usual, there was much splashing of water and hustle and bustle permeated with the odor of osier and the beauty parlor. Flora, dressed in a huge sun hat, walked along the edge of the beach. Mena, holding arrows in the air (the bow lay not far from her), called Barbara's greyhoud so that, beside the huge animal, she would look more like Diana. Sylvia and Jeremy were paddling a canoe and singing, "Rrrum-bus the glorious dance of great Colum-bus. . . ." On the syllable *bus* their paddles struck the water simultaneously. Paul and Gigi were waving their feet in the air. Madzia stood beside them and struck their calves with a rod whenever they bent their knees. The summer residents flocked in the water and crowded the beach. They peeped at the artists and gossiped about them. They made fools of themselves attempting to dazzle them.

Simon had made an impression. His friends surrounded him.

"Hello," they cried. "Simon! We like you in this little costume! How did you manage to get yourself up as such a Mohammedan apparition? It's true, 'a grandma is no longer a grandmother and a Jew is no longer Jewish!' "

Singing this song they led the Arab to the ladies.

A few days later Simon, his bliss almost making him ill, made a date with Madzia. He was to come to her. Alone. There were to be just the two of them. He . . . and the Slavic nebula.

And the afternoon had come. Simon, filled with delirious feelings, began to dress. He ran around the room. He kept muttering. He delighted in the few words that Madzia pronounced as though she were speaking Russian. She did not even say "Wyspianski" but "Wishpianski." From her narrow, childish lips these words flowed so gracefully. . . . Simon was dying of the wish that today she would wear no lipstick. Let her lips be pale. Let them yield, their strength gone, in a kiss. Let them tremble with pain. Let her fair eyelids flutter on her white cheeks.

The feeling of sweetness overwhelmed the painter. After three mornings on the beach he had learned by heart even the smallest veins on Madzia's hips and all the intonations of her voice. Now he was to drink the very essence of her femininity.

He put on his saffron shirt, crumpled it and opened it deep on his chest, and at last, flashing a smile, he walked out abruptly, like a storm.

Madzia lived in a hut in a large plum orchard owned by some fishermen. It was there that Goldman had seen her the first time. She stood then with Paul among the plum trees. Down below shone the river. On the sides, nets were perched on poles to dry. They looked so harmonious, so simple, so happy, like two healthy stems of the same plant. It was then that Simon had begun to hate Paul—and himself.

But now everything was different. The turban had changed the ugly strangeness into a miracle. Now the man of Yemen was able to reach for what had been a vain dream not only of Chaja's son (15 Zamenhof Street) but also of the blue-eyed Paul of Kujawy.

Simon walked with large strides across the marketplace. Two boys ran behind him, shouting:

"You nigger! Tell us how far it is to hell? Look at him, a Turk! Give us some halvah, you disease!"

Then they fell to quarreling, trying to figure out who that fellow with a towel on his head could be.

Simon stopped at the gate. He sighed deeply. He was almost faint with tenderness. Now . . . in half a minute he would be grasping her pearly hand in his swarthy paw. In a half hour . . . perhaps . . . he would be pressing the breasts of this siren of the Vistula with his heavy, brown body. And then at last he would be able to throw away his hated Arab pretense. After having cheated away the anti-Semitic prejudice, he would be able to kiss this flaxen girl and weep with her in wonderful, all-human bliss.

He pushed the gate. Once again desire filled his veins. Simon ran through the orchard and reached the hut.

Near the steps to the porch he suddenly halted. . . . On the banister, perched like a bird on the branch of a tree, sat a wild woman. Feathers fluttered round her head; wild colors flared on her body. Abashed, he hurried to bypass the spectacle. Then, however, the woman jumped down from the banister and barred his way.

He looked . . . and was dumbfounded. It was Madzia—the actress. From under the black eyelids, thick with mascara, Simon felt her eyes rapaciously boring into him. The whites of her eyes and her teeth gleamed in the chestnut-colored face, while her bare arms and legs tensed like straps of dark leather.

Simon groaned:

"What's this? What is this?"

Madzia replied, "It's me . . . my true self. I can't stand insipid beauty. Mine is purely exterior, accidental. Inside I feel I am a dark, wild woman."

Then she added passionately, "You are fond of me, aren't you? And you are also a fierce, splendid, and exotic man. For you I want to be beautiful and my own true self!"

Simon was silent. He felt a painful emptiness replacing his blissful passion. He broke into laughter. Then he shuffled his feet. At last, hardly able to speak, he said:

"A terrific, wild couple . . . indeed. Shouldn't we go to have a picture taken? It would be a fine vacation souvenir!"

Translated by George J. Maciuszko

Eliza Orzeszkowa
(1841–1910)

Eliza Orzeszkowa was a master of the Polish realistic novel. Her father left a library that enabled Orzeszkowa to become one of the most educated women of her time. At sixteen, she married a wealthy landowner, Peter Orzeszkowa. They both cooperated with the movement of democratic youth that organized the insurrection of 1863 and, after the uprising was quashed, he was exiled to Siberia. In Grodno, where Orzeszkowa moved, she wrote articles and pamphlets and became an advocate of social equality. She worked toward full rights for peasants and Jews and criticized the gentry's intolerance.

Although of the positivist generation, she differed from them in not condemning the uprising and in her emphasis on man's moral predicament. Her fifty volumes of novels and short stories reveal a social awareness and a knowledge of the Polish people at the close of the century.

The short story "Powerful Samson," excerpts of which follow, typifies Orzeszkowa's interest in the unsophisticated mind and the way art and idealism open it up.

Powerful Samson

Shymshel, the son of a water carrier or woodcutter, a poor student at a free school, possessed no fortune except the two hundred zlotys collected by public donation. He was, nevertheless, deemed such a good match in the eyes of young girls and their parents that, when his marriage with Tsipa was announced, everyone was astonished at the luck of the little *gizelka* or salesgirl whose old mother carried heavy baskets of fruit in the streets and whose sisters had married cobblers, carpenters, and the like, men of the unrefined trades and low estate. It is true that these cobblers and carpenters owned houses and large workshops, and had steady incomes. Shymshel did not own a house nor did he have a workshop, or an income, but he was educated. Moreover—or therefore—he was so beautiful and delicate.

Shymshel and Tsipa married, possessing a joint capital of thirty rubles. Besides this, Tsipa also had a trousseau, that is, three undershirts, two feather beds, two dresses and one quilted jerkin.

They had nothing more at the time of their marriage, and yet somehow they had lived twelve years. . . . During that time, nine children were born to them. Four died, five lived. No doubt they will have five more; three of them to die and two to grow up, and yet they will love on. . . . It may seem strange, or even improbable to you, that a family affluent in such magnificent, or to be more explicit, numerous results could live on a capital of thirty rubles. I myself was greatly astonished at this until I got to know Tsipa a little better.

In appearance she is a little Jewish woman, and as they say, very simple. At twenty-eight she looks more than forty. Her small figure straining forward, her back covered with a quilted jerkin that is humped and shining, not with the richness of the material but with age, she moves through the crowd with short, hurried, and yet shy and seemingly stealthy steps.

She seems to be constantly troubled, numbed, stultified, and only her black eyes, darting frequent flashes, move very quickly in her dark, wilted face. These flashes betray a constant and intent quest, a pursuit for something, and at times take on a malicious expression. They are then in perfect harmony with the low forehead covered with uncountable lines running from the thick brows to the edge of the black wig.

But please do not laugh at this small and simple Jewish woman who does not look attractive or wise. She has accomplished something quite important. She has resolved in actual practice a certain social problem that the world has found extremely difficult, namely the question of feminine equality in the right to earn. Tsipa has reached an ideal solution to this question, for her earnings have been supporting her husband and five children for the past twelve years. All her enterprises that led to this objective are founded on the capital of thirty rubles.

With these thirty rubles, which represented the foundation of her family's existence, Tsipa opened a grocery store. However, she did have an additional credit, equal to this sum, promised by the shop in which she had previously worked. The most important task of any kind of enterprise whose aim is to earn a profit is to find customers. Tsipa began to look for customers from the very first day that her shop opened. She is looking for them to this very day, not because she cannot find them, but because having found them she loses them and must look for new ones. She loses them for a variety of reasons, among which the most inferior part is played by certain mysterious activities that Tsipa performs in the evening after the shop is closed, in the right corner of that very shop, between the cupboard, counter, and wall. A specific rustle can be heard issuing from that corner as if something were being sealed and then sealed again, as if something were being sifted and poured.

Although these activities, to which the proprietress of the shop devotes herself at this hour, may appear mysterious in the dim light of the lamp that burns on the floor behind the counter, it would, nevertheless, be an exaggeration to ascribe a tragic significance to them. Tsipa does not belong to any kind of Jewish plot to the detriment or for the destruction of the Christian population. She is not preparing in privacy and secret any kind of injurious activity against her *meropia** for I can vouch for it that she does not possess any *meropia* of her own, and I even doubt that she ever in her whole life heard the sound of that word. She is acting absolutely on her own, and not in compact with her own people. Her *meropia* is a collective being, carrying the names of the buying public, and the powerful authorities that impel her to sift and pour in order to turn high-quality goods into mediocre and medioce into inferior are the educated husband, the five children, and the thirty rubles that is the principal invested in her enterprise. Tsipa's *meropia*, the buying public, seems to possess a sense of taste and an exquisite sense of smell. For scarcely do its members become acquainted with her goods when they soon stop buying, and that after numerous but unfortunately justified reproaches, much shouting and beating. Hence, Tsipa's search for new customers constitutes a chain of never-ending trials and endeavors. Her trials and endeavors are varied: a pleading wail, hand kissing, performing every service that anyone may demand. In order to gain the good graces of the public and to make additional money from time to time, she becomes everything in turn: a public messenger, a letter carrier, an agent for house servants, a go-between for borrowers and lenders, for sellers and purchasers. She is at the shop infrequently, only now and then. Her mother, one of her sisters, or a neighbor will replace her while she runs up and down stairs the whole day long, toting heavy bundles under her arm, carrying piles of old clothing on her back, standing humbly on the threshold of houses

---

*Victim of exploitation (according to the anti-Semites of Orzeszkowa's time, *meropia* was designated by the Jewish community council).

with a basket in each hand, one with dried fruits and nuts and the other with tea and bottles of wine, quarreling with cooks and janitors who do not want to admit her to her benefactors, softening their severity with a pair of figs or a handful of nuts. At times she grows impatient with persons of her own sex who create an onerous competition for her and induce her by the force of their fists to leave the battlefield. Once, a large piece of the once-velvet collar that had adorned her quilted jerkin remained in the hands of these uncouth representatives of a great idea.

Having lost the magnificence of her dress in this manner, Tsipa wept plaintively. . . . This moment of emotion was exceptional with her. On the whole, she never complains of anything, and if sometimes someone meeting her mournful gaze asks with more or less sympathy: "Well, Tsipa, are things going very badly with you?" she never even answers in the affirmative but says: "As God wills, so it is." There are some who, knowing Tsipa's situation at home a little better, will say to her as they look at her dark, wrinkled face, so often moist with perspiration and exhaustion and quivering with involuntary, nervous twitches:

"And what is your husband doing all his life? Why doesn't he help you?"

Then the dejected expression leaves Tsipa's face and is supplanted by something resembling anger.

"He has his work!" she answers sullenly. "He cannot help me in trading."

"You are very fortunate, Tsipa, to have such a clumsy husband."

Hearing this Tsipa raises her head:

"If I had ten daughters, I would pray God to give them all the happiness that I have."

It now gives me great pleasure to present Shymshel to you, in person this time, of whom you have heard so much from me! I am sure that once you have looked at him, you will confirm Tsipa's statement that he is very beautiful and delicate. He is tall and slim. His hands are as white as those of a woman of great quality and high birth. They are narrow and very shapely, though thin. His face, lean and pale with its long, curly raven-hued beard, possesses a strange purity and delicacy of features and a calm and most kind expression. When he happens to lift his eyes from the book, his face becomes suffused with the light of deep and mysterious dreaminess; it is apparent that those black eyes, with the fiery depths and moist surface, weep at times at the Babylonian enslavement and destruction of Jerusalem, and often gaze upon the flaming hieroglyphics that wreathe the proud head of the archangel of knowledge and upon the diamond teardrop that burns in the eye of the angel of prayer. Something of the calm pride of that angel Sar-ha-Olam [angel of knowledge] and of the strange goodness of Sandalfon [angel of prayer] is mirrored and remains in Shymshel's fiery and yet mild eyes. If his lips, outlined in a thin and scarcely pink line amidst the black beard, did not belong to an uneducated and simple Jew, they would have infallibly signified a sensitive, nervous, even artistic nature, so exquisite is their shape, so eloquently do they tremble as they move from time to time, and so understanding, yet mild and tender is the smile that appears upon them.

I agree entirely with Tsipa's opinion of her husband's appearance, and discover that by looking at her with eyes that contain something of the light of the angel of knowledge and the angel of pity one can think, surmise, and regret a great deal. . . .

If you have taken as great an interest in this Jew as I have, then you may look at him as much as you will and as often as you may wish if you come at the same hour to the same yard. For every day, without fail, he sits of an evening, at a table, his face turned toward the window with the dim lamplight falling on it. He either bends over a book or gazes somewhere on high. At times you will see him with little Esther as she jumps on his knees or with little Lezer, who climbs on his back and buries both hands in his raven hair. He is very happy then. He forgets the slavery in Babylon and Sandalfon, and laughs at his children and presses loud kisses on their cheeks. . . . .

We shall not look at him longer now, for the door to the sign-painter's home is opening and a group of dark figures, having come out, moves under the orange hand that seems to threaten their heads, and in noisy talk passes through the yard and enters Shymshel's room.

Let us follow them.

You know the room from my previous description. It is crowded now. Six men have entered. I present them: Itzek, the tinker; Moishe, the sign painter; Yosel, the furrier; Meyer, the son of Yosel the furrier; and two others I do not know.

It is for these people that Moishe had lighted his house *a giorno* [brightly]. It is they who had talked so noisily with him. But what do they want from Shymshel? They are bowing with a respect so great that it is immediately apparent that these simple craftsmen feel the learned man's great superiority. Shymshel greets them politely, gently, but with a composure befitting his dignity. Yosel, the furrier,

steps out of the center of the small group (being either the oldest or
the most eloquent), and with some timidity launches upon the subject and says that the whole company has decided. . . .

Decided . . . what? Have we guessed? They have decided something. What could they have decided? Naturally, something that is to
undermine or painfully wound the Christian world, as the pamphlets
would have us believe. I vow that it was written by a man of great
wisdom and adapted to the Polish language by a man of still greater
wisdom. It is called: "World Conquest of the Jews."

They (they, a militant nation!) wish to and try to conquer the
world, and now they must have decided something that will lead to
this aim.

So Yosel, the furrier, says that he and his companions have decided
on the day of the nearest Purim . . . to give a play.

Is that all?

Only this.

. . . To give a play for the benefit of the poor. . . .

Rebe Shymshel has a beautiful voice for singing, a very beautiful
voice. No one else can sing the main part better than he.

The cantor himself has advised them. The cantor, who, as everyone
knows, sings so magnificently and who knows the voices of the whole
community as well as his own.

Rebe Shymshel is a learned man, a very learned man. No one but
he can arouse the people's eager sympathy for this undertaking; no
one but he can add dignity to it. Rabbi Boruch himself, whose great
zeal in caring for the poor is known, begs . . .

What are they to play? They are to perform a play called *Powerful
Samson*, which Rebe Shymshel knows (for what is not known to the
wisdom of Rebe Shymshel?), and in which there is such beautiful
singing and such beautiful scenes, that—ach!

. . . Shymshel, or Samson, thinks for a long while upon the propo-
sition put to him. The thing they have asked of him is no longer
meditation or contemplation, but action, a thing that Shymshel has
not yet come in contact with.

Action terrifies him. It will be hard for him to walk, move, try—in a
word: to act. And a thing as flighty as giving a play: will not this
offend his dignity, will it not lower his authority?

He thinks for a long time, then he rises and says:

"If the cantor says that I have a beautiful voice for singing, and if
Rabbi Boruch begs me to do this, and if it is for the poor, then I agree
to take part in this."

Delilah sat behind a curtain on a Viennese chair. Her azure gown was spread over a large crinoline and a small pink fan was in her hand. She sat and her great childish eyes, which looked out of her face like forget-me-nots in a bouquet of peonies, gazed straight at the audience. Then she rose and came out from behind the curtain. She began to sing.

A very nice bass voice.

She sang that she must lure Samson with her charms in order to extort from him the mystery of his strange strength. . . .

Delilah found it a little awkward to move in the long dress and iron hoops. Besides, she was much troubled by the implement in her hand, not knowing what to do with it.

The woolly locks that flowed about her brow and down her back increased the warmth that one feels at the sight of so many eyes riveted to one's face. Her bass voice trembled and fell to so low a register that it was not at all appropriate to a delicate, feminine bosom. Her azure eyes were moist with tears of unutterable suffering.

But this was nothing.

Never in all his life had Shymshel seen so beautiful a woman.

As he walked on stage, did he see the Delilah who was really there? No one knows. However, I did hear afterward that as Shymshel walked on stage, instead of Meyerek's crimson face, forget-me-not eyes and woolly locks, he saw a snow-white countenance in a garland of gleaming raven braids, gazing at him with eyes shining like two stars.

He saw a musing tear, a passionate fire in those black eyes, and the figure which faced him was tall, lissome, and as the heavens are warmed by the eastern sun so it emanated a breath of the sultry raptures of the East.

Never before had Shymshel experienced the sensation that he now felt, nor could he name it. But as he approached the charming apparition that stood before his eyes, and as he began to sing to it, his voiced possessed such soft and fervent, plaintive and violent shades that Delilah opened her eyes wide with amazement and when later she was to give him her hand, as the part called for, she did so with evident trepidation.

With a gesture of violent joy Shymshel caught her hand, not the one holding the fan but the other, and drawing Delilah to his bosom, placed a kiss on her lips. Completely frightened by this kiss, Delilah broke away from his embrace and sat down on one of the two Viennese chairs placed in front of the porch of her palace.

Having calmed down somewhat, Shymshel sat on the second chair and the duet began.

Samson's fate was sealed in this duet. He was reticent and not easy to draw out, but Delilah's charms succeeded in overcoming the most determined resistance. Standing before her, in vain did he sing to her in his most convincing, most supplicating voice: *"Dus is nit dein gescheft."* The beguiling seductress knew well that this was an important business for her and so long did she sing in her bass voice (Shymshel heard the most beautiful mezzo-soprano instead of the bass), so long did she open wide her tired childish eyes with the effort (Shymshel saw two black burning diamonds instead) that, worn out by the battle and overcome with love, he grasped his locks with both his hands, and showing them to the sorceress sang out: "My strength is in them."

The Philistines arrived. But what was this? They were the same who had died at Samson's hand in the third act. Having risen from the dead, their wrath against their murderer must have been all the greater. They were waiting for Delilah. They stole to the palace door, peeked through its only window and exchanged mysterious signs. But there she was.

She emerged from behind the curtain and, holding the pink fan in one hand, carried a large strand of long raven hair in the other. The joy of the Philistines was indescribable. The king himself shook Delilah's hand in token of gratefulness. The knights took their swords out of their scabbards, and with a shout of furious vengeance, fell upon Samson as he came out of the palace. Samson had changed. Without the helmet and hair, without the white coat, he fell into the enemy's hands and without much ceremony they blinded him in both eyes.

The curtain fell. A silence of deadly awe fell upon the auditorium; only sobs could be heard in the darkness.

They were right—these compassionate souls—to shed tears. Dressed in his theatrical costume, Samson sat on the bench where the Philistines had placed him. He was deathly white, breathing heavily and his eyes were closed.

"Rebe," Moishe spoke to him, "look at the palace, which you are to topple on the stage. . . . Maybe it is too heavy for you. . . . We can make it smaller . . ."

But only a hollow moan rattled in Shymshel's chest.

"My enemies have taken the light of my eyes," he whispered in anguish, "I am blind and my eyes will never see the great works of the Eternal."

"Herste, do you hear!" the Philistines said to each other as they

exchanged surprised glances. "He thinks that we have really gouged out his eyes."

Suddenly Delilah moved through the dressing room. Shymshel heard the rustle of her dress and raised his eyelids.

His eyes hurled bolts of anger and despair, a dark flush covered his pale face.

"What have you done to me? What have you done to me? You have ruined me! I have lost my eyes through your great cunning, I have been captured and ruined!"

Shouting these words with increasing violence and force, he clenched his fists and made a rush toward Delilah, who dropped her pink fan in fear and ran into the farthest corner of the dressing room where she hid behind a long, flowered robe of one of the Judaic elders. Moishe also shielded her with his wide shoulders, and not daring to lift his hand to the learned man, stretched both his hands in front of him and called in a persuasive voice:

"Rebe! Ay, ay, Rebe!"

Shymshel's wrath lasted but a short while and quickly changed into a deep and gentle grief. He fell on the bench, lowered his hands, closed his eyes and began to moan:

"Oy! Oy! I looked upon your face as on a flower of paradise. Your lips were to my lips like a brook of honey. Your eyes burned like a great flame and all my heart melted before them. . . . And you have wronged me so. For I am lost, Delilah."

No longer was anyone paying attention to the plaintive lament of the blinded hero except Delilah, who baring her head of the locks and roses, looked at him with fear.

On the stage stood a palace. Different from the one before. It was composed of two pasteboard pillars joined at the top with a pasteboard cornice. The Philistines were feasting around the pillars. They were happy and singing. For their greater joy, they commanded the blinded prisoner to be brought under the monarch's roof. Samson, led by two soldiers, stood with his eyes closed. He was not frightened; only mortally sad.

Look closely at him: it would seem that within this one hour his face had become thinner. His pale cheeks seem to have fallen in, and his closed eyes are surrounded by dark circles. One could say that this face has been wasted by passion, love, hatred, despair. . . .

The Philistines laughed, mocked him in all sorts of ways, telling him of the destruction and vengeance that they were sowing in his country. And he, a prisoner, a blind, helpless athlete, could no longer defend it. . . .

In vain were the Judaic elders crying there somewhere, in vain did the Judaic women fill the air with their lament, and the most valiant men stain with their blood the seared wastes of Judaic fields. . . . Samson would no longer shield his native land with his chest, the strength of which has been taken away, he would not see his arms raised against the enemy with eyes dispossessed of their light. . . .

Shymshel listened to the ridicule and triumphant tales of his enemies and slowly began to lift his head. . . . Feeling his way, he left the palace with faltering steps, stood on the other side of the pillars and began to sing. How deep and boundless was the pain with which his voice swelled! What great heights it climbed! With what desperate calls and invocations it was filled! He called to Jehovah for strength, for that old strength, which he desired for only a moment, only one moment, for one instant. . . . Calling thus, he lifted up his trembling hands and his pale face with its closed eyes and lips, surrounded with a tormented expression.

Standing thus, framed by the pasteboard pillars in the light of the lamp with a long funnel, which one of the Philistines held close to his face, he bore the semblance of a martyr, but a martyr who suffered "with the suffering of millions."

This lamp, held close to his face (probably to light the scene), burned his cheek. He thrust it away with an energetic and irate gesture, seized the pillars with both hands, shook them and toppled them upon the Philistines who, too, fell upon the ground with a great noise. . . .

They were all killed and Samson was killed.

The inanimate bodies of the dead lay under the palace ruins, and the scarlet, yellow, and green colors of their robes shimmered amidst the crushing pillars. The curtain fell and the public broke into frenetic shouts.

There, through the dark street, lighted by a weak flame of an infrequent street lamp, strode a lonely, slim male figure. As it passed beside the occasional lamp post, the figure glowed with a sheen of the scarlet, gold, and diamonds that covered it. When it was engulfed by darkness, its long cloak falling in folds grew white and unfurled like the arms of a phantom. The figure was alone, but by no means sad. The dignified stride indicated lightness and force, and from its chest, once in a muted and once in a loud burst of tone, flowed the magnificent aria of triumph.

Shymshel, having crushed the Philistines and himself under the capsized palace walls, had risen from the dead, had comprehended, had forgotten all the past humiliations and anguish. But not for one single second had he stopped being the "Powerful Samson." True, walking now from one street to another, between the brick walls with the dark or only infrequent windows dimly lit here and there, he ran in his mind through all the great deeds he had performed and was filled with joy and pride.

At times a recollection of the beguiling and faithless Delilah flashed through his mind . . . then longing and regret wrung his heart. Yet quickly he called to mind his native land, Judea, which he had saved from blood, tears, and conflagration; he raised his head high, sang louder and more joyously, and trod on the uneven pavement of the dark street as on laurel wreaths. . . .

In this manner Shymshel passed the boulevard and entered the side lane. Automatically, out of habit, he turned toward his home, and without giving a thought to his actions and still singing, he touched the latch of his low door with his hand and stood on the threshold of his room.

He stopped and stood for a few minutes in numb immobility.

In the room, a lamp burned on the table that stood at the window. A foul, yellowish smoke curled upward from its long cylinder. Farther the gray, low walls, beds with feather covers, old clothing, torn and dirty, strewn over the floor and chest, several smaller and larger human figures lying here and there in slumber had created a chaos in the dim light that was completely incomprehensible to his eyes and mind. He understood after a few minutes—and awakened.

. . . He lowered his head and looked at his clothes.

A strange smile appeared on his lips.

Samson's white cloak fell over his knees and feet in soft folds; the scarlet robe radiated a golden luster in the light of the lamp; the beads of his necklace covered his chest with the sparkle of rubies, emeralds, and silver; and on his forehead he felt the soft touch of the crest that hung from the knight's helmet. He smiled strangely for a long while, until lifting his arms he slowly removed the golden helmet with the crest from his head. He placed it on the table and gazed at it with flaming eyes from which after a while two large tears rolled down his pallid cheeks.

"Farewell, powerful Samson, great among men! You have taught me that there are heroic deeds in this world, a great love toward people, beautiful Delilahs and . . . small, weak, unhappy Shymshels."

He had learned that never had he been great, or wise, or happy . . . and he wrung his hands with such vehemence that the bones cracked in their joints, and then he placed them on the back of his neck and began to unclasp his necklace of rubies, emeralds, and silver. He unfastened it and took it off and held it in both hands, stretched in front of him. From beyond that net of shining strings gleamed his black eyes, brimming with large tears.

"Farewell, powerful Samson, great among men . . ."

He then raised his eyes and his hands holding the necklace dropped to his knees. He saw before him a picture of which he at first did not know the meaning. Before him, the gloomy depth of the room was strewn with six pairs of lively, glistening points. These points were human eyes and they shone at various levels and at various distances from each other, but the human figures to which they belonged were completely hidden in the dark. The six pairs of eyes were staring at Shymshel's face and expressed admiration, wonder, and joyful astonishment. As he lowered his hands which held the necklace to his knees, these points, black, blue, gray, but all burning with a shining luster, began to move toward him. Above, at the highest point, he noticed two other lights. They were golden like two ducats and a monotonous, loud purr issued from the spot from which they shone.

It was the gray cat, which sat high in the opening of the oven, looking at the master of the house and purring. Lower, was the family group, asleep when Shymshel had arrived, but which awoke later and, sitting on the floor, each in the place where the awakening had found him gazed at the radiant costume of husband and father. . . .

Thus they all sat and had been looking for some time, holding their breath in order not to startle the vision in crimson and gold that seemed like an apparition from their dreams. Tsipa was first to slip out of the gloom, furtively, very quietly, crawling rather than walking toward her husband's knees.

She sat down again as she reached his knees, lifted her dark, wrinkled face enclosed by the rim of a black round cap worn at night instead of the wig, laced her hands over the quilted skirt with the blue stockinged feet showing from under it, opened her mouth and looked at his face with eyes suffused with the honey of tenderness.

Behind her the fiery-haired heads of little Mendel and Esther emerged out of the gloom. Enoch strained forward his wan, thin face, above which appeared a crumpled rim of a hat pushed to the back of his head. Liba stood up behind all of them with her braid undone to half its length, holding little Lezer in her arms.

All were silent.

And Shymshel was silent for a long while, looking in turn at the figures that now surrounded him closely.

Then his eyes encompassed them all, and quickly hiding his face in both his hands, he was shaken with a loud wailing.

Crying thus he said:

"My poor children! Oh, my poor, poor little fish, my diamonds. What am I to do for you? What can I do for you? I myself am so poor, weak, small, and so—ignorant, and so—stupid. And you will always be poor, small, and ignorant, and stupid."

Suddenly he stopped crying and moaning and sprang up from the stool. Standing at the window, he gazed deep into the darkness. He stood thus for a while until he saw again . . . a great and long band of gold that against the dark backdrop of night formed a golden ladder, its rungs filled with angels and at the peak, weaving garlands, the white, the merciful angel of prayer, crowned with suffering.

Shymshel turned toward his family and snatched little Lezer from Liba's arms. . . .

Had someone stood in the cramped dark yard outside the window in which the dim lamp was shining, he would have seen a singular scene:

A the back of the gloomy room, at its farthest corner, still shone the golden eyes of the cat as if suspended in midair. Closer, the thin, wan faces of Liba and Enoch, their lips opening in astonishment, rose out of the gloomy background. Closer still, little Esther and Mendel stood holding hands, their wide-open blue eyes almost hidden by the great masses of fiery locks that fell on their brows. Near them, Tsipa in the round cap that clung to her head, frightened and saddened at her husband's weeping folded her dark hands over her bosom; and closest of all, just by the window, a tall Jew with tousled, black hair, wearing a scarlet robe that shone with gold embroidery, bending over the table, holding in both his outstretched hands the two-year-old child in a gray shirt. Almost touching it to the window pane, and sending his beseeching, tearful look somewhere high above, he cried in a loud voice:

"Sandalfon! Sandalfon! Pray that Jehovah make him a 'Powerful Samson!' "

Translated by Krystyna Cekalska

Joseph Wittlin
(1896–   )

In all of the previous selections the themes were resistance, struggle against poverty, patriotism, collaboration; but along with these there were some glimpses of the everyday, even if that everyday occurred during a war. The hero drawn by Wittlin in his brilliant novel *Salt of the Earth*, the hero in the context of the ethos of Polish history, is the antihero. He is a human who wants only one distinction from life—to be recognized as a human. Wittlin, who is best known for his poetry and for his marvelous Polish translation of the *Odyssey*, wanted to show that a Pole, or not even a Pole but anybody living in Poland, has the right to live in the fullness of the dignity due any human.

Two short stanzas from Wittlin's poetry will make the point, illustrate his world view through the ex-soldier:

> *Within my lungs, gas, dust, the world ablaze*
> *Still strangle each word that forms in my throat*
> *Today is purgatory—yesterday was hell;*
> *Endure, my friends, till evening endure.*
> *Tomorrow Eden comes into being.**
>
> *And you are lying in the field that is fallow*
> *For you were told to go to war by the chiefs.*
> *And they were told by the kings,*
> *And the kings were told by their pride and by God*
> *All power comes from God,*
> *He places kings upon the thrones,*
> *That is why you are lying dead.***

Wittlin uses a humble Huzul (a Pole living in the eastern regions of the Carpathian mountain range) as the antihero because such a person is un-

---

* Quoted from Zoya Yurieff, *Joseph Wittlin*, trans. Dorothy Meller (Boston: Twayne Publishers, 1973), p. 23. Reprinted by permission.
** Quoted from Yurieff, *Joseph Wittlin*, p. 25. Reprinted by permission.

spoiled by sophistication. Through him, the author can set straight some basic human values and defamiliarize what the sophisticates take for granted. Here it is not self-evident that the right hand is the right hand and the left hand the left. What is self-evident is that both belong to a human and therefore deserve to be respected.

Salt of the Earth

Through forgotten corners of the Huzul countryside, where the smell of mint rises on summer nights, past dream villages nestling in quiet pasture lands, where shepherds blow their long reed pipes, runs the train. It is the train, shut in between wooden fences, that alone links these quiet lands to the outer world. It stains the darkness with the dazzling glare of its headlight; it outrages the virgin stillness of the night's deep peace. The gleam of its lighted carriages tears through the veils of the mist; the long shriek of its whistle startles the hares, and wakens the sleepy curiosity of men. Like some monstrous iron ladder bolted down over the stones, the shimmering rails, on their black wooden ties, stretch out forever in either direction. The tiny, white railway stations, surrounded by hedges, little gardens, shrubberies, and flower beds, brightened by balls of colored glass on long white stakes; the countless iron bridges flung over countless streams; and the little signal boxes, set at frequent intervals, give the comforting assurance that the passing train was not, as one might have fancied, a devil bidding the world goodnight.

For twenty years a man, whose origin was the dark, had been handling wood and grain, potatoes and casks of spirit from the local distillery on the little station of Topory-Czernielitza.

Darkness was his home and his element, as water is the element of the fish, and earth the element of the mole. Like a mole, Peter worked in darkness and burrowed in subterranean passages essential to his well-being. In the upper air he could only gasp desperately, like a fish out of water.

He cleaned the station lamps, filled them with oil, and swept out the so-called waiting room. If need arose he helped on the permanent way, taking out rotten ties and scattering ballast; and every now and then he rode on the inspection trolley with the engineer. Fast trains never deigned to honor Topory-Czernielitza even by slowing down. They swept disdainfully through it, flinging a contemptuous cloud of smoke into its face. But in summer the train occasionally brought visitors from town. Schoolboys would arrive with wooden boxes too heavy for them to lift. The train stopped only three minutes in Topory-Czernielitza, and the helpless young gentlemen would shout "Porter!" in the authoritative tone of old travelers to hide their nervousness. Then Peter, though he was no porter, though he had no railway cap, and didn't even wear the brass badge of the railway men, would jump into the carriage, collect the luggage, and carry it out to "the horses," waiting outside the station. Sometimes the Ruthenian priest took the train to town and had to be helped into his carriage. At times, too, there was hunting in the nearby forests; and some of the gentry would come by train, so as to spare their horses. On such occasions there was a chance of picking up good money and stowing some count's cigarettes into one's cap. Those were fine days!

Harvest was a good time also; to begin with, sacks of oats, and, later, sacks of corn. One could, now and then, make a hole in a sack, and then swear that the sack had been full of holes before. Besides, the sacks had no lead seals. And the stationmaster was human; he would box your ears, of course, but he would not discharge you. When the stationmaster boxed your ears it was good policy to kiss his hand at once, and to say, striking your breast: "I swear to God, on my honor, I'll never do it again!" But you had to put back what you had stolen. It was a hard life.

To say that he carried burdens epitomized Peter's life. Even in childhood he carried within him seeds of that malady that it is the fashion to attribute to the French; its symptoms were discernible in the typical nose and in certain defects of vision, which, however, grew no worse with the years. And as if the French influence was not enough, Peter's childish organism was subjected to an English influence as well—rickets.* Thus it came about that France and England, whose centuries of war had filled history, were reconciled at last in the body of a Huzul child. To the end of his life Peter was bandy-legged.

In addition, it was Peter's lot to carry on his back the weight of his father's sheepskin coat, and also to bear his name. He had never known his father. His mother was a Huzul and smoked a pipe into her old age. She held herself straight, had small feet, a few beautifully embroidered shifts, some fur jackets, and a great many children, most of whom died soon after birth. The only ones who had lived were Peter and that Parashka who, in the opinion of most serious-

---

*Rickets in Poland was commonly known as "the English sickness."

minded folk, would have done much better not to live. The mysterious father was believed to have been a Pole. His name was Neviadomski [of unknown origin]. It is the name that, out of deference to the susceptibilities of the gentry, is usually given to the children of a *pater incertus.* But Peter himself was the fruit of a lawful marriage bed. The bed in question was still standing in a hut, now much decayed, at the far end of the village of Topory. And it was because of this hut, with its thatching of straw, that Peter had spent his whole life in Topory, and had never even been led astray by the "Saxons"* often though they had tempted him. A fruit garden of half an acre went with the hut. Of the two apple trees one had long been barren. And naturally, for it belonged to that Parashka who took the train to town, and "rotted," as the parish priest used to say, in a house where the door was always open. On the other hand, the plum trees, which belonged to Peter, bore so rich a harvest that all the children in the neighborhood could eat their fill. Peter had no other land, but the railway company had given him the use of a little plot quite close to the viaduct. Here he cultivated potatoes, corn, cabbages, and a few sunflowers, or, rather, it was not he who cultivated the sunflowers, but a certain orphan, by the name Magda. Sunflowers were a passion with her. After the death of old Mother Neviadomska in the year 1910, she had begun to hang about Peter's hut. It was common talk among the gossips in the village that Magda, when she took the milk to Peter in the evening, would often come back only in the morning, just in time for milking. Peter had no cow. As a child he had driven his mother's cow and his mother's geese to pasture; but no sooner was his mother dead than he sold the cow at the fair. Half of the money he sent to Parashka; that was only right. The rest he spent on drink. The geese he presented to the stationmaster's wife. But he plucked some feathers first and kept them for himself. His entire livestock consisted of a dog, but what a dog! A dog like that was more an angel than a dog. True, he could not be milked, but he was a real dog, properly dangerous. His mother had been a sheepdog, his father a wolf. Peter attached little importance to pedigree, being a mongrel himself. The dog was called Bass, because of his powerful voice. As Bass grew older, he became, if not gentle, at least indifferent, and in the end nobody in the village feared him any longer. This dog was Peter Neviadomski's true and only love.

Why didn't Peter marry Magda? People who approved of the mar-

---

*"Saxons" was the designation invariably applied by Galician peasants to those who, before the war, journeyed in search of work to Prussia, Westphalia, or Saxony itself.

riage sacrament often asked this question, and the Ruthenian priest once put it to Peter at his Easter confession.

"I haven't had any children by her," Peter protested, "and I shan't have any."

And though the priest threatened the most terrible consequences in the life to come, and, in an endeavor to save a hardened sinner's soul, even offered to take a reduced marriage fee, Peter declared outright: "I won't marry her, because she is not a virgin!"

But Peter had other reasons for not wishing, for the moment at least, to adorn his head with the plated crown that the Greek Catholic rite prescribes for a bridegroom. Peter Neviadomski was a visionary. He was dreaming of a head covering quite other than a marriage crown, but it could be worn all through life, and not only at a wedding. And if it was a question of resembling the great ones of the world, Peter was showing good judgment in preferring a particular cap to a plated symbol of doubtful value, even though the symbol was meant to render him, in his wedding hour, the equal of crowned kings. It was Peter's belief, by the way, that kings wore golden crowns only on playing cards. Peter was an authority on playing cards.

A great while ago, maybe as far back as Metternich's time, some clever state official in Vienna designed the Austro-Hungarian kepi [a military hat with a round flat top and a visor]. He fixed its shape, settled the form of the crown, laid down how it should be cut, decided how it should be trimmed, and, after obtaining the approval of the All-Highest, forced it on the heads of all who desired to serve the emperor. By way of setting an example, the emperor, as his own chief servant, adopted it himself; it was worn by the emperor's relatives, by his marshals, his generals, and his commissioners; by officers; by gendarmes, even in retirement; and by the conductors of military bands. It was also the proud wear of petty officials, postmen, school ushers, prison warders, and of all railway servants right down to signalmen. It was the imperial cap. It was in this cap that his majesty, the emperor, showed himself to his people on the palace balcony or in his carriage: he lifted his shaking, white hand to its shiny black peak whenever his subjects greeted him; and he had so many subjects in the sixty-six years of his gracious reign! Naturally, the cut and the trimming had undergone endless changes in the long years. Many a Hapsburg victory and many a Hapsburg defeat had left its mark on the imperial cap. To accord with the rank of the wearer and the nature of his service, the intelligent inventors and improvers of the cap had introduced the subtlest variations, not always perceptible to the lay eye. For instance, the officer's cap was of black felt edged at the base with a gold cord, round which ran a fine black line. The cord for inferior ranks was not gold, but yellow thread; yet they had one thing in common: the imperial monogram. Worked or stamped, it appeared in the place of honor on every cap. The emperor's servants were marked like the imperial handkerchiefs, or the imperial forks and spoons, to keep them from being stolen, sold, or pawned.

Peter, too, was a servant of the emperor. He never lost consciousness of that service. He might seem to be carrying loads for the landed proprietors, or serving the Jews, who, in these parts, were the principal dealers in potatoes and grain. But in reality he carried all these burdens for the emperor, and in return the emperor paid him and protected him by special laws. Let one of these hucksters only dare to touch him while he was on duty! That would be an offense against an imperial and royal official, and no laughing matter. It was an offense chargeable before a criminal court.

Nevertheless, Peter was sometimes assailed by doubt, and somber bitterness crept into his heart. After all, why was he not entitled to wear an imperial cap like the other railway men? Why shouldn't he be able to command respect? Why, in spite of his long years of devoted service, did he still look like the merest civilian? Why did he get no promotion? Was he perhaps of so little moment that anyone could step into his place? Perhaps he was a mere kitchen spoon, considered unfit to figure in the government plate?

At such moments Peter was overwhelmed with self-pity; he began to think that it would be better to get out of the whole show, throw up this railway job, which brought only a bent back, and not much pleasure. Perhaps it would be better, after all, to sell the house (naturally with Parashka's consent, though she wasn't coming back, anyhow) and go to "Saxony"? Yet such bitter thoughts never troubled him for long. Soon his doubts would be replaced by the belief that one must not despair, that the emperor was kind, the Good Lord just, and that neither would harm their own people. All one had to do was to wait patiently, work patiently, bear patiently the insults as well as the jeers of railway conductors and senior railway porters. One had even to put up with the wrath of the stationmaster. An imperial servant had the right to strike another imperial servant, for in doing so he was acting in the name of his imperial majesty. But civilians had no such right—hands off!

So, for many a year, Peter went on hoping that one day he would receive promotion, a bigger wage and a railway cap. Perhaps these dreams of the imperial cap were echoes from his wretched childhood, when an old chamber pot, found on a garbage heap, had served him for a shako [stiff military cap with a high peak and plume]. And the possibility that so childish a memory may have operated in the mind of forty-year-old Peter is surely borne out by one fact, which must be revealed—the fact, in short, that it would have given Peter Neviadomski exquisite pleasure to be able to salute people, instead of lifting his cap to them like a civilian. It would have pleased him most to be a "real" railway porter or a brakeman on a freight train. Service on the railway had one attraction for Peter: it brought him into close touch with railway cars, rolling past to far-off destinations.

The cars came roaring through Topory-Czernielitza station, bringing in their wake that distant world of which Peter had heard in travelers' tales. Peter had seen coaches where you slept under blankets, as comfortably and safely as in a bed, and other coaches where gentlemen sat at white-covered tables, eating and drinking and making merry. Once, an express, with curtains and flowerpots at the windows, streaked past Peter like a flash of lightning, leaving him bemused. Leaning against the glittering metal fixtures was a fat cook, all in white, with a white cap, mixing something in a copper pan.

And Peter saw other coaches that came from Turkey, where the sea is, and where the people are heathen and can have several wives all at once. And he saw coaches that came from Vienna where the emperor lives. It is true that he had little personal contact with such coaches, for Topory-Czernielitza was not one of their stopping places; but there were occasions when it was Peter's duty to take a hammer and go along sounding wheels that were used to rolling over foreign tracks. When he touched such wheels with his hands, wheels that traveled so far and to such distant countries, it seemed to him that he was touching the very secret of the world, that secret that he would never learn.

Why should he not become a signalman or take a freight train to the Rumanian frontier? Even if he could not read he could see colors, distinguish green from red. He could also look after the railroad ties. Did they say he was stupid? And supposing he was, what then? The saints use no glue pots and King Solomon wasn't a railway porter. If Peter became a signalman. . . . Oh! how everything would change! He would no longer avoid the marriage altar, although Magda would have less chances than ever. Peter, the signalman, would be an excellent match for some respectable widow; or even for an elderly spinster, perhaps a farmer's daughter, though, of course, he would not take her without a dowry. Then he would set up a real house for a real housewife. He would renovate the hut, mend the roof, through which the rain leaked now, and cover it with fresh straw. He would repair the rotten rafters of the ceiling and scrub the bedstead with a rough brush. Over the bed he would hang a row of holy pictures, the Immaculate Virgin, the Mother of God of Poczajow, the Lord Jesus of Mylatin, and one or two others, and over the pictures he would put paper roses on wires. At the fair he would buy a cuckoo clock, a mouse trap, and a stew pan; fuchsias would stand in the windows and he would paint the whole room in blue. The wife would surely be presented by her people with painted chests in which they would keep shirts, sheepskin coats, money, and prayer books. Magda, if she wanted to, would be allowed to stay on in his service, but he would get his milk from his own cow, which would be part of the dowry. No, he would not fling Magda out of the house, neck and crop. Heaven forbid! But she wouldn't be allowed to sleep with him, that was obvious. But no matter, she would find someone else. Thoughts like these, which Peter concealed from the priest in the confessional, kept him at Topory and prevented him from taking any decisive step with regard to Magda.

Such thoughts combined, in one joyful vision, his two ideals: a cap and a house. With the eyes of fantasy Peter saw his tumble-down house blooming and transformed, and filled, in the absence of children, with hens, ducks, and sucking pigs, all living with Bass in the harmony of paradise. He always thought of his house as a place of happiness. And then, at Easter, he would have sausages from his own pig, fat for the whole year, and for his marriage bed—goose feathers, which he would have no need to steal.

One morning the stationmaster of Topory-Czernielitza called Peter into his office at twenty past five. As a rule, at that hour the stationmaster was still sleeping. But today, though unshaved, he was fully dressed, and an empty cup and a half-eaten roll on a tin tray showed that he had already breakfasted. Why, Peter wondered as he entered the office, had the stationmaster left his breakfast unfinished? And then, after a considerable delay, a second question presented itself: Why had "the old man" called him in so early?

The stationmaster, in his service cap, the red of which contrasted startlingly with his pale face, which was covered with dark stubble, was sitting at the ticking telegraph machine. He took no notice of Peter. He was entirely absorbed in culling the secrets of the long strip of paper that was sliding through his fingers. The telegraph ticked without intermission. In the unbroken silence that filled the office and brooded over the lonely station in the fields, the dull and obstinate clicking of the instrument began to frighten Peter. Helplessly, he turned his eyes from the figure of his superior to the little window, which framed a patch of blue sky and some peaceful trees. The sight of the sky and the trees reassured him. Suddenly the ticking ceased. This seemed even more ominous. The stationmaster raised his head, a change seemed to come over him. From his dry, cold, self-satisfied countenance there had vanished overnight that hard, mocking expression, which had disconcerted Peter for years. How many bad moments of his life could he not put down to those eyes, which went through a man, even stabbed, when mercifully closed! Those eyes could stop the beating of Peter's heart and probe into the most secret places of his conscience. Before those eyes, Peter would squirm and writhe until he had achieved that false smile with which poor devils seek to shield themselves against the burden of contempt. Peter had so many burdens, and to feel the glance of the stationmaster resting on his back seemed to him at times the heaviest of all. Today the eyes of the stationmaster looked guilty; they were like the gaping breech barrels of a double-barreled gun, empty of cartridges. What has come over the stationmaster? Peter wondered. He doesn't look at me as he usually does. He looks at me as if he wasn't the stationmaster any longer. Can he have been transferred and an end put to all his high-and-mightiness at Topory-Czernielitza? Peter began to think about his chief as he would about an equal. And, in fact, to judge by the expression on his face, there was not much to choose between the stationmaster and Peter Neviadomski. In his eyes could be seen the helplessness, the dumb helplessness, of those who try in vain to fathom the cruel laws of existence. Today the stationmaster was displaying the essence of his humanity—his weakness. And the peasant stock that had been successfully hidden under his official frock coat stood suddenly revealed. There are moments in life that make an end of years of effort to deceive oneself and others. They put a stop to all the continuous imitation and copied gestures. In such moments, by some chemical process, race comes suddenly to the surface and betrays itself in a single unconscious movement of the hand, in a twitching at the corners of the mouth, an inflection in the tones of the voice. Something unprecedented must have occurred that night to have changed the stationmaster so utterly. He had, perhaps, suffered some family loss? Or been accused of some dereliction of duty? Or had it, perhaps, been thrown in his face, in those circles to which he was climbing on the ladder of railway hierarchy, that he was basely born? No! No misfortune had fallen on his home, no breach of duty had been alleged against him, and no one had reminded him that his father was a wheelwright over in Rohatin. Quite other matters had been afoot that night.

That night, the entire timetable, the timetable that for uncounted years had been the decalogue of the Lemberg-Czernowitz-Itzkány line, had fallen. It had been broken in pieces suddenly, and there was no hope that it would ever recover from the catastrophe. In a moment there had come into force those mysterious instructions "in case of war," which the stationmaster, who had taken the oath to the state, used to keep sealed in an iron box, in the innermost compartment of the safe. These instructions were issued, not by the lawmakers who receive their commandments on that Mount Sinai of the railways, the Ministry of Transport, but by the general staff. Thus, the strict article of faith that the railway had so long observed had lost all meaning. Civil transport had stopped.

The stationmaster looked up at Peter in a helpless, almost beseeching way, and handed him two large, white sheets of closely printed paper tightly rolled.

"Neviadomski," he said, in a voice that sounded strangely gentle, "it's war!"

It was a long while before the significance of this word got through to Peter's consciousness. War! The word crashed down on his head like a landslide. It pierced his cranium and passed through the membrane into the brain. And, instantly, Peter's brain was a flood of memories. A picture flashed up of the maneuvers, which he had watched in this very place, two years before. There had been a great host of soldiers, all taking aim. They lay along the railroad tracks, out there by the viaduct, and there was shooting, first from one side of the line, and then from the other. They were fighting for the railway line: but nobody got killed. And then, when the bugles blew, they all got up, lit cigarettes, laughing, and marched off into the forest, headed by the band. Peter knew that men killed each other in real war. In a colored magazine print of the battle of Tschataldja that a tobacconist had shown him over in Snyatin, he had seen the dead bodies both of Serbs and Bulgars. And there were other pictures he remembered of the Russo-Japanese War. And suddenly the word *war* turned a somersault in his brain and dropped into his bloodstream, which would have burst had not the blood swept the dread word back to his heart. From there it worked its way down into his belly, where it finished up with a pain as sharp and sudden as the stab of steel. For one instant Peter knew the fear of death. But, gradually, the heavy blood, exhausted by its sudden rush, began to flow back into his brain, carrying with it the poor remains of the spent word *war*. Peter regained his balance. He remembered that only soldiers died in war, and that he wasn't a soldier. Calmly he listened to the words next spoken by the stationmaster.

"Take these posters and put them up in the waiting room under the clock, not too low and not too high. Do you understand, Neviadomski?" While he was giving the order, the stationmaster suddenly realized to whom he was speaking and strove to invest his defenseless voice with some semblance of its usual severity: "Be careful not to tear them. And see that you put them up straight!"

Peter went out. He softly closed the door with its legend: "Entrance strictly forbidden to strangers," and stood a moment in the dim corridor, holding the war in his hand. The war in his hand was not yet unfurled. It was shut tight like new buds in spring.

Peter only unfurled it in the waiting room.

As Peter went out, the stationmaster again glanced anxiously at the great clock on the wall under which hung a large loose-leaf calendar. In his excitement he had been looking at the clock every five minutes. The stationmaster's first job every morning was to tear a leaf off the calendar. But today, though the stationmaster had been over an hour in his office, the calendar still showed July 27. Here, in this office, yesterday still reigned instead of today. The calendar had not been touched. Why didn't the stationmaster of Topory-Czernielitza remove yesterday from the world? Was he clinging still to the vanished time when the railway was ruled by the codes and regulations of its own administration, and not by "theirs"? Was he loath to part with yesterday and the world order that it knew? Or had he simply overlooked his daily custom in the rush of work that had overwhelmed him in the night? It was already half-past five. Six o'clock went by, and still the stationmaster could not tear off yesterday's leaf.

At 6:25 A.M. there was a knock at the door. The stationmaster jumped up; coils of white paper covered with the signs of the Morse code twisted themselves, like snakes, around his feet. Like a dancer at a carnival ball, a gallant entangled in paper streamers, the stationmaster disengaged himself from the clinging strips whose contents he had already deciphered. He shook the war from his feet, and was free.

"Come in," he cried.

The assistant who relieved him at seven appeared in the doorway. The sight of his deputy recalled the stationmaster to reality. Quickly he stepped up to the calendar and tore off the leaf bearing the date of the twenty-seventh of July. He crumpled it in his hands and threw it into the overflowing wastepaper basket, as into a common grave of fallen soldiers. In such fashion did Topory-Czernielitza station say good-bye to the last day of peace. The waiting room was still empty. The ticket office was still closed. Twice every day people came rushing to this little window, hurrying to catch their train. Today there was no more need to hurry. No one knew whether the little window would open at all. It was shut like the mouth of the dead; it would take in no more money and issue no more tickets, unless someday it was opened again by the same power that, in this night, had destroyed the foundations of faith.

On the left-hand wall of the ticket office, over the wooden benches, there was still hanging a big, imposing-looking sheet, divided into sections for the main and side lines. It was the timetable of the Imperial and Royal State Railways of West Galicia. Folk who could read would go up to it in perfect confidence, and find out the sacred hours of arrival and departure. Today they would find there nothing but dead memories. The official timetable hung there, useless, as inconsequent as a printed funeral notice left hanging outside a house that had buried its dead yesterday.

There were other documents and bills on the waiting-room walls. An announcement, in faded colors, of the Eucharistic Congress still issued its invitation to past and forgotten celebrations. Some magnificent turkeys and hens invited the attention of visitors to the Third Provincial Poultry Exhibition. A portly, smiling waiter in evening dress, with a foaming beer tankard in either hand, witnessed to the excellence of the Lemberg brewery. A sinuous, sphynxlike woman, with a lovely olive complexion and large hoop earrings, was smoking a cigarette "Rolled with Abadie Cigarette Paper." Years ago, Peter Neviadomski had made it his job to brighten up the walls of Topory-Czernielitza Station with these posters, which he had stuck up with his own hands, and which had hung there ever since.

The two new posters had been drying for an hour on the waiting-room wall. They were large, and white, and serious-looking, with no pictures, no smiling waiters or sphynxlike women. They were exactly alike and joined together on one side, like Siamese twins, and it was Peter who had stuck them on the wall. Their freshness was provocative.

About seven o'clock the earliest passengers began to arrive: a gamekeeper in a green hat, one or two peasant women with their baskets, some red-trousered Huzuls, and the usual Jews in black kaftans. They all crowded around the new poster, talking noisily. It seemed there was something they couldn't understand, and they were quite impatient about it. Presently the stationmaster appeared. He wanted to inform the passengers himself that there would be no train; that the line was in the hands of the military. As he came in, his eye fell on the posters he had ordered Peter to put up, and at once he lost his temper.

"Where's Neviadomski?" he shouted. "He deserves to have his ears boxed!"

Neviadomski was staggered: he could see no reason for this outburst.

"Damned fool! He's got the imperial proclamation upside down!"

It was a long while before he calmed down. But finally he went off to his office, fetched two new posters, and put them up himself. And then the little group in the waiting room began to spell aloud the words of the proclamation, "To my dear peoples . . .," at first one at a time, as their capacity for reading permitted, and then in chorus, those who could not read joining in. They repeated every word, like the litany in church. In these remote provinces belief in the Emperor Francis Joseph united Roman Catholics and Greek Catholics, Jews and Armenians, in a common and universal church. Involuntarily, Peter removed his hat, and listened open-mouthed to the dolorous plaint of the emperor. For the emperor had sent his plaint all the way to the farthest frontiers of his realm, so that good people, simple people, should pity him and make their own the wrong that had been done to him. And his faithful subjects did not disappoint their emperor. In the emotional atmosphere that filled the little waiting room in the station of Topory-Czernielitza, Peter Neviadomski forgot his own disgrace, for, though thick-skinned, he had a very soft heart. And in the proclamation, the emperor complained in liturgical and pathetic phrases of the wicked and infamous Serbs, who had obliged him to draw the sword, when all he asked was to be allowed to die in peace. What is a sword? Peter wondered. It must be some kind of long silver pocket knife. His majesty carries it about with him in his pocket and takes it out when war comes.

Two days later, the stationmaster once again summoned Peter into his presence. Peter expected to be accused of lese majeste for having put the proclamation upside down. The only excuse he could think of was that he couldn't read, and that there were no pictures on the imperial proclamations to show him which was the top and which the bottom. However, the stationmaster received him in his most gracious mood. Apparently he had forgotten the scandal Peter had caused. The mobilization had obliterated everything else and extended a welcome and unexpected amnesty to many a criminal.

"Neviadomski," said the stationmaster, "you are a fool! But I have nobody else. The army is taking one man after another. You, Neviadomski, are now to take over signal box number 86: Signalman

Banasik has been called up for the special reserve. You are to go down the line now, take his cap and flag, and in the future look after the gates in his place. Banasik will show you the work. The war will not last long—three or, at most, four weeks. In a week we shall march into Belgrade, in two weeks we shall take Warsaw, and in three weeks, with the help of God, we shall be in Moscow. In a month we shall all be back home, and Banasik too, unless he gets killed meanwhile. But until then you'll have to stay in 86 and carry on. I only hope I shall get no complaints about you. Remember we are at war now, and this is no time for fooling about. If you do, you'll be thrown out, and not even a dog will bark."

When he said: "We shall march into Belgrade" and "we shall take Warsaw," the stationmaster was in no way implying that he intended taking any personal part in the campaign, being, for the present at least, exempt both because of his calling and his age. He was merely using the popular plural with which, in all wars, those who stay at home emphasize their unity with those who go to the front. But such nice metaphors, which the civilized have used for centuries, were quite beyond Peter. He took every word, every expression, at its face value. Consequently, he imagined that the stationmaster and the signalman were both going to the war. And this idea drove personal considerations temporarily into the background. If Peter had been capable of thinking like civilized people, he would have wished either that the war should last as long as possible, or else that signalman Banasik should not come back at all. In either case he would have the chance of staying in signal box number 86 for ever. But Peter couldn't rise to such elaborate calculations. He accepted the passionately longed-for change of his fortune with a calm that bordered on renunciation. After being obliged to listen to all the stationmaster had considered fit to say to him, he felt that this unexpected and conditional promotion was almost a humiliation, for he was being made a signalman, not because of his ability and long service, but because the stationmaster couldn't help it.

And that was how Peter Neviadomski achieved his ambition and acquired the imperial cap, the cap of his dreams. True, it was not black, but blue, and the button with the imperial monogram had somehow got mislaid, but, on the other hand, it was ornamented with a beautiful brass carriage wheel, everlastingly revolving, with wings, like the wings of an angel, sprouting out at both sides. It was a sad pity! Received under these conditions, the cap was no longer a sign of promotion, and it brought Peter no joy. At the very moment when he was allowed to wear it, the enchanted vision faded. Peter was the victim of his own imagination.

The news that Peter Neviadomski had a railway cap left the world unconcerned; and Peter himself was not so naïve as to think that the changes that had taken place since the twenty-eighth of July had resulted from his own promotion. But, all the same, he was surprised to notice that even his immediate entourage, who had not been let into the secret of how his promotion had come about, paid him no deference whatsoever. Even Magda remained completely unimpressed. His feelings were much like those of the young author who, when he first sees his name in print, wonders why all the people in the street do not point him out to each other. Peter, indeed, asked very little of the world. But it hurt him that he should have reached the great moment of his life, and that it made no impression, that it was attached to an unpleasant and even humiliating memory, and that, in the confusion and distress of memorable days, it had gone completely unnoticed. Before long, his head became so filled with thoughts about the changes that were taking place in the world that there was little room left for thoughts about his own share in the matter. But even then the new privilege of saluting people was no pleasure to Peter now; he was surrounded by men in uniform for whom saluting was a duty.

He locked the door of his hut, took Bass with him, and went off down the railway line. The signalman's wife remained in the signal box a few days longer, but soon left with the children to join relatives in town. After that Neviadomski was alone. But every day, about noon, Magda came and brought him his dinner. The signal box stood in the open fields, high up on an embankment, and one climbed up to it by steps like a ladder. And now trains, endless trains, crowded with soldiers, or laden with war material, began to pass rapidly in front of Peter's weary eyes. For ten nights he got no sleep, so busy was he with the gates. Once he nearly got into trouble: through some blundering of his, a Jew with a horse and cart was almost run over. And the imperial cap he now wore could not save poor Peter from losing his head. The cap was rather large for him and slipped down over his ears, those poor ears that were deafened by the sound of war, the roar of passing trains, the clanking of guns lashed down on open trucks, and the many-tongued babble of soldiers' talk.

But after ten days and ten nights of this, the military trains passing in this direction grew fewer and fewer, the singing of soldiers more and more rare. Finally, transport stopped altogether, and quiet reigned. Gradually, the passenger trains began to run again, though the ticket office in the little waiting room of Topory-Czernielitza Station opened only once a day and no timetable could be relied upon. At nighttime, now, there were only passenger trains to waken Peter. And often the track was so still, and the air so clear, that he could hear the song of the telegraph wires and the voice of the engine in the distant sawmill.

Translated by Pauline De Chary

Slawomir Mrozek
(1936–   )

An architect and painter who contributed to literature in its rarest of forms, satire, Mrozek's plays have been translated and performed and his humor is universal.

No picture of Poland, however, could even approach completion without that magnificently irreverent Polish humor—part of which was the Yiddish humor that has been lost in the smoke of Auschwitz, but part of which is still alive.

Mrozek, in the introduction to his play *The Police*, an excerpt of which follows, emphasizes that the work is not a metaphor for anything but is naked. But he portrays police mentality, and although this mentality is not unique to Poland, neither is it absent in a country where every citizen, meeting another citizen on the street, begins to whisper.

The Police

The action takes place in the home of the agent provocateur. On the wall are the well-known pictures of the infant king and his uncle the regent. There is a wedding photograph of the agent provocateur sergeant and his WIFE. *A door and a window are in clear view, and there are two chairs, a table, and a tailor's dummy dressed in a very elaborate uniform of a police sergeant with a large number of medals. Nearby is a small screen, under which a pair of jackboots can be seen. There is a fig plant, or possibly a palm, and a small table carrying a pair of dumbbells. The agent provocateur's* WIFE *is on stage, as is the* CHIEF OF POLICE, *who is disguised with a coat and hood thrown over his uniform. He is wearing his sword.*

CHIEF OF POLICE (*his hood pulled over his eyes*): Good morning. Is your husband at home?

WIFE: No, I'm afraid he's not back from work yet.

CHIEF: Not back from work? Today's his day off, isn't it?

WIFE: He doesn't like days off. What do you want to see him about? (*The* CHIEF OF POLICE *moves into the center of the room and throws off his hood.*) Colonel! I didn't recognize you.

CHIEF: Shhh. . . . Not so loud! Did your husband say when he'd be back?

WIFE: No. He went into town to do some voluntary provoking. I don't know when he'll be here.

CHIEF: Please don't let me interrupt you. You're sewing, I see.

WIFE (*ashamedly putting down her work*): Er . . . yes. It's just some gold braid for my husband's underpants. He feels so terrible in civilian clothes these days and always likes to wear some tiny piece of military dress, even if it's underneath everything. (*Suddenly changing her tones, imploringly*) Colonel!

CHIEF: Yes. What is it?

WIFE: I wish you'd take him off this job. Don't make him do any more provoking in civilian clothes.

CHIEF: Why not?

WIFE: You've no idea how thin and pale he's got since he's had to go about in civvies. He can't exist out of uniform. He's withering away.

CHIEF: I'm afraid that's just too bad, madam. Provoking is always done in civilian dress.

WIFE: Couldn't he just wear his helmet? He always used to feel much better then.

CHIEF: No, madam. A helmet would attract attention.

WIFE (*in a confidential tone*): Oh yes, of course. It's such a long time since he's had anyone to arrest. He probably doesn't show it in front of you, Colonel, but at home he's become moody and quite intolerable. One new arrest would put him right again.

CHIEF (*pompously*): You can't make arrests without an agent provocateur.

WIFE (*dully and sadly*): I'm afraid I've just given up hope.

CHIEF: *You* don't know anyone that we could arrest?

WIFE: No! All the people I know are loyal as hell. And if there was anyone, my husband would be the first person I'd tell, just to give him a bit of peace of mind. He's always asking me.

CHIEF: Any neighbors, then? Any distant relatives?

WIFE: No. They're all law-abiding citizens. There was an old man on our street who used to complain, but with him it was the gout, not the government. He's just died, probably of being too careful.

CHIEF: Yes, nowadays it's all so peaceful, all so quiet. Tell me, how did you first meet your husband?

WIFE: Oh, that was ages ago, Colonel. He reported me to the secret police and I reported him. That's how we got to know each other.

CHIEF: Have you got any children?

WIFE: Two. But they're locked up now. Shall I get them down?

CHIEF: No, please. I don't want to inconvenience anyone. I just dropped in to have a word with your husband.

WIFE: He may be back by now. He always listens at the doors on the way upstairs. I'll go and have a look.

(*Exit. Light footsteps are heard on the stairs. The window opens and through it enters the* SERGEANT *in civilian clothes. He is carrying a raincoat and a small green hat.*)

SERGEANT: Colonel! Fancy seeing you in my house. How wonderful!

CHIEF: Psst! I'm here unofficially. I'll tell you why later. Why didn't you come in through the door?

SERGEANT: I was walking on the tops of the houses. When it was time to come home I thought I'd come back across the roofs. It's one way of getting here and there could have been something going on. Anyway, down in the street it couldn't be quieter.

CHIEF: What did you find?

SERGEANT: Nothing at all, Colonel. Just a few birds. Is my wife here?

CHIEF: She went out on to the staircase. She thought you were there.

SERGEANT: She always listens at the doors when she goes down those stairs. You don't mind if I change now, do you, Colonel? I feel naked without my uniform on.

CHIEF: No, do change if you like. You're in your own home, and it's your day off anyway.

SERGEANT (*going behind the screen*): Yes, I know. But you see, I thought maybe today would be my lucky day, and I went out. I did a bit of provoking before lunch, but as usual it was no good. They just said hello and walked on.

CHIEF: Sergeant, if it hadn't been for you perhaps we'd never have lived to see this alarming drop in the crime figures. That is to say, I mean, thanks to you we now have this perfect state of law and order. I must recommend you for promotion.

SERGEANT (*all this time changing into uniform behind the screen*): It's nothing, Colonel. I just felt I had to go and try once more. I like doing, it really. (*Pause. The* SERGEANT *finishes changing.*)
(*He comes out in full uniform with sword and medals. He stretches himself luxuriously.*)
Ah, what a relief. At last I feel I can relax. Coming home from work,

changing into uniform, you've no idea how marvelous it is. Oh . . . er, excuse me, Colonel. (*Realizes he has been behaving a little too informally. Comes to attention.*) This is what comes of working in civvies. Civilian clothes are very bad for morale. You see, sir, I've got to get a grip on myself.

CHIEF: Oh, don't worry about that. I've got an important matter to discuss with you. Find some excuse to send your wife off; she mustn't come in here. I'm sure she's quite reliable, but what I have to talk to you about is most secret.

(*The* SERGEANT *exits. His footsteps die away on the stairs. The* CHIEF OF POLICE *takes off his coat and sits down. More footsteps. Enter the* SERGEANT.)

SERGEANT: I sent her off to get some waterproof glue.

CHIEF: Couldn't you think up a better pretext than that?

SERGEANT: It wasn't a pretext, Colonel. I really need it. My raincoat got torn when they beat me up last time.

CHIEF: Oh, all right. Has she gone far?

SERGEANT: She won't be back for three-quarters of an hour.

CHIEF: I suppose you're surprised by my visit.

SERGEANT: Just as you say, sir.

CHIEF: You're surprised, then?

SERGEANT: Yes, sir. The chief of police here in my house! I'd sooner have expected a revolution.

CHIEF: No wishful thinking now, Sergeant. And a keen sergeant must always be prepared for a revolution. No, I didn't really mean that. Your service record is irreproachable.

SERGEANT: But of course, Colonel.

CHIEF: Still, in your exemplary conduct there is something more than ordinary conscientiousness and sense of duty. (*The* SERGEANT *comes to attention*). No, don't bother about that. Sit down.

SERGEANT: With your permission, sir, I'd rather do my exercises for a bit—that is if you don't mind, Colonel.

CHIEF: Your exercises?

SERGEANT: Always at this time, as soon as I get home, I do a little weight lifting or spring exercises. I must be able to cope with any situation that crops up. They're good for my muscles. (*Bends his biceps*) You want to try them?

CHIEF: No, thank you. I can see from here. If you want to do your exercises, do them.

(*The* SERGEANT *tucks up his sleeve, takes the dumbbell from the table and returns to his place in front of the* CHIEF OF POLICE. *All the while listening to his boss, he performs a few rhythmical lifts of the dumb-*

bell every now and again. Every now and then he checks his biceps to see if they have hardened. He then tries the other arm. All this time he is engaged in conversation with the CHIEF OF POLICE.)

As I said, you are not only an excellent policeman. I have found that you are something more than that.

SERGEANT (*in a very disciplined manner*): Sir!

CHIEF: I find that you have given me an idea.

SERGEANT (*as before*): Sir! Yessir!

CHIEF: You put on civilian clothes, do you not, when your job requires it, even though you can't stand wearing them?

SERGEANT: Yessir! Anything for my job, sir.

CHIEF: Exactly, in other words you sacrifice your personal likes and dislikes on the altar of service to the state. But that's not important. In examining your case I have come to the conclusion that your keenness, readiness, and devotion to duty are quite out of proportion to the tasks you fulfill so admirably, even though these tasks are certainly not easy.

SERGEANT: Yessir!

CHIEF: You give me the impression of a Hercules who spends his time cutting wood and carrying water. Of course, this sort of work is difficult and useful, but it is not the work of a Hercules. In you there is strength, Sergeant, a strength that is only partly finding its outlet in ordinary work. For you are something more than a civil servant. You are inspired by the idea of order and general discipline. You are the mystic of the police force, the saint of the police. Why have you got so thin lately, Sergeant?

SERGEANT: It's my insomnia, Colonel.

CHIEF: Oh, I see. Tell me, do you have dreams?

SERGEANT: Well, I do sometimes, but they're silly.

CHIEF: Tell me about them.

SERGEANT: Often, I don't know why it is, but I dream that there are two of me.

CHIEF: Bravo! Bravo!

SERGEANT: One in uniform and another in civilian clothes. We are walking across a big field; the birds are singing, it's warm—and then I, that is both of us, or both of me, feel in my soul that I am being carried far, far away . . . and somewhere out there . . . and there's a smell of fresh grass, you know, like in the spring—and then I feel such a desire, such a longing to arrest someone, to arrest someone even if it's just a hare sitting under a ridge, or a little bird. Then I look, or rather we look, all round the field; we strain our eyes and there's nobody there, nobody to arrest, and then I throw myself on the soft earth, beat my head and the tears pour out. And it's then that the stupidest part of my dream comes.

CHIEF (*in great suspense*): Tell me! Tell me!

SERGEANT: Then I dream that I arrest myself. That is to say—the I that's in uniform arrests the me that's in civilian clothes. Then I wake up covered in sweat.

(*The recounting of the dream has been a severe effort for the* SERGEANT. *While he is telling it he stops doing his gymnastics.*)

CHIEF: This is very interesting, what you say, very interesting. Now, Sergeant, when was the last time that you made an arrest?

SERGEANT (*heavily, despondently*): Oh, Colonel. I'm ashamed to tell you.

CHIEF: Well, listen carefully to what I say.

SERGEANT: Yessir.

CHIEF: Do you realize that we shall never have the chance to arrest anyone again?

SERGEANT (*letting the weight fall from his hand*): What did you say, sir?

CHIEF (*gets up from his chair and begins to walk about the room*): I'll tell you something else. Not only will we never arrest anyone ever again, but your son, your grandson, and your great-grandson—they won't arrest anyone either. The whole police force is standing on the edge of a precipice, on the eve of a catastrophe. What is the function of a policeman? It is to arrest those who offend against the existing order. But suppose there aren't any people like that left. Suppose that as a result of the operations of our improved and reconstituted police force the last trace of rebelliousness in our people has disappeared and they have become universally enthusiastic for the regime. Suppose that they have formed once and for all a permanent love for our (*stands to attention*) infant king and his uncle the regent. What is there for the police to do then? I did my best to improve matters and that is why I advised you to carry on provoking people to criticize the government, but, as you see, even this last resort has come to nothing. Not only were you unable to provoke anyone, but when you started on your antigovernment slogans they beat you up.

SERGEANT: That's nothing. It's healed up already.

CHIEF: That is not the point. We are dealing here with more general matters. For a long time I have been expecting and dreading the moment that has now arrived. Our last political prisoner has just signed the act of allegiance, has been released from prison and has begun to serve our infant king and his uncle the regent. I tried to keep him back; I promised him stamps for his collection; it was no good. Do you know what this means? It means that we have beautiful prisons constructed at great expense; we have a highly trained, devoted staff; we have courtrooms, offices, and card indexes—and we now have not one single prisoner, not one single suspect, not one single clue to follow up. The people have become, wildly, cruelly, bestially loyal.

SERGEANT: That's true, Colonel. That's a fact. I'd—

CHIEF: Soon the time will come when we'll have to take off our uniforms; and then you'll toss and turn in bed at nights, longing hopelessly for one little interrogation. Your gold braid sewn on to your underpants won't be much good to you then. Already you're suffering from insomnia, and for the moment you've still got your job. Think what it'll be like soon, eh?

SERGEANT: No, no!

CHIEF: But yes, yes! They'll take away your uniform; they'll give you some sort of sports jacket, walking shoes, and a pair of flannels. You'll be able to go out into the fields or onto the water, with a fishing rod or a shotgun if you like, and enjoy your spare time exactly as you wish. You'll be able to arrest hares and sparrows, so long as it isn't the mating season.

SERGEANT: Is there nothing we can do, Colonel?

CHIEF (*putting his arm round his shoulder, warmly*): I have come to you not only in my capacity as chief of police, not only as your superior officer. At this dreadful time we are both of us just simple constables. In the face of the ruin that is facing our life's work we must give each other our hands and offer brotherly advice for its solution.

(*Gives the* SERGEANT *his hand. He is very much moved and squeezes it, at the same time wiping away a tear with his left hand.*)

And now listen to me. The man who can even now save the situation—is you.

SERGEANT: Me?

CHIEF: Yes, you. Pay attention to what I'm saying. What do we need? What we need is one person whom we could lock up, whom we could arrest for something that could in some very slight degree be described as antigovernment activity. Having several times attempted to find this man, it has become apparent that we shall not find him in the ordinary course of events, or in what we might call a natural manner. We must, so to speak, compose this man ourselves. My choice has fallen on you.

SERGEANT: I don't understand, sir.

CHIEF: What don't you understand?

SERGEANT: What I have to do.

CHIEF: Exactly the same as you've been doing all along: shout something against the government, but with this difference—this time we won't let you off; we'll lock you up.

SERGEANT: Me?

CHIEF: I assure you that the fulfillment of the task I have set you is far more admirable from the point of view of police morality than simply provoking any old citizen to criticize the government and arresting him. That would simply be carrying out your ordinary daily work. Here it is a question of fulfilling an act that is not without a certain poetry of its own, an act that belongs only to a policeman who is specially selected, inspired, pierced right to the marrow of his bones with the spirit of the police force. This is what I was thinking of when I said that I saw in you the fire of a policeman's vocation, something that is rare even among the best of us. I said that there was something in you that had not found its proper outlet, that had been eagerly awaiting the assignment that I can only now reveal to you. You are going to be our sergeant redeemer.

SERGEANT: Colonel, I'll always—anything I can do, sir—sir, I've got a headache.

CHIEF: Don't worry about that. Now change back into civilian clothes.

SERGEANT: What, again? What for?

CHIEF: You can't act as your own provocateur wearing uniform.

SERGEANT: All right, shall I change now? This minute?

CHIEF: Yes, of course, we've no time to waste. When you've changed we'll open the window so they can hear you better from the street. Then you can stand by the window and shout out something as loud as you can against our infant king and his uncle the regent. (*Both stand to attention.*) Then I'll draw my sword, arrest you, and that's that.

SERGEANT: My God, but I'm supposed to be a policeman!

CHIEF: You are more a policeman than anyone else in the world. To be a member of the police and to pretend to others that you're not a policeman—that makes you a double policeman; but to be a policeman and to pretend to *yourself* that you're not a policeman—that makes you a policeman deep down, luxuriously, in the depths of your heart. We might say that you're a superpoliceman, unlike any other policeman, even a double-police policeman.

(*The* SERGEANT *goes behind the screen. There, groaning and sobbing, he changes into civilian clothes. The screen is low so that his head is visible and, at the bottom, his calves too.*)

CHIEF: Before today is out I shall send a report to the general. Tomorrow morning our infant king and his uncle the regent will be informed that we have discovered and arrested a revolutionary. We shall be saved.

SERGEANT (*doing up his buttons*): What do I have to shout?

CHIEF: Haven't you got anything prepared from your previous experience?

SERGEANT: Shall I say that our regent, the uncle of our infant (*stands to attention*) king, is a swine?

CHIEF: That's not direct enough. It must be something strong and forceful, with no understatement, so that I can arrest you one hundred percent.

SERGEANT: Well then, what about—dirty swine?

CHIEF: That's much better. We'll open the window. (*They open the window.*) Now . . . one . . . two—

SERGEANT: Just a minute!

(*Runs away from the window and takes out a brush from behind the screen. With one careful movement he removes a speck of dust from the uniform that is now hanging again on the tailor's dummy. Puts down the brush and returns to the window.*)

All right, now! (*Fills his lungs with air.*)

CHIEF: One . . . two . . . three . . .

SERGEANT: (*shouts*): Our regent, the uncle of our infant king, is a dirty swine.

CHIEF (*drawing his sword, loudly*): I arrest you in the name of our infant king and his uncle the regent.

SERGEANT'S WIFE (*enters the room suddenly*): Good heavens! Still trying to provoke people. Can't you ever take a rest?

CHIEF: Silence, woman! At last he's made a success of it!

Translated by Nicholas Bethell

THE PEASANTS

The peasants share the fate of the downtrodden all over the world. They are subjects of extensive studies; their memoirs, like those memoirs of slaves, have been published. They are occasionally glorified, yet they remain oppressed and mysterious. No one can explain how they survived so many adversities and still cling to a lifestyle they could choose to abandon—what keeps them tied to the land even if it gives them only an economically marginal existence. According to official Polish statistics, today less than fifty percent of the population are peasants, on whom—the statistics do not tell us— the other half of the population depends.

Wladyslaw Reymont
(1867–1925)

Reymont was one of a family of ten poor peasant children. What set him apart from his brothers and sisters was his talent to see the peasants. He saw them not like Staszic as near animals in human form, or even like Mickiewicz as beasts of burden who were mistreated regardless of who ruled Poland. Rather, he saw that underneath their very real coarseness, under the dirt and indescribable poverty, were people filled with the whole range of emotions so unique to all of humanity. He saw it and wrote about it. He lived on the edge of poverty until he wrote his major four-volume work, *The Peasants*, for which he received the Noble Prize in 1924.

The excerpt that follows is taken from the last volume, entitled *Summer*; the other three are, appropriately for peasant life, *Autumn*, *Winter*, and *Spring*. Reymont's story is one of love, jealousy, adultery—all occurring amid the very complex setting of peasant life.

Reymont was alone among all of Poland's writers in his ability to universalize the complexities of peasant existence. To begin with, peasants are completely at the mercy of the unpredictable rhythms of nature—too much of anything and they starve. Being on the bottom of the social pyramid, peasants have to deal with more officialdom—most of whose purposes they cannot understand—than the members of any other social strata. And as if that were not enough, peasants have to deal with their friendly enemy—their neighbor. They have to learn how to hide, dissimulate, cheat, lie, while all they really want to do is work and live according to the only thing they have ever learned—the catechism. The catechism is the Virgin Mary and the Virgin Mary is Poland and for the preservation of this simple equation peasants are willing to resist—providing they have their piece of land.

Reymont understood and captured the triadic world of the peasant: the Virgin Mary, Poland, his land. If any of these were attacked, the peasant would resist with a cunning absent from either the intelligentsia or the proletariat. Being on intimate terms with nature, peasants would fight with the weapons of nature—they had the ultimate power: they could withhold food from their enemies.

Noteworthy in the following selection are the fine characterizations, the clarity of the characters, motivations, and the warm human morality. Yagna is the mistress of Antek, who is married to Hanka. The villagers know this, but no one refers to it. The problem confronting them is how to aid the escape of an enlightened peasant who had come to their village to tell them of their rights—the rights that are obviously disregarded by the police and the other officials.

This excerpt illustrates the resistance of the majority of the Poles in the reality of their setting. Note that the peasants succeeded in saving their "wise man," although most of the gentry only knew how to die bravely and, too frequently, pointlessly.

The Peasants

On entering the village, Yagna at once could see that something out of the ordinary was going on. The dogs in the farmyard were barking in great excitement; the little ones, hiding in the orchards, peeped out from behind the trees and hedges; the people, though it was yet far from sunset, were fast coming in from the fields; women were whispering together in groups; every face bore an expression of disquietude, and in every eye there was a look of alarm and suspense.

"What has come about?" she asked the Balcerek girl, peering round the corner of her hut.

"I cannot say; belike soldiers coming from the forest."

"Jesu Maria! Soldiers!" And her knees trembled with terror.

"Young Klemba," added the Prychek girl, as she ran by, "says they are cossacks from Vola."

In great dismay, Yagna hurried on to her cabin, where her mother, sitting on the threshold, and spinning, was in earnest talk with several women.

"We have both seen the same thing—the men sitting in the porch, and their leader with the priest inside the house."

"And they have sent the organist's lad Michael to fetch the Voyt."

"The Voyt [village elder, supervisor]! then it can be no trifle. Ho, ho! Something is in the wind!"

"It may be they have only come to collect the taxes."

"With such a number of men? No, they come surely for something more than that."

"Perhaps; but, mark my words, they are here for no good!"

Yagustynka came up. "I," she said, "can tell you why they have come."

All crowded round her, stretching their necks out like so many geese.

"They have come to take us women into the army!" she cried with a croaking laugh that no one took up; and Dominikova remarked sourly:

"Ye must always be making some wretched joke!"

"It is you that are always making mountains out of molehills! You quake so, your teeth are well nigh falling out of your heads; yet all are greedy to hear that something is to hap! Much do I trouble about the gendarmes!"

Thereupon Ploshkova, pushing forward her portly figure, began telling them how "something had come over her as soon as she saw those carts . . ."

"Be quiet! Here comes Gregory and the Voyt, running at full speed toward the priest's house."

Their eyes followed the two moving figures on the farther side of the pond.

"Aha! Gregory too is wanted!"

They were wrong. Gregory only pushed his brother in, but stayed himself to look at the carts drawn up there, and to question the drivers who were sitting in the porch. Then, in great distress, he ran to Matthew, who was working at Staho's cabin, and sitting astride on one of the roof beams, while cutting hollows in it to fix the rafters.

"Not gone yet?" he asked, cutting away as before.

"No; and the worst is, we cannot tell for whom they have come."

"Some evil thing is certainly at hand," old Bylitsa stammered.

"Perchance they come about our meeting. The district official threatened us then, and the gendarmes have been to and fro, seeking to find out who it is that eggs on the Lipka folk," Matthew said, slipping down to the ground.

"Then they are likely to have come for me!" Gregory rejoined, suddenly breathless with apprehension.

"No, I think they mean to seize Roch!" Staho asserted.

"True, they have inquired about him once already; how could I let that slip my memory?" He felt relieved for himself; but at once said, in distress for the other's fate:

"No doubt, if they have come for anyone, 'tis for him!"

"Well, but shall we let him be taken?" shouted Matthew. "Him, that is so truly a father to us all!"

"Alas! We cannot resist them, it is not to be thought of."

"Let him hide somewhere—and first let us warn him instantly."

"But peradventure," Staho remarked diffidently, "they may have come on some other errand—the Voyt's business, for instance."

"He must at all events be warned," cried Gregory; and, rushing out into the rye, and working around several gardens, he soon reached Boryna's hut.

Antek was sitting in the porch, putting jagged edges to some sickles on a small anvil. On hearing what the matter was, he started up in alarm.

"He has only just came in. Roch!" he cried. "Here, we want you."

"What is it?" the old man asked, putting his head out of the window; but before they had time to speak, in dashed Michael, the organist's lad, panting very hard.

"Know, Antek, that the gendarmes are coming to you now, and are already at the mill pond!"

"For me!" Roch bowed his head with a sigh.

"Jesu Maria!" Hanka shrieked from the threshold, and burst into tears.

"Oh be quiet!" Antek whispered; he was thinking very hard. "We must hit upon something."

"Roch!" vociferated Michael, breaking off a large branch and looking daggers. "I'll shout the news through Lipka, and we will not give you up!"

"No fooling! Roch! Get behind the haystack and into the rye this instant. Wiggle into some furrow, hide yourself well, and stay till I call you. Quick! Ere they are here!"

Roch snatched up some papers he had in the room and handed them to Yuzka, who was in bed:

"Hide them under yourself, do not give them up," he whispered.

And just as he was, without hat or capote [long, hooded overcoat], he darted into the orchard and vanished like a stone in the waters: they could just see the rye undulating slightly beyond the haystack.

"Now, Gregory, off with you! Hanka, to your work! Go, Michael— and not a word of this!" Antek commanded, sitting down again to his interrupted labor. Again he set to notching the edges of his reaping hooks, evenly and calmly as before. Now and again he would hold the edge up to the light, glancing the while in every direction about him; for the barking of the dogs was growing louder, and in a little he could hear the heavy tread of the approaching gendarmes, the jingling of their sabers, and the sound of their voices.

His heart was palpitating, his hands were shaking; yet he managed to go on, notching evenly, regularly, with rhythmical strokes, never raising his eyes till the men were standing before him.

"Is Roch in your hut?" asked the Voyt, mortally afraid.

Antek looked around at the group, and replied with great deliberation:

"He must be in the village, I suppose: I have not set eyes on him since this morning."

"Open your doors!" thundered the commanding officer.

"Why, they are open!" Antek growled, getting up from his bench.

The officer and some of his men went in, while the others watched the orchard and outhouses.

About half the village was now outside in the road, looking on in silence, while the cottage was searched and ransacked thoroughly. Antek had to point out and open everything, while Hanka sat by the window with the baby at her breast.

The search was of course fruitless; but they sought everywhere, and were so careful to overlook nothing that one of them even peered under the bed!

Some little books, strapped together, were lying on the table. The officer pounced upon them, and set to examine them with the utmost care.

"How have ye come by these?"

"Belike Roch has left them there . . . and there they lie."

"The mistress here cannot read," the Voyt explained.

"Can anyone amongst you read?"

"No," Antek returned; "they teach us at school so well that now no one is able even to spell out the words in our prayer books!"

The officer handed the little books to a subordinate, and passed round to the other side of the hut.

"What's here? A sick child?" he said, taking a step towards Yuzka.

"Yes. She has been lying there for a couple of weeks: smallpox."

He retired hurriedly into the passage.

"Was Roch a lodger in this cabin?" he asked of Voyt.

"In this or any other, according as it struck him: 'tis the *Dziads'* [old men] wont."

They peered into every hole and corner, even looking behind the holy images; while Yuzka followed their movements with eyes full of dread, trembling all over. One of them having approached her, she cried out wildly:

"Oh, have I hidden him under me? Seek him then here, do!"

When they had done, Antek went over to their officer, and said very humbly, with a deep bow:

"Has Roch stolen aught, I should like to know?"

The other, putting his face close to Antek's, replied with a stare, and laying stress on each word:

"Be it but found that you have concealed him, and ye shall go on a journey together, both of you! Do you hear?"

"I hear indeed, but cannot think what all this means." And he scratched his head, as if much perplexed.

The officer shot an angry look at him, and left the cabin.

They went round to many another, looking here and there, asking questions of many a one, until sundown; when, the roads filling with home-driven cattle, they went back empty-handed.

Now the village breathed freely, and people began telling of the searches—at the Klembas', at Gregory's, at Matthew's—and how each had seen things better than anybody else, and had not been frightened in the least, but had annoyed and bantered the gendarmes to the utmost!

But Antek, once alone with Hanka, said to her, dropping his voice:

"This is a wretched business, I see: there will be no keeping him in our cabin any longer."

"What, turn him out? So holy a man? One that does so much good?"

"A curse on it all! I am sick of it!" he cried, unable to find any way out of the quandary. But Gregory came presently, along with Matthew, and they held a consultation, locked up together in the barn: the cabin, continually full of callers for news, was no fit place.

When they came out, it was quite dark. Hanka had milked the cows, and Pete was back from the forest. Antek got the britzka [a long, horse-drawn carriage] and directly, while Gregory and Matthew went out, ostensibly to look everywhere for Roch, in reality to mislead the people of the village.

They were indeed all surprised at the quest, having made sure that Roch lay somewhere concealed on Boryna's premises. But the two friends gave out that he had left Boryna's directly after dinner and had not been heard of since.

"Lucky for him, or he would be journeying in chains ere now!"

So it became generally known (as they had planned) that Roch had not been seen in Lipka since noon.

People were glad, and said amongst themselves: "He guessed what was awaiting him, and is off 'to the land where pepper grows.'"

"Let him not come back, I say; we do not want him," old Ploshka growled.

Matthew snarled back at him: "Is he in your way? Has he wronged you in aught?"

"He disturbed the peace and troubled Lipka not a little. We all may yet suffer on his account."

"Then why not seize on him, you, and give him up?"

"Long ago we should have done so, had we any understanding!"

Matthew uttered a curse, and would have flown at him; they held him back, but with difficulty. And then, it being late, they went each man to his own cabin..

Antek was awaiting this moment, when the roads were deserted, and everybody was supping at home, and the scent of fried bacon was wafted abroad with the sound of merry talk and the tinkling of spoons in the dishes; then he brought Roch to the room where Yuzka lay; but he would not have a candle lit.

The old man snatched a hasty meal, put on what clothes he had left in the hut, and said farewell to the women. Hanka fell at his feet, and Yuzka wept and wailed piteously.

"God be with you! We may meet once more!" he said in a tearful voice, pressing them paternally to his breast, and kissing them on the forehead; but, Antek urging him to make haste, he once more blessed the women and children, crossed himself, and went out to the stile by the haystack.

"The britzka is waiting at Simon's hut in Podlesie, and Matthew will drive for you."

"But I must still pay a visit here in Lipka. Where are we to meet?"

"At the crucifix by the forest, whither we are going at once."

"That's well, for I have yet many things to speak of with Gregory."

And presently he was unseen and inaudible.

Antek put the horses to, placed a bushel of rye and a whole sack of potatoes in the britzka, conferred for some time apart with Vitek, and then said, for all to hear:

"Vitek! Drive over to Szymek's hut with the cart, and then come back. Do ye hear?"

The lad's eyes blazed, and he started off at such a pace that Antek called after him:

"Slower, you rogue, or you'll lame the horses!"

Roch had meantime crept stealthily to Dominikova's, where he had left a few things, and shut himself up in the inner room.

Andrew was on the watch by the roadside, and Yagna every now and then looked out into the enclosure, while the old woman, sitting in the front room, listened, trembling all over.

It took him some time before he came out to talk a little with Dominikova by herself; then he wanted to take up his bag and start off. But Yagna insisted on carrying it for him, at least to the forest. He agreed, and, taking leave of the others, went out into the fields, and slowly along the narrow pathways, with noiseless caution.

The night was clear and starlit; the lands lay hushed in slumber, with only now and then a sound of fitful barking.

They were nearing the forest, when Roch, coming to a standstill, took Yagna's hand.

"Hear me, Yagna," he said in a kindly tone, "and take to heart what I am going to say."

She lent an ear, though agitated by an unpleasant sense of foreboding.

Then, just as a priest might speak in confession, he talked to her of her doings . . . with Antek . . . with the Voyt . . . and most of all with Yanek.

She listened in deep humiliation, with averted face covered with blushes; but when he named Yanek, she raised her head defiantly.

"With him I have done no evil whatsoever!"

He pointed out gently to her the temptations to which they were exposing themselves . . . the sins and scandals to which the Evil One might give occasion thereby.

But she hearkened to him no longer; her mind was full of Yanek only: unconsciously her bright red lips were murmuring with ardent and frenzied love:

"Yanek, O Yanek!"

Her glowing eyes gazed afar, and circles in fancy over his adored head.

"Oh, I would go with him to the ends of the earth!" she declared, not knowing what she said. At the words, Roch shuddered, cast one look at those wide-open eyes, and held his peace thenceforward.

At the edge of the wood, just by the crucifix, several capotes were seen to glimmer white. Roch stopped, full of misgiving:

"Who is there?"

"Only we—your friends!"

"I am tired, and must rest awhile," he said, sitting down amongst them. Yagna gave up the bag to him, and seated herself not far off, at the foot of the crucifix, in the deep shadow of the branches.

"Well, may your troubles at least come to an end here!"

"The worst of all will come," said Antek, "now that you go from us."

"But it may be, it well may be, that I shall return one day!"

Here Matthew exploded. "Blood of a dog!" he cried; "to hunt men down so . . . . as if they were mangy curs!"

Gregory moaned. "And why, Lord God, why?"

"Because," Roch declared with solemn emphasis, "I want truth and righteousness for the people!"

"Hard is every man's lot; but that of the righteous is harder!"

"Do not mourn, Gregory; evil will be changed into good."

"So I think; 'tis hard to fancy that all we do is in vain."

"While we're awaiting the summer, the wolves will eat up our horses," Antek sighed, peering into the darkness at the white blot which was Yagna's face.

"But I say unto you: 'Whoso plucks up the weeds and sows good seeds, great riches shall win, when harvest comes in!' "

"And if he fail? Such things have been."

"Yea, but he that sows, sows in the hope of gathering in a hundred-fold."

"Surely, for who would care to lose his toil?"

And they pondered these things deep in their hearts.

The wind was up now, the birch trees murmured above them; a rustling sound came out of the forest, while the voice of the waving corn rose up to them from the fields. The moon floated along a pathway in the sky, made up of a double row of white clouds; the trees flung shadows mingled with patches of brightness; goatsuckers passed over their heads with a noiseless circling flight. Their hearts were very full of sadness.

Yagna shed tears in silence: she could not have said why.

"Wherefore do you sorrow?" he asked, laying his hand paternally on her head.

But the others too, all gloomy and cheerless, sat with their eyes fixed upon Roch, whom they now held for a man of God. He was sitting beneath the cross, from which the Crucified seemed to bend forward to bless his white weary head.

Then he spoke these words to them, full of hope and confidence:

"Fear naught for me. I am only a unit—one blade of corn in a fruitful field. If they take me, and I perish, what of that? So many more remain! Each of us ready to die for the cause! . . . And the time cometh when there will be thousands of them, from town and country, from cottage and from manor, all incessantly giving up their lives, one after another, piled and heaped together, the stones that are to form into the Holy Church of our desire! And that Church, I say unto you, shall stand and last for ever; and no power of evil shall prevail against it, because it will be built up completely with blood and loving sacrifice!"

Then he told them how no drop of blood, nay, not one single tear, would fall in vain, nor any endeavor be without its fruit; and how on every side, as from a soil abundantly manured, new forces, new defenders, and new victims would spring forth, until that blessed day should dawn—that sacred day, the day of resurrection and of justice and of truth for all the nation!

He spoke with glowing enthusiasm; often, too, of such high matters that they could not understand all that he said; but his fire inflamed them also, and their hearts leaped up and were exalted by his words in mighty faith and longing. Antek said at last:

"O God! Be ye our leader: I will follow you even to death!"

"We all will follow you and trample down whatever may resist us!"

"Who can withstand us and prevail? Let him but try!"

So they all spoke, till he was forced to hush their violent words and, drawing them still closer, and whispering, say what that longed-for day would be, and how its coming would be hastened by their labors.

He told them many a thing they had not dreamed of, and they listened breathless, full of dread and joy at once; and every word of his gave them the thrill of faith which one feels at the communion table. He opened heaven before them, and made paradise appear visibly to their eyes; their souls fell prostrate in deep ecstasy, their eyes beheld ineffable wonders, and in their hearts the sweet, sweet hymn of hope was heard.

"And it is in your power to realize all this," he ended, when quite tired out. The moon was just eclipsed behind a cloud; the sky was gray, the landscape murky; the woods gave forth their inarticulate utterances, and the cornfields rustled and shook as if with fear. Afar there was a noise of dogs that barked. And still they sat there, silent and subdued, listening in rapt attention, inebriated with the words he had said, and feeling as one who has just taken some great vow may feel.

"It is time: I must go!" he said, and, rising embraced each of them, pressing them to his heart. They could hardly keep back their tears when he knelt down, said a short prayer, and prostrated himself with both arms on the breast of that holy mother—the land that he might perhaps never see again. Yagna sobbed aloud, and the others were struggling with deep emotions.

Such was their parting.

Antek alone went straight back to Lipka, along with Yagna; the others disappeared in the shadows at the edge of the forest.

They long walked on in silence. Then he said: "Beware and say naught to anyone of that which you have heard."

"Am I, then, a peddler of news from hut to hut?" She was offended.

"And," he added, with stern significance, "God forbid that the Voyt should ever hear anything of this!"

She answered only by hurrying on; but he would not let her go, and strode on by her side, again and again glancing at her indignant face, bedewed with tears.

Translated by Michel H. Dziewicki

THE
EPILOGUE
AS
PROLOGUE

Karol Wojtyla
(*Pope John Paul II*)
(*1921–   *)

Karol Wojtyla was steeped in Polish history past and present. He knows the romantic anarchism of the Poles, their exaggerated notion of individualism, their charming Don Quixotism, their uncritical love of their country together with a paradoxical distaste for all authority, even that which they themselves created. He knows their penchant to swing from unrealistic optimism to deep depression. Yet he obviously loves his country and, above all, the peasant whom he understands at least as well as did Reymont. It was this love that radicalized him. He could not accept any system, capitalist or socialist, that alienates the peasant from his land and, by extension the worker from his means of production.

Wojtyla saw that what happened in Poland is a universal phenomenon. The world is actually divided among socialist and capitalist systems, neither of which serves the human person.

He looked again at his country, in which every form of government has been tried and none has worked. Yet he was always conscious of the fact that early in the fifteenth century the Polish Kingdom attempted to create a system of government based on Christian humanism, which has its roots in the evangelical commandment to love.

This perception led him in the late 1960s, as professor at the Catholic University of Lublin, to begin to formulate a new theory of social change that was neither explicitly anti-Marxist nor anticapitalist. His theory so transcends both systems that the Polish communist censors could not prevent him from publishing his lectures, nor could the United States take exception when, as John Paul II, he voiced a massive critique of corporate capitalism. Wojtyla, who was very much a realist, proposed a theory of social change that could be subscribed to by all people regardless of their ideological preferences—as long as they understood the principle of the common good. If they do, then they can work "jointly with others" to implement that goal.

The selection that follows gives the highlights of his theory; an attentive reader will also find in it echoes of Ostrorog, Mickiewicz, and Reymont. Wojtyla, whose writings are primarily directed at the Poles, asks them to work in solidarity.

More than ten years have passed since Wojtyla articulated his theory. Today's Poland, under the banner of Solidarity, is attempting to create a front of national unity for the first time since the Parliament of 1791 promulgated the Constitution of the third of May. The constituent parties of this front are the Communist party, the independent labor union Solidarity, and the Roman Catholic church—quite different in its method of operation from the rapacious and morally indifferent curialists of Rome. The fact that Wojtyla became the vicar of Christ on earth, the Pontifex Maximus, is not the essential factor that makes the Polish experiment universal in its scope and importance. Undeniably, the pope does bring its universal importance to the attention of the world; but the universality is in the event.

By implementing Wojtyla's theory of participation, which in itself is a major contribution to political philosophy, the Poles are proving that the survival of the human person in its full individual and collective dignity can be achieved by a commitment to social and economic justice.

What is required is the understanding that the evangelical commandment to love is the ability to be tolerant to the point of accepting the intolerance of others.

Toward a Philosophy of Praxis

Analysis of Attitudes: Authentic Attitudes

On the basis of reflections of the real meaning of the common good . . . of the relationship that occurs between participation as a quality of the self and the good of the community, one should scrutinize characteristic attitudes of acting and being "jointly with others." *Primary emphasis should be placed on the attitudes of solidarity and opposition.*

Both of the labels *solidarity* and *opposition* get their meaning from their relationship to a commonality of action as well as the common good. Related to these labels is a certain qualifier, which, in the final analysis, is an ethical one. In our analysis, we will focus on the personalistic meaning of those two attitudes, and therefore their qualities will contain not so much their ethical meaning as a *preethical* one. We are still primarily concerned with rendering a sketch of the very structure of human action and the values relevant to the accomplishment of an act. We are not primarily concerned with the value of the act stemming from a relationship to an ethical norm.

. . . We desire to continue solely with the subjective accomplishment of acts and with their immanent value, which is a personalistic value. In this context, we will find the key to the explanation for the proper

dynamism of the self within the confines of a variety of communities of action and existence. For this reason, the categorization of attitudes that we intend to analyze will be primarily personalistic and, in that sense, *preethical*. In this chapter, however, we are fully aware that we are proceeding on the border between ontology and ethics brought about by the axiological aspect—that means by the wealth of values that is difficult to exclude from an ontology of the self.

We will join the analysis of the attitudes of solidarity and opposition because each is needed to understand the other. The attitude of *solidarity* is a "natural" consequence of the fact that a human being exists and acts together with others. Solidarity is also the foundation of a community in which the common good conditions and liberates participation, and participation serves the common good, supports it, and implements it. Solidarity means the continuous readiness to accept and perform that part of a task that is imposed due to the participation as a member of a specific community.

Because of solidarity, a person performs what is expected of him . . . "for the good of the whole"—thus, for the common good. . . . Solidarity, in a certain sense, prevents transgression into the field of someone else's obligation. . . . This attitude corresponds to the principle of participation because participation, *understood objectively and "materially," indicates certain common structures of human action and existence.* The attitude of solidarity respects the limits imposed by the structures and accepts the duties that are assigned to each member of the community. Assuming responsibility for a duty that has not been assigned to me is fundamentally contrary to the concepts of community and participation.

There are instances, however, when solidarity demands such a contrariness. In such instances, restricting oneself to the assigned duty only could be tantamount to a lack of solidarity. This is indirectly proven by the fact that in solidarity the attitude toward the common good has to be always present, active, and dominant to such an extent that a human being must know when he has to undertake the performance of a task that is beyond his usual action and responsibility. A specific sensitivity to the needs of the community . . . . is expressed by the readiness to move beyond the partial and particularistic . . . *the readiness to "complete" by my act that which others complete jointly.* This quality enters . . . into the very nature of participation—which we now understand subjectively as a quality of the self and not only objectively as a division of tasks that fall upon everyone in the cooperative structure of acting and existing. This is why it can be maintained that the basic expression of participation as a quality of the self is the attitude of solidarity. On the basis of this attitude, a human being finds the fulfillment of himself by adding to the fulfillment of others.

The attitude of solidarity, however, does not exclude the attitude of opposition. *Opposition is not a fundamental contradiction of solidarity.* One who expresses opposition does not remove himself from participation in the community, does not withdraw his readiness to act for the common good. Naturally, it is quite possible to have a different understanding of opposition. Here, however, we understand opposition basically as an attitude of solidarity. We understand it not as a negation of the common good or a denial of the need for participation, but as a confirmation of both. The content of opposition is primarily a method of understanding the common good and, most important, perceiving the way in which it is to be realized. Experience with diverse forms of opposition . . . teaches that people who oppose do not wish to leave the community because of their opposition. They are searching for their own place in the community—*they are searching for participation and such a definition of the common good that would permit them to participate more fully and effectively in the community.* There are countless examples of people quarreling—thus, assuming the attitude of opposition—precisely because they have in their hearts a concern for the common good, for example, parents who oppose their children because they want the best possible upbringing for them, or statesmen who oppose . . . because they are concerned with the good of a nation or a state, etc.

Perhaps these examples do not show the entire picture of opposition, but they point to it. The basis for opposition results from the personal view of the community and its common good. Opposition is also an expression of the vital need for participation in the community of existence, but especially in the community of action. Such an opposition has to be viewed as constructive. . . . We are concerned with such a structure of community that permits the emergence of opposition based on solidarity. Moreover, the structure must not only *allow the emergence of the opposition, give it the opportunity to express itself, but also must make it possible for the opposition to function for the good of the community.* . . . A human community only then has a correct structure when a rightful opposition not only possesses the right of citizenship but is also endowed with the potential for effectiveness needed by the common good and demanded by the right of participation.

It is evident . . . that the common good has to be perceived dynamically and not statically. The common good depends basically on solidarity, but it cannot close itself off or cut itself off from opposition. *It seems that the principle of dialogue is an effective countermeasure to a restrictive structure of a human community and participation.* The concept *dialogue* has many meanings. At this point, we emphasize only one—that which is applicable to the formation and deepening of human solidarity even through opposition. Opposition might make living and acting together more difficult but should neither ruin it nor render it impossible. A dialogue may lead to the comprehension of what is real in a given confrontational situation by eliminating the subjective attitudes and preferences of the participants in the dialogue. It is those elements that are the germs of infections, conflicts, and fights among people. Whatever is real and right always deepens the self and enriches the community. The principle of dialogue is so vital because it serves to *avoid tensions, conflicts, and fights,* which can be seen in so many communities. Moreover, dialogues *attempt to reveal what is real and right in those communities and could be a source of good for the people.* The principle of dialogue should be accepted regardless of the difficulties that emerge on the way to holding it.

Analysis of Attitudes: Inauthentic Attitudes

. . . In considering the possible loss of authenticity that threatens the attitudes of solidarity and opposition . . . *it is important to indicate here certain inauthentic attitudes.* We shall describe them through the use of labels that are rather more popular than scientific: These are *conformism* and *avoidance.* . . . Both of these attitudes are inauthentic for very basic reasons and not because they are simply deformations of solidarity and opposition.

. . . The label *conformism* denotes similarity and assimilation with others—a normal process and, under certain circumstances, even a positive one. Nonetheless, the concept *conformism,* despite its positive association, indicates something negative. *It indicates the absence of a basic solidarity and an avoidance of opposition.* When it indicates assimilation to others in the community, it does it only in external, superficial manifestations devoid of a personal reason, conviction, and election. Conformity primarily contains a certain surrender, a specific variety of apathy in which a human being is only the subject of a "happening" and not the instigator of his own attitude and his own engagement in the community. The human being does not create the community but somehow "allows himself" to be included in the collectivity. Hidden within conformity is a limitation—if not a denial—or at least a weakness of self-transcendence, self-determination, and selection. . . . We are not concerned here with a simple submission to others in a community. This could have, in many instances, a positive connotation. It is something else that concerns us here: It is a *basic resignation, a giving up of self-fulfillment in acting "jointly with others" and of acting itself.* The human self agrees that the community takes the self away from him.

At the same time, the person takes himself away from the community. *Conformism is a denial of a participation in the real meaning of that term.* Real participation is replaced by the illusion of participation. It is a superficial assimilation to others without conviction and without an authentic engagement. In that way the human capacity of creative structuring of a community is as if suspended or even counterfeited. This must have a negative consequence for the common good whose dynamism flows from real participation. Conformism means something opposite. It creates the condition of indifference for the common good. Conformism is a special variant of individualism. It is a flight from the community through the subterfuge of external posturing. Conformity is more like *uniformity* than unity. Under the surface of uniformity exist differentiations, and it befalls the community to create for it the conditions necessary for participation. Conformism is unacceptable. In a situation where people only externally assimilate or acquiesce to the demands of the community, and they do it only to avoid unpleasantness, the self and the community suffer irreplaceable losses.

The attitude we describe as avoidance *seems indifferent to illusions of being concerned with the common good, an attitude that was part of* conformism. In a certain sense, avoidance is more authentic, but basically it also suffers from inauthenticity. Conformism avoids opposition; avoidance avoids conformism. This, however, does not change avoidance into an authentic opposition to conformism. . . . Avoidance is only a retreat. Perhaps it is even a sign of protest but without an attempt at engagement. Avoidance is an absence of participation and therefore an absence from the community.

Avoidance can be expressed through absence. . . . In such instances, avoidance gives a human being a substitute method of not expressing solidarity or opposition. Since avoidance or absence can be consciously chosen, one cannot deny that it has a personalistic value. If, however, there are reasons that justify the attitude of avoidance, then the same reasons form an accusation of the community. The basic good of a community is the potential for participation. If participation is not possible—which explains the reason for avoidance—then the community does not properly function. It lacks a common good, thus avoidance or absence become venues of "exit" for the member of the community.

Despite all of these reasons that might rationalize avoidance as a *sui generis* substitute attitude, it still remains impossible to ascribe to it an authentic character in the area of acting and being "jointly with others."

. . . In conformism and avoidance, the human being is convinced *that the community is taking away his self, and that is why he attempts to take his self away from the community.* In the case of conformity, he does it by maintaining the appearances; in the attitude of avoidance, he seems not to care about appearances. In both instances, something very vital is taken out of the human being. It is that dynamic quality of the self that enables it to perform acts and authentically fulfills the self through these acts in the community of being and acting "jointly with others."

Translated by Alfred Bloch

Acknowledgments

Grateful acknowledgment is made to the following for permission to reprint selections in this book:

Elizabeth Kridl Valkenier for "Treaties on Improving the Republic" by Jan Ostrorog, "Improving the Republic" by Andrzej Frycz Modrzewski, and "A Warning for Poland" by Stanislaw Staszic, from *Anthology of Polish Literature*, edited by Manfred Kridl.

J. M. Dent & Sons Ltd., Everyman's Library series, for the excerpt from *Pan Tadeusz* by Adam Mickiewicz, translated by George Repell Noyes.

Twayne Publishers for "The Underground People" by Andrzej Strug, "Dream of a Sword" and "Forest Echoes" by Stefan Żeromski, and "Powerful Samson" by Eliza Orzeszkowa, from *Introduction to Modern Polish Literature*, edited by Adam Gillon and Ludwik Krzyanowski, copyright © 1960 by Twayne Publishers.

The Wayne State University Press for "A Turban" by Marie Kuncewiczowa, from *10 Contemporary Polish Stories*, edited by Edmund Ordon, copyright © 1958 by The Wayne State University Press.

Stackpole Books and The K. S. Giniger Company, Inc. for the excerpt from chapter one of *Salt of the Earth* by Joseph Wittlin, translated by Pauline De Chary, copyright © 1970 by the Estate of Joseph Wittlin.

Grove Press, Inc. and Dr. Jan Van Loewen Ltd. for "The Police," from *Six Plays* by Slawomir Mrozek, copyright © 1967 by Nicholas Bethell.

Alfred A. Knopf Inc. for the excerpt from *The Peasants* by Waldyslaw Reymont, translated by Michel H. Dziewicki, copyright © 1924 and renewed 1952 by Alfred A. Knopf Inc.